The Who's Who roster of singles in *A Singular Devotion* includes:

- George Frederick Handel — composer
- Amy Carmichael — missionary
- Dietrich Bonhoeffer — theologian
- Susan B. Anthony — reformer
- Thomas A. Dooley — humanitarian
- Wilbur and Orville Wright — aviation pioneers
- Barbara Jordan — member of Congress
- Judith Resnick — astronaut

and a myriad of perhaps lesser known, but nonetheless noteworthy singles who made enduring contributions to our world:

- Clara Dutton Noyes — nurse
- Thomas Nuttal — botanist
- Carrie Chapman Catt — suffragist
- Nicholas Biddle — naval officer
- Julia Johnston — churchworker and hymnist
- Pierre Charles L'Enfant — architect
- Abraham Baldwin — political leader

Harold Ivan Smith invites you to meet these and hundreds of other fascinating singles in *A Singular Devotion*.

D1509161

BY Harold Ivan Smith

Movers and Shapers

A Singular Devotion

A
SINGULAR
DEVOTION

Harold
Ivan
Smith

Fleming H. Revell Company
Tarrytown, New York

Library of Congress Cataloging-in-Publication Data

Smith, Harold Ivan.
   A singular devotion / Harold Ivan Smith.
      p.   cm.
   Includes bibliographical references.
   ISBN 0-8007-5367-4
   1. Single people—Prayer-books and devotions—English.
2. Devotional calendars.   3. Single people—Biography.   I. Title.
BV4596.S5S626   1990
242'.64—dc20
                                                      90-35348
                                                          CIP

In a day of an overabundance of celebrities
but a conspicuous absence of heroes,
on June 5, 1989, Wang Weilin, a Chinese single adult,
dared to step in front of a column of army tanks
advancing on Tiananmen Square. The tanks stopped.
And the world gawked in disbelief at such a display
of courage. To that courageous
young man, I dedicate this book.

Special Appreciation

A book like this requires a great deal of research and assistance. I am particularly indebted to Bonnie Perry, who took a 750-page manuscript and helped make it into the readable draft submitted to Revell. Without her capable editorial help and perspective as a woman, this book would still be only a manuscript and a dream.

Where do I begin to express my appreciation to those librarians who went out of the way to trace facts, dates, and marital statuses for me. The following were especially helpful:

The Library of Congress, the State Library of Missouri, the State Library of New Mexico, the Boston Atheneum, the Library of the American Nursing Association, the Historical Society of South Carolina, the Tennessee State Archives.

The libraries of the University of Missouri at Kansas City, University of Kansas, University of Nebraska, Seattle Pacific University, Olivet Nazarene University, Southern Nazarene University, University of Southern Mississippi, University of North Florida, Vanderbilt University, Baylor University, John Brown University, Emory University, Biola University, University of Washington, University of South Florida, the Air Force Academy, George Washington University, University of Georgia, University of Michigan, Portland State University, University of Louisville, Brevard College, Scarritt College, Point Loma College, Trevecca Nazarene College, Southern Methodist University, Greenville College, College of Charleston, Anderson University, Columbus College, Avila College, Rockhurst College, and the University of Tulsa.

The libraries of the Southern Baptist Theological Seminary, New Orleans Baptist Seminary, Luther Rice Seminary, Midwestern Baptist Seminary, St. Paul's School of Theology, Nazarene Theological Seminary, Fuller Seminary and the Joint Theological Union in Berkeley, the Library of the Baptist Sunday School Board of the Southern Baptist Convention, and the Baptist School of Nursing in Kansas City.

Public libraries are a great heritage and provide not only the reader but also the writer with worlds of free information and data.

Public libraries that offered assistance included the Kansas City Public Library, Johnson County (KS) Library, Dallas Public Library, Jackson (MS) Public Library, Louisville Public Library, Hamilton County (OH) Public Library, San Francisco Public Library, Chicago Public Library, Colorado Springs Public Library, Orlando Public Library, Tampa Public Library, Key West Library, Memphis–Shelby County Public Library, Phoenix Public Library, Miami Library, Daytona Beach Public Library, Sarasota Public Library, Saint Louis Public Library, Meredian (MS) Public Library, Jacksonville (FL) Public Library, Palm Springs, Nashville Public Library, and the Gatlinburg Library.

Introduction

Andy Warhol, a single adult and pop artist, may be as well remembered for one quote as for his art. He once foretold of a world where "everyone will be famous for fifteen minutes." No wonder we're hooked on celebrities.

Our media offers a daily parade of fresh faces that are notorious today and forgotten tomorrow.

Anne Burford, former administrator of the Environmental Protection Agency in the Reagan administration, was shopping in a market one day after she was fired. Another shopper noticed her and stared. Finally she walked up and said, "Didn't you used to be somebody?"

Everybody wants to be a somebody.

In this age of celebrities, we forget the quiet heroes and heroines who lived without pomp, fanfare, or exposure on the six o'clock news. Oh, we have a place in our hearts for a Mother Teresa. "Isn't she something!" we say, but we see no link between her example and our everyday lives. In the age of celebrities, we occasionally ask, "Whatever happened to so-and-so?" as if it were a potential question in a trivia game.

Further, our heroes don't last. We expect too much from them, so presidents resign, TV ministers fall, athletes cheat on drug tests, and we throw up our hands in despair while eagerly searching for a replacement for the pedestal. No wonder we're skeptical. We view our celebrities with a "yes, but" in our mind, if not in our voice. We've been around the block before.

Unfortunately, we have few unmarried heroes or heroines in this age, so many single adults have concluded that life begins when (and only *if*) you get married. Many single adults live their lives on hold, waiting for the tardy appearance of a charming prince or princess, who had better have a good excuse for showing up so late.

This book of devotionals was inspired by a series of

experiences. On a visit to a monastery in Dubrovnik, Yugoslavia, a few years ago, I discovered a tradition called the *martyrologum,* or the writing of short histories of the saints. That visit prompted my book *Movers and Shapers: Singles Who Changed Their World.* However, that book provided an in-depth study of only nine single adults.

For some time I have been troubled by the words of Rabbi Samuel Dresner,

> We who dwell in the twentieth century are experiencing the collapse of faith. . . . Poets applaud the absurd, novelists explore the decadent, and men prostrate themselves before the deities of lust and power. Our obsession is with human flesh. . . . Daily we are bombarded by lurid reports of the mass-killer, the rapist, and the corrupt bureaucrat. The fantasies of even little children are now peopled with perverts and the radiated dead. Who will speak of those who do justice, love mercy and walk humbly?

From Dresner's *I Asked for Wonder*

This book attempts to do just that.

Finally, as part of a Christian education course I taught in a large church, I passed out a who's who matchup list of single adults and their achievements. The most that anyone matched was fifteen out of forty. Today's single adults have no consciousness of the legacy of single adults who lived and achieved when it wasn't acceptable to be unmarried, when "old maid," "unclaimed blessing," and "spinster" were painful labels.

Those three experiences prepared me for Daniel Taylor's important article, "The Fear of Insignificance," in *Christianity Today.* I was overwhelmed by his central question: "Who will remember me one hundred years from now?"

That question is even more haunting for those of us who realize we may never marry. Yet, as Taylor said, "we want to feel we can say at the end of our lives, 'My life was worth living. Things are [at least slightly] better in the world because I was here.' "

Clearly, the people in this book merit our consideration, lest we forget that they lived, sacrificed, and

8

opened doors for us—lest we doubt that *we* can make a difference.

I hope that you, as a result of spending the next year with these devotionals, will gain inspiration and some guidance for coming to grips with the challenges that you face.

Remember, we can see singleness as either an opportunity or a problem. These 366 single adults saw and seized their opportunities.

There are plenty of books and seminars that can teach you how to do something *about* your singleness, but I hope these single adults will encourage you to do something *with* this season called singleness.

A Word on Method for Inclusion

A book of this nature is a challenge for any writer. Thousands of dates must be checked and verified, then rechecked. It's not that the individuals change their dates of birth, but sometimes even reputable reference sources can be wrong. For example, Humphrey Bogart is listed in reference books under five different birth dates.

So I relied on three "Rock of Gibraltar" reference works as final authorities:

- *The Dictionary of American Biography*
- *Notable Women in America*
- *The National Dictionary of Biography*

I have also consulted encyclopedias, biographical dictionaries, chronologies, almanacs, biographies, and archival materials. I owe a great debt to a legion of librarians who aided my research and encouraged my efforts.

But the question remains: "Why didn't you include so-and-so?"

Some that I wanted to include, such as Francis Marion, "the Swamp Fox," were excluded because of the absence of a verifiable date of birth or death.

I also excluded members of religious orders who took vows of celibacy.

On some days it was feast or famine. I remember how difficult it was to find individuals born on the last four days of the year, while on other days, I had a baker's half-dozen candidates to choose from.

Certainly, not all of those included here were spiritual giants or paragons of virtue. Some biographers only offered a passing mention of faith, some apparently thought the issue too private or personal.

Such a project sets the author up for stern rebukes from irate readers who may be far better acquainted with the individual than I. "Why did you include X? Don't you know about . . . ?" and they then offer me a delicious tidbit or a skeleton from the closet. There is also a risk of misunderstanding subtle nuances of language, since words change over generations—particularly words dealing with intimacy and relationships.

In some cases, I have mentioned a contributing factor *to* a person's singleness: illness, death of a fiancée or fiancé, or financial reverses. It should be noted that earlier Americans took an engagement quite seriously. If it was broken, a party could be sued for breach of contract, and many expected that even the innocent party would never marry. If a fiancée died, the survivor was obligated by honor not to marry, as happened with James Buchanan, Judge R. E. B. Baylor, and Catherine Beecher.

In other cases, the person's singleness remains a mystery, and I will not speculate.

Some of the people in this book never caught the eye of a potential spouse, but they caught the eye of God. Some were never married; some were widowed; some were divorced; a few were single parents. I did not assume to decide the innocence or guilt of those who were divorced.

Finally, some may question the scarcity of contemporary single adults. A rule of thumb in this type of writing is to give time for a person's record to "set."

I suspect that a century or two after their deaths, some people in this book would be surprised that they have been remembered. Some would protest, "But all I did was. . . ."

I have relied on this scriptural guidance: "a righteous [single adult] will be remembered forever" (Psalm 112:6).

A
SINGULAR
DEVOTION

January 1

Frank Bigelow Tarbell, anthropologist
January 1, 1853–December 4, 1920

Frank Tarbell was described by his peers as frail, shy, and reserved. Yet, over the years, this unassuming man established a reputation as a fastidious and accurate scholar, becoming one of the most respected anthropologists in the world. Tarbell began his brilliant career at Yale and then spent two years in Europe before beginning work on his Ph.D., which he completed in 1879. For the next thirteen years he taught Greek and logic at Yale, then took a position at Harvard.

After spending 1892 to 1893 at the American School of Classical Studies in Athens, Tarbell joined the faculty at the newly established University of Chicago. He was one of the first American scholars to achieve prominence in the field of classical archaeology. Tarbell was widely published (*A History of Greek Art,* 1896; *Illustrated Catalogue of Carbon Prints on the Rise and Progress of Greek and Roman Arts,* 1896), and he prepared the catalog on the bronze sculpture in Chicago's Field Museum. But Frank Tarbell's major contribution was in the classroom. This shy man, perhaps an unlikely success, trained a generation of young anthropologists. Those who knew him praised Frank Tarbell as a man who consistently followed the path of his own ideals.

"Set a guard over my mouth, O Lord; keep watch over the door of my lips."

Psalm 141:3

Key Point: Significance is not always achieved by intellect. Many of us, like Tarbell, will be remembered for the lives behind the intellect.

January 2

Thomas Whittemore, archaeologist
January 2, 1871–June 8, 1950

Thomas Whittemore trained to become an English professor, but his real love was the history of art. He began to teach art history in 1906, when he was thirty-five years old.

"Enlarge the place of your tent, stretch your tent curtains wide, do

13

Whittemore worked with the French Red Cross during the early years of World War I. In 1915, he was in the Balkans and witnessed the devastation caused by the German advance that resulted in thousands of Russians becoming refugees. Whittemore organized a relief program called Refugees in Russia and directed the organization's activities until 1918.

After the Bolshevik Revolution in 1919, he focused his energies on refugee camps outside Russia. Using a route through Sofia or Constantinople, Thomas Whittemore helped many anti-Bolshevik youths escape. He used his own wealth to finance his relief work. In 1927, Whittemore returned to the United States to teach art history at New York University.

In 1930, he organized the Byzantine Institute to spotlight Christian art in the Near East, which he thought was superior to Western medieval art. He worked on and copied Coptic frescoes near the Red Sea and helped uncover the grand mosaics of a church in Constantinople built by the Emperor Justinian.

For the rest of his life, Whittemore spent half the year in Istanbul and the other half raising money, publicizing his work, and strengthening the institute's Library of Byzantine Studies in Paris.

A deeply committed Episcopalian, Whittemore appreciated the rich heritage and liturgy of the church. His work with Russian refugees and his efforts to promote Byzantine art made a lasting impression on many.

not hold back; lengthen your cords, strengthen your stakes."

Isaiah 54:2

Father, so much beauty in our world is lost because we are unaware of it. Help us to see the world through Your eyes.

January 3

Sophia Packard, college founder
January 3, 1824–June 21, 1891

Sophia Packard began teaching in rural Massachusetts schools at the age of fourteen. In 1855, as a teacher at New Salem Academy, she met Miss Harriet E. Giles, who was to become a lifelong friend and companion.

In 1870, when Sophia was forty-six years old, she became an assistant to the Reverend George C. Lorimer of Boston's Shawmut Avenue Baptist Church. When he moved to another pastorate in 1873, she took a salaried position on his staff, an unusual accomplishment for a

"Sing, O barren woman, you who never bore a child; burst into song, shout for joy."

Isaiah 54:1

woman in those days. Her responsibilities included overseeing a women's prayer meeting, teaching Sunday classes, and visiting the sick.

Out of her concern for ex-slaves in the South, Sophia founded the Women's American Baptist Home Mission Society in 1877. In 1880, she traveled to the South to analyze the needs of blacks there. Sophia returned to Boston determined to organize a college for black women in Georgia. She and Miss Giles moved to Atlanta in 1881.

On April 11, 1881, they opened a school in the basement of the Friendship Church. Although the basement "college" was damp, cold, and dark, and although her first students were of all ages, Miss Packard taught them all enthusiastically.

Sophia eventually bought a small campus, formerly headquarters for the Union army. She attracted the attention of John D. Rockefeller, who gave generously to the school, and in honor of Mrs. Rockefeller's mother, the college was named Spellman College.

By 1883, the school had four hundred students and Sophia was continuously raising funds. The two women were ostracized by most Southern white women but continued to educate a generation of future Southern leaders.

Father, by the world's standards, Sophia Packard was barren. But by her vision, she trained a generation to make a difference. Remind us through her example. Amen.

January 4

William Goebel, governor
January 4, 1856–February 3, 1900

To what length should a man go to achieve his political ambitions? William Goebel's political career began with his election to the Kentucky Senate in 1887. Previously he had studied law in the office of former Governor John W. Stephenson.

Goebel was not a spellbinding orator; he relied on biting vindictiveness for success on the political stump. Biographers say that, despite five election campaigns, he had almost no friends. His political rise was attributed to his skill and risk taking.

In 1899, he ran for governor and secured the nomination of the Democrats through back-room deals that split the party and alienated his opponents. After a vi-

"God gives a man wealth, possessions and honor, so that he lacks nothing his heart desires, but God does not enable him to enjoy them, and a stranger enjoys them instead."

Ecclesiastes 6:2

cious campaign, William S. Taylor defeated Goebel by a slim margin.

Goebel charged the Republicans with fraud, and the election went to the state legislature for resolution. On January 30, 1900, Goebel was shot as he approached the statehouse. In the emotion of the hour, the legislature declared him the winner of the 1899 race; he served four days before he died.

Father, remind us that some prices are too great to pay.

January 5

Thomas Nuttall, botanist
January 5, 1786–September 10, 1859

As a young man, Thomas Nuttall traveled from England to Philadelphia in 1808. Not long after his arrival, Nuttall met botanist Benjamin Smith Barton, who nurtured in the young immigrant the pleasure to be found in the serious study of plants. Nuttall traveled across Delaware, New Jersey, Maryland, and into North Carolina, collecting plant specimens. Between 1809 and 1811, he accompanied John Bradbury, a Scotch naturalist, on his expeditions through the Arkansas and Louisiana territories. Nuttall's description of plants appeared in a variety of publications.

In 1822, Nuttall became curator of the botanical gardens at Harvard University, a position he retained for ten years. Although he occasionally gave lectures, he spent most of his time caring for rare plants and exploring a new interest, ornithology. Because of his outstanding contribution in this area, the first ornithological club in America was named for him. His *A Manual of the Ornithology of the United States and Canada* gained him a wide reputation. He also worked at recording the music of birds by writing the sounds.

In 1842, Nuttall returned to England to accept an estate willed him by his uncle. He became a recluse and spent much of his last years growing rhododendrons and other exotic plants.

Nuttall made lasting contributions in botany, mineralogy, and ornithology. Because of his work, we are more able to appreciate the beauty of the earth.

"The land produced vegetation: plants bearing seed according to their kinds and trees bearing fruit with seed in it according to their kinds. And God saw that it was good."

Genesis 1:12

Father, this is a beautiful world. We praise You for creating it and for endowing men like Thomas Nuttall with the capacity to help us admire Your handiwork.

Sam Rayburn, Speaker of the House
January 6, 1882–November 16, 1961

Mr. Sam, as he was called, was a Texas Democrat "without prefix, without suffix, and without apology." When Sam Rayburn spoke, Congress listened.

When Sam Rayburn went off to East Texas Normal College in 1899, he took with him twenty-five dollars (his family's life savings) and an ambition to be Speaker of the United States House of Representatives, a longing he'd had since the age of twelve.

At age twenty-four, "with a pony, a smile, and determination," Sam Rayburn visited every house in his district, campaigning for the Texas legislature. He won, and between sessions he studied law at the University of Texas. Rayburn served six terms in the Texas legislature. In 1912, he was narrowly elected to the House of Representatives from Texas's Fourth Congressional District.

In 1940, Mr. Sam became Speaker of the House. His influence was seen in one prophetic vote. Just four months before World War II broke out, the House passed a bill extending the Selective Service Act. The vote was 203 to 202. On such close votes, it is routine to request reconsideration. In a bold, courageous act, Rayburn gaveled down all motions to reconsider. As a result, the United States narrowly avoided a disastrous shortage of military manpower on the eve of war.

Sam Rayburn's office in the Capitol was called "the Rayburn Board of Education." One of its many ambitious students was a young Texas congressman named Lyndon Johnson.

Some Rayburnisms include:

- "To get along you've got to go along."
- "You cannot lead people in order to drive them."
- "Persuasion and reason are the only ways to lead them."

Speaker Sam was called "the greatest compromiser since Henry Clay." This may explain why he served as speaker longer than any other man: eighteen years.

Sam Rayburn was "a Texan without a ten-gallon hat, an officeholder who didn't slap backs, a politician with

"What does the Lord your God ask of you but to fear the Lord your God, to walk in all his ways, to love him, to serve the Lord your God with all your heart and with all your soul, and to observe the Lord's commands and decrees."

Deuteronomy 10:12, 13

Father, Mr. Sam gave his life to public service. Many of the things we take for granted have his fingerprints on

no instinct for publicity, and a doer who is shyly modest." Mr. Sam was a member of the Primitive Baptist Church.

January 7

Louise Imogen Guiney, author
January 7, 1861–November 2, 1920

Louise Guiney loved "grubbing for facts." The library was a second home to her. She began writing in 1879 to assume financial support for her widowed mother. *Songs of the Start* (1884) and *Goose Quill Papers* (1885) won her recognition and friends in the Boston literary world. Her writing was influenced by Tennyson and Hazlitt.

Guiney's *A Little English Gallery* contained her best writing. *Happy Ending*, first published in 1909 and revised in 1927, represented her best poetry.

Louise was postmistress of Auburndale, Massachusetts, between 1894 and 1897, and also worked for the Boston Public Library. In 1901, she moved to England and lived at Oxford, spending joyful hours exploring the Bodleian Library. In order to have money to buy books, Louise scrimped on food and coal for heating. Such habits eventually weakened her health.

Louise died with her two major literary projects unpublished: a biographical study of Henry Vaughn and an anthology of Catholic poets. Her manuscripts, which included comprehensive biographic and bibliographic notes, demonstrated her intense skills as a researcher.

"... much study wearies the body."

Ecclesiastes 12:12

Father, sometimes life runs out. Thank You for tasks that demand the most of us. Help us to enjoy this day.

January 8

Elanor Chestnut, physician
January 8, 1868–October 1905

Elanor Chestnut was consumed by the idea of becoming a doctor. Without the support of her family, she moved to Chicago, lived in an attic, and existed on a diet of oatmeal through medical school.

In 1893, Elanor was appointed as a missionary physician to China. Soon after her arrival, she set out to build a hospital, investing most of her monthly salary in

"While they were stoning him, Stephen prayed, 'Lord Jesus, receive my spirit.' "

Acts 7:59

18

building supplies and budgeting only $1.50 per month for herself. When the mission board discovered her sacrificial giving, they offered to reimburse her, but Elanor refused, saying, "It would spoil my fun."

Once Elanor operated on a Chinese man many dismissed as a good-for-nothing. Finally, she had to amputate his leg. However, the stump would not heal properly. Later, people noticed the doctor limping. Elanor had taken skin from her own leg (without anesthesia) and had grafted it onto the patient's stump. He improved.

When other Americans fled China during the anti-American Boxer Rebellion, Dr. Chestnut refused to leave her hospital. When a rioting crowd set the hospital on fire, she quickly went to the police, then returned to the hospital, thinking she could quiet their rage. Instead, Elanor was pelted with rocks and assaulted.

As she lay dying, Elanor tore strips from her dress to bandage a young injured boy lying near her. The physician died in the smoke of her burning hospital.

Elanor Chestnut chose China at the expense of a comfortable American practice and paid the price with her life.

Father, sometimes love and commitment are costly. We may lose things we hold dear. Test my commitments. Help me to face the real answer.

January 9

Carrie Chapman Catt, suffragist
January 9, 1859–March 9, 1947

If it weren't for Carrie Catt, women might not have gained the right to vote. What many take for granted was the lifetime goal of this widow.

Carrie's first husband died eighteen months after their marriage; four years later, she married George Catt, a prosperous engineer. In 1895, at age thirty-six, she became chairman of the Organizing Committee of the National American Women's Suffrage Association (NAWSA). In 1900, she succeeded Susan B. Anthony as president but resigned in 1904 because her husband became ill.

After George's death, the young widow became active in the New York women's suffrage movement, trying to secure passage of a statewide referendum to give

". . . But because of the way you are going about this, the honor will not be yours, for the Lord will hand Sisera over to a woman."

Judges 4:9

19

women the right to vote. The campaign was completed in 1917, two years after Carrie Catt resumed the presidency of the NAWSA.

Carrie Catt immediately recruited fresh leadership, designed a six-year campaign, and built a financial war chest. She encouraged supporters to picket the White House and to hold the political party in power responsible for the delay in giving women the vote. When the proposed Constitutional amendment finally passed Congress, Catt launched an intense state-by-state battle for ratification.

Catt gained a reputation as a persistent lobbyist. In one case, when her train wrecked in Colorado and she was likely to miss her next speaking engagement, Carrie commandeered a handcar and pumped her way up the tracks to her destination.

Once women had the vote, Carrie encouraged them to use it aggressively. Go through "the locked door," she urged, to the real seat of political power: holding office.

"You will have a long hard fight before you get behind that door," she said. "For there is the engine that moves the wheels of your political machinery. . . . If you really want women's votes to count, make your way there."

Carrie Catt worked to open the door of opportunity offering women full citizenship of the republic. Today her legacy is seen in the women who serve in Congress and state legislatures, or as governors and mayors— someday, perhaps, as president.

Father, remind me today of ways that I can make my life count. Dispel my cynicism about the slowness of change. Strengthen my commitment to the important issues of the day.

January 10

Katherine Burr Blodgett, chemist
January 10, 1898–October 12, 1979

In an era when women were not thought to be scientifically oriented, Katherine Blodgett made people scratch their heads. This Bryn Mawr graduate had heard many say that the coming war would open up new opportunities for women. General Electric had expressed an interest in hiring her but said she needed more science, so she went to the University of Chicago, where she wrote her master's thesis on the interaction of certain gases in gas masks.

After her return, General Electric did hire Katherine

"For now we see through a glass, darkly; but then face to face: now I know in part; but then shall I know even as also I am known."

1 Corinthians 13:12
KJV

and assigned her to the labs of Dr. Irving Langmuir, who would eventually win the 1932 Nobel Prize in physics. As a result of their work, they published several journal articles together.

Langmuir used his influence to have Blodgett considered for the Ph.D. program in physics at Cambridge University, which was reluctant to admit a female. Katherine was admitted and studied with Nobel laureate Sir Ernest Rutherford. In 1926, she became the first woman to receive a doctorate in physics from Cambridge.

Later in her career, Katherine began experimenting with an oily substance that Langmuir had discovered and discarded fifteen years earlier. When spread on water, the substance would form a film only one molecule thick. Of what practical use could that be?

None, until she discovered that when she applied the substance to a sheet of glass, all reflection was eliminated. Katherine Blodgett had just invented transparent nonreflecting glass.

On that morning in December 1938, hundreds of newspapers carried the story of the discovery and the single-adult scientist who discovered it. Her discovery had enormous application: windshields, showcases, cameras, and measuring light. Katherine's reaction was humble:

> You keep barking up so many wrong trees in research. It seems sometimes as if you're going to spend your whole life barking up wrong trees. And I think there is an element of luck if you happen to bark up the right one. This time I eventually happened to bark up one that held what I was looking for.

Key Thought: Keep barking!

January 11

Stella Dysart, miner
January 11, 1878–January 16, 1966

Life was not easy for Stella Dysart. After a divorce and several career changes, she decided to try the oil and gas business. Stella bought almost 150,000 acres in New

"If any of you lacks wisdom, he should ask God, who gives

Mexico and fought to succeed in a male-dominated field. Stella had especially high hopes for one particular well. However, when a driller disobeyed her specific instructions, the well was lost, along with $150,000 of Stella and her investors' money. Many of us would have wasted time thinking of what *might* have been; Stella asked God for guidance instead.

Stella began to wonder if she might be looking for the wrong natural resource. Maybe she should be mining for uranium. She decided to pursue this idea, and on March 17, 1955, at 292 feet, Stella's crew hit pay dirt. They didn't find oil, but uranium—the mother lode. The Atomic Energy Commission has estimated that 72 percent of the nation's proven uranium ore is on Stella Dysart's property.

At age seventy-seven, Stella knew she would never have financial worries again, yet she worked on for years, tracing people who had invested in earlier ventures and sharing her bonanza with them.

What kept Stella going after her failure in the oil business? Her faith in God. Stella never asked God for things, but rather for guidance. "Insistence on certain things, or certain results, or specific requests can result in disaster," she said. "But guidance has never failed."

Stella lived her life by the following principles. They make sense for single adults today:

- The Bible has always been my guide.
- If it can't be helped, it must be endured.
- Always turn immediately from failure to success.
- Discouragement never won anything.
- When you pray, ask for guidance, strength, and inspiration.

Stella Dysart is a vibrant example of persistence despite adversity.

generously to all without finding fault, and it will be given to him."

James 1:5

Father, when our dreams vanish before our eyes, remind us of Your faithfulness. Teach us to ask You not for things but for guidance.

January 12

Samuel Porter, teacher
January 12, 1810–September 3, 1901

Samuel Porter graduated from Yale University and studied for the ministry, but before graduation he suffered a

"Do not curse the deaf or put a stum-

partial loss of hearing. Porter decided to seize the opportunity and become a teacher of the deaf. From 1832 to 1836 he was an instructor of the American Asylum in Hartford founded by Thomas Gallaudet. After more graduate study at Yale, Samuel worked at the New York Institution for the Deaf until 1846, when he returned to the American Asylum.

Samuel Porter wrote skillfully and was frequently published in prestigious journals of the day. He wrote articles on the teaching of English, the formation of vowel and consonant sounds, as well as the mental processes of the deaf. Perhaps his greatest contribution was through the *American Annals of the Deaf*, which he edited from 1854 to 1861.

Through his friendship with Thomas Gallaudet, Porter was invited to join the faculty of what is now Gallaudet College in Washington, D.C., teaching science and English. After his retirement, Samuel Porter taught the deaf who lived in his neighborhood.

bling block in front of the blind, but fear your God."

Leviticus 19:14

Father, thank You for the life of this man who turned his handicap into an opportunity to enrich the lives of others. Give me that kind of courage.

January 13

Horatio Alger, writer
January 13, 1832–July 18, 1899

"Holy Horatio," as he was nicknamed by his friends, graduated from Harvard and, influenced by his clergyman father, decided to become a minister. Horatio's father broke his son's engagement because he disapproved of the girl, and Horatio never married. After graduating from Harvard Divinity School, Horatio spent a year in Paris, trying to find himself.

He returned to the United States and was ordained in 1864. However, after pastoring for two years, he resigned and moved to New York City to write.

While in New York, Horatio developed a friendship with the director of the Newsboys' Lodging House, which provided shelter for the city's homeless boys who sold newspapers on the street. Alger became acquainted with many of the newsboys, and their stories influenced his sentimentalized writing about their lifestyle. Alger once stated his philosophy: "Every boy's life is a campaign, more or less difficult."

"Of making many books there is no end . . ."

Ecclesiastes 12:12

Ragged Dick was his first series of tales about news-boys; it was followed by *Luck and Pluck* (1869) and *Tattered Tom* (1871). The stories focused on poor boys trying to survive in a cold, heartless world. All of the books sold well and generated a great deal of money for Alger.

Horatio gave away most of the royalties from his books, using the money to sponsor boys he met, to buy them food and clothing, and to provide them with educations. He also set up several of the young men in business.

In his career, Alger wrote 119 books, some of which he completed in less than one month. All his life he wanted to write serious novels, but he couldn't escape the popularity and easy money of his rags-to-riches stories.

Eleven of Alger's books were published after his death. Most of the stories remained popular reading for boys until the Depression.

Key Point: It is possible to so spend our lives doing good things that we never get around to the great things.

January 14

Katherine Prescott Wormeley, author and philosopher
January 14, 1830–August 4, 1908

Although her father was a rear admiral in the British navy, when Katherine Wormeley was eighteen, her family moved to the United States. Katherine was accustomed to the best of British society.

During the Civil War, Katherine served as a nurse for the army and was superintendent of a hospital for recuperating soldiers in Rhode Island. She wrote a book on the wartime activities of the United States Sanitary Commission. After the war, she founded and financed a vocational school for girls in Rhode Island.

Katherine Wormeley won her first literary recognition for her translations of several French writers such as Balzac, Alexandre Dumas, P. Bourget, and Molière. Her translations were well received and praised for their technical precision and enthusiasm. She wrote *A Memoir of Honoré de Balzac*.

Katherine greatly influenced the American recognition of French literature.

"They read from the Book of the Law of God, making it clear and giving the meaning so that the people could understand what was being read."

Nehemiah 8:8

Father, give us the strength to be enthusiastic in our world, just as Miss Wormeley was. Keep us from "getting by" and prompt us to make excellence a priority.

January 15

Elizabeth Cole, nurse missionary
January 15, 1911–

A leprosy colony in Swaziland is a long way from a ranch in Montana, but Elizabeth Cole, R.N., made the adjustment. Elizabeth loved horses and thought she would have to give them up to work on the mission field. But when she got to the Raleigh Fitkin Memorial Hospital in Manzini, Africa, Elizabeth found her riding skills useful in reaching patients in outlying clinics.

In 1948, the British opened a new leprosy colony and the Nazarene missionary was given permission to live there. Dr. Samuel Young, a general superintendent of the denomination, later reported, "I heard a small lady testify that God had given her the desire of her heart. He had let her do what she wanted to do more than anything else on earth. I knew that she was stationed alone at the leprosy colony, where her only visitor for weeks at a time was the medical doctor who came once a month."

In 1960, to honor her work with lepers, Queen Elizabeth made Elizabeth Cole a member of the British Empire, the first American in Swaziland to receive the honor.

One other American had a chance to visit the colony and observed Miss Cole cleansing a leper's wound.

"I wouldn't do that for a million dollars!" the visitor declared.

"I wouldn't either," Elizabeth Cole responded. "Not for a million dollars, but I would for Christ."

"A man with leprosy came to him and begged him on his knees, 'If you are willing, you can make me clean.' "

Mark 1:40

Father, wherever we find ourselves can be heaven, if You are with us. Anywhere You lead us, You can keep us. Give us the courage to love those the world casts aside.

January 16

George Kelly, playwright
January 16, 1887–June 18, 1974

How long does the applause last? What should we do when it stops?

George Kelly was born into a prominent Philadelphia family (his niece was Grace Kelly). As a teen, Kelly followed his older brother, Walter, into the theater. In 1915, he turned to vaudeville and began writing, producing, and acting in short plays.

"The crucible for silver and the furnace for gold, but man is tested by the praise he receives."

Proverbs 27:21

In 1922, his first full-length play, *The Torchbearers*, was produced on Broadway, to less than glowing reviews. Two years later he wrote a success, *The Show-Off*, and his reputation as a dramatist was established.

In 1925, he was the darling of New York theater and won the Pulitzer Prize for *Craig's Wife*, but then Kelly's reputation was tested by four successive flops. He went into a writing exile for five years and returned to Broadway in 1936 with *Reflected Glory*, which the critics trounced. Years passed. Once more he offered plays that failed.

Without the applause, Kelly couldn't continue. He retired, dying long after the audiences had forgotten him.

Father, give us courage to keep praise and applause in perspective in our lives. Help us to see them as the dessert, not the entrée.

January 17

Thomas Anthony Dooley III, humanitarian
January 17, 1927–January 18, 1961

By the time Thomas Dooley was thirty-three years old, he was, according to the Gallup organization, one of the ten most admired Americans.

His fame came as a result of a best-selling book, *Deliver Us from Evil*, in which he recounted his experiences as a naval physician in Vietnam. Dooley supervised some 600,000 Vietnamese in refugee camps as the former French territory was split into north and south.

After his book's publication, Dooley resigned from the navy and established a hospital in Laos. In 1958, he turned that hospital over to the Laotians and started another one at Muong Sing. In 1958, he founded MEDICO to provide medical care in more remote areas.

President Eisenhower paid tribute to the young bachelor, saying, "It must be a source of heartened gratification to realize that in so few years you have accomplished so much for the good of distant peoples and have inspired so many others to work for all humanity."

Few Americans realized that the faraway world of Dr. Tom Dooley would soon become a preoccupation with America. American military involvement in Vietnam

"Even if I go through the deepest darkness, I will not be afraid, Lord, for you are with me . . ."

Psalm 23:4 TEV

Key Thought: "I believe that it behooves those of us who attempt to aid in a foreign land to be content with small achievements. We must not attempt to build dynasties. We must try to build at the level of the people, or just one step ahead, always planning it so that the

26

was just around the corner. Dr. Dooley had gone with a stethoscope and penicillin; the next Americans would bring the instruments of war.

Asian can ulti-mately take over"

Thomas Dooley, III

January 18

Emil Alexander de Schweinitz, biochemist
January 18, 1866–February 15, 1904

Born to Moravian parents (his father was a bishop) in North Carolina, Emil Schweinitz attended the University of North Carolina and received his Ph.D. in 1885. He did additional study at the University of Berlin and Göttingen, earning a second doctorate in chemistry.

In 1888, Schweinitz joined the United States Department of Agriculture as a chemist. Two years later, he was chosen to direct the government's research in biochemistry, which he did until his death in 1904. The Department of Agriculture asked Schweinitz to find ways to protect farm animals from diseases like hog cholera and tuberculosis. Schweinitz was the first scientist to produce immunity in animals by inoculating them with attenuated human tubercle bacilli.

Dr. Schweinitz published several scientific papers and reports and encouraged researchers across the United States. He also served as dean and professor of chemistry at Columbia University Medical School, where he contributed to the development of a major teaching hospital.

In Jesus' days there were no biochemists. Instead, He healed people. Scientists like Schweinitz have helped prevent the illness of many people. He, too, was a healer.

"Jesus went throughout Galilee . . . healing every disease and sickness among the people."

Matthew 4:23

Father, we thank You for the brilliance of this great scientist. Bless today all those single adults who are scientists, peering hour after hour into microscopes and using their findings to improve our health.

January 19

William Otto, jurist
January 19, 1816–November 7, 1905

William Otto began practicing law in Brownstown, Indiana, in 1836. By 1844, at age twenty-eight, he presided over Indiana's second judicial district and held the dis-

"David reigned over all Israel, doing what was just

27

tinction of being the last judge to be appointed by the legislature; after Otto, all judges were elected. Otto did not campaign well and lost the election in 1852. After his defeat, Otto faced a turning point in his legal career; he moved to southern Indiana and began building a reputation as one of the state's most competent lawyers.

He was defeated in a bid for state attorney general but was chosen as a delegate to the Republican National Convention in 1860. Because Otto supported his candidacy, Abraham Lincoln appointed him assistant secretary of the interior. In that position Otto worked tirelessly to improve the status of the American Indians.

Between 1871 and 1875, Otto served as an arbitrator for the United States in its dispute with Spain concerning mistreatment of American citizens in Cuba. In 1875, he became reporter for the United States Supreme Court, responsible for publishing the court's decisions for the legal profession. In 1883, he resigned but returned to government service two years later as the United States representative to the International Postal Union. Otto continued to practice law until his death at age eighty-nine.

and right for all his people."

2 Samuel 8:15

Key Point: There are always opportunities for a skilled, resourceful single adult.

January 20

Oliver Smith, philanthropist
January 20, 1766–December 22, 1845

Oliver Smith grew up in a single-parent home in Hatfield, Massachusetts. Although he came from poor beginnings, by the time he died, boys in the town boasted that they wanted to grow up to be as rich as Oliver Smith.

Smith made his fortune by farming, selling cattle, and investing in Wall Street securities. When it came to *spending* money, though, Smith was a Scrooge. "He wasted nothing, spent little, and rarely gave anything away," one critic said. Another claimed that, in the thirty years he had known Smith, Oliver had always worn the same clothes.

Smith opposed education, and he avoided paying taxes, fearing the money would be ill spent. When his church decided to install stoves, Smith quit.

"Whoever loves money never has money enough; whoever loves wealth is never satisfied with his income."

Ecclesiastes 5:10

Ironically, his will directed that his entire estate go to charity. He created a trust fund to provide grants for indigent children and widows. He designated provisions that placed worthy orphan boys with good families, taught them a trade, and at age twenty-one provided five hundred dollars to launch their careers. Girls, under similar provisions, received three hundred dollars as a marriage dowry. He also provided a means to grant cash to girls to set up housekeeping after marriage and to care for needy widows without dependents. Finally, a large grant established a state agricultural school.

Famed attorney Daniel Webster defended the will against the relatives who challenged it in court. The will and Oliver Smith's belated charity were upheld.

Key Point: In matters of charity, better late than never.

January 21

Julia Johnston, church worker
January 21, 1849–March 6, 1919

For Julia Johnston, life centered around the First Presbyterian Church of Peoria, Illinois. She went there as a seven-year-old girl when her father became pastor. For forty-one years she was the superintendent of the children's department of the Sunday school, and she also taught the infants' class.

Missions was a strong interest in her life; for twenty years Julia was president of the Presbyterian Missionary Society of Peoria. She also wrote curriculum for children for the David C. Cook Publishing Company and wrote such books as *School of the Master, Bright Threads, Indian and Spanish Neighbors,* and *Fifty Missionary Heroes.*

She also wrote about five hundred hymns to tunes composed by many hymnists. Only one of them has remained popular: "Grace Greater Than Our Sin."

"How great is the love the Father has lavished on us, that we should be called the children of God! And that is what we are!"

1 John 3:1

> Marvelous grace of our loving Lord,
> Grace that exceeds our sin and our guilt!
> Yonder on Calvary's mount outpoured—
> There where the blood of the Lamb was spilt.
>
> Grace, grace, God's grace.
> Grace that will pardon and cleanse within;
> Grace, grace, God's grace,
> Grace that is greater than all our sin!

Father, we thank You for the reality of Your grace in our lives—that Your grace is greater than all our sin. Give us the confidence to believe that.

29

Catherine Wolfe Bruce, philanthropist
January 22, 1816–March 13, 1900

Catherine Bruce was born into a wealthy New York family; her father had made his fortune in the printing plate industry. After a private education, she traveled extensively in Europe and became fluent in five languages. A painter, she also collected art, antiquities, and typography.

Over the years, affected by frequent illness, she lived as a comfortable recluse with her younger sister.

At age seventy-three, she became interested in funding astronomical research. Biographers say she had long been intrigued with the subject but was prompted to action in 1888 when she read an article by a noted American astronomer, Simon Newcomb, who argued that most astronomical discoveries of significance had already been made.

"We'll see about that!" Catherine responded, reaching for her checkbook. "Such a blow from a friend!" she chided Newcomb. "I think we are [only] beginning. . . . The world is young."

Her first grant of $50,000 established the photographic telescope at Harvard. Later, she added another $125,000. She made many grants of $1,000 to young scientists and scholars at crucial points in their careers. For many years, a significant portion of the world's astronomical and astrophysical research was conducted on equipment financed by Catherine Bruce. Without her money, astronomy would have remained little more than stargazing.

Her desire as a single adult: "to be useful to Astronomy now and always."

"Let your astrologers come forward, those stargazers who make predictions month by month, let them save you from what is coming upon you."

Isaiah 47:13

Key Point: To be useful, whatever the field of endeavor, is a good goal for any single adult.

Amanda Smith, evangelist
January 23, 1837–February 24, 1915

Life was hard for Amanda Smith, a black woman born into slavery in Maryland. At seventeen, she married her first husband, who deserted her and their little girl. She

"You will receive power when the Holy Spirit comes

described her struggle as a single parent: "I boarded my little girl, here a while, there a while. . . . I found that often people do things just for the little money they get out of it; and when I would go and see the condition of my poor little child, and then had to turn away and leave her and go to my work. I often cried and prayed; but what could I do more? I had not yet learned to trust God fully for all things."

After the Civil War, Amanda moved to Baltimore and married a Methodist preacher, James Smith, but he did not encourage her desire to preach. After his death in 1869, Amanda decided to become an evangelist. She was viewed with great skepticism when she attended the Africa Methodist Episcopal Church's general conference in Nashville in 1870. Since women were not permitted as delegates, many males were suspicious that she was there to lobby for female ordination.

Preacher Woman, as she was dubbed, said, "The right of ordination had never once entered my mind, for I had received my ordination from Him, who said, 'Ye have not chosen me, but I have chosen you, and ordained you, that you might go forth and bring forth fruit.' "

She became a popular speaker at camp meetings all over the country, but faced a great deal of racial prejudice. Nevertheless, thousands heard her and made decisions.

In 1876, Amanda Smith left the United States to preach in England and India, later spending eight years in Liberia. She returned to the United States in 1890 and opened Amanda Smith's Orphan's Home for Colored Children in Harvey, Illinois.

Concerning the prejudice she faced daily, Amanda said: "Even among my own people, in this country, I have not always met with the pleasantest things. But still I have not backslidden, nor felt led to leave the church. His grace has been sufficient. And all we need today is to trust him."

on you; and you will be my witnesses in Jerusalem, and in all Judea and Samaria, and to the ends of the earth."

Acts 1:8

Key Thought: "I belong to Royalty, and am well acquainted with the King of Kings, and am better known and better understood among the great family above than I am on earth."

Amanda Smith

January 24

Mary N. Murfree, author
January 24, 1850–July 31, 1922

Writing about the Tennessee mountains made Mary Murfree's reputation as a "colorist." She wrote eighteen novels and six volumes of short fiction under the name Charles Egbert Craddock and knew tremendous popularity during her lifetime. Murfree established Southern writing as "respectable" to the Eastern literary establishment and critics.

Born into a family whose ancestry went back to the American Revolution, Mary's parents were avid readers and cultured people. After Mary finished college, her family moved back to Grantford, the family estate destroyed during the Civil War; Mary began writing.

Her break came when the *Atlantic Monthly* published "The Dancing Party at Harrison's Cove." In 1884, her first novel, *In the Tennessee Mountains,* was published, and by 1890 six more had followed, including her best, *The Prophet of the Great Smokey Mountains* (1885).

Murfree's writing is sprinkled with mountain dialect, local color, and mountain customs. When the literary world's fascination with "local color" diminished, she wrote several successful historical novels. In her last years, Mary was confined to a wheelchair and was blind.

"Do not move an ancient boundary stone set up by your forefathers."

Proverbs 22:28

Father, thank You for all the bits of color in our lives.

January 25

Corazon Aquino, president
January 25, 1933–

For almost twenty years, Corazon Aquino had been the wife of Begnino Aquino, who had led opposition to Ferdinand Marcos, president of the Philippines. Corazon had remained in the background as mother to their five children and hostess at her husband's political gatherings.

When Marcos declared martial law in 1972 and imprisoned her husband, Corazon came into the political limelight, working tirelessly to encourage her husband

"The king asked her, 'What is troubling you?' She said, 'I am indeed a widow; my husband is dead.' "

2 Samuel 14:5

and to keep his name alive. Under pressure from President Jimmy Carter, Begnino was released from prison, and he and Corazon came to the United States. She became a typical suburban housewife while Begnino taught at Harvard and M.I.T. But in 1983 the Aquinos decided to return to the Philippines and challenge Marcos in the parliamentary elections.

On August 21, Begnino was assassinated in Manila. Corazon Aquino led 1 million people in the funeral procession and at her husband's grave promised to continue his fight.

Overnight, the little woman in yellow became the worldwide symbol of opposition to Marcos. When Begnino's supporters suggested she run against Marcos, she replied, "Gosh, what do I know about being president?"

On December 2, Philippine courts overturned the convictions of those charged with her husband's assassination. Corazon Aquino secluded herself in a convent for a day of prayer and fasting. When she entered the sanctuary, she prayed, "as I had never prayed before, saying, 'Please, Lord, tell me what to do.'"

Corazon decided to run for president. The election was hotly contested—ballot boxes were stolen and voters were harassed by army troops.

On February 25, 1986, both Marcos and Aquino held inaugurations. Under pressure from the Reagan administration, Marcos went into exile in Hawaii.

When asked by *Time* reporters, "Do you believe God has a plan for you?" Mrs. Aquino answered, "God has a plan for all of us, and it is for each of us to find out what that plan is. I can tell you that I never thought the plan was for me to be President. But it seems it is."

So a woman whose last office was sixth-grade valedictorian is president of the Philippines today. Prayer is still an important element in her decision making.

Father, Corazon Aquino reminds us of the reality that, with You on our side, we can accomplish more than we imagine. When life gets tough, remind us of her courage.

January 26

Julia Morgan, architect
January 26, 1872–February 2, 1957

Julia Morgan was one of the first women ever to enroll at the School of Engineering at the University of California at Berkeley. She became the first woman archi-

"By wisdom a house is built, and through under-

33

tect licensed in California and, in 1921, the first woman admitted to the American Institute of Architects, based on her accomplishments.

While studying in Paris, Julia met Mrs. Phoebe Apperson Hearst, mother of publisher William Randolph Hearst. Her friendship with Mrs. Hearst, who was a strong supporter of Mills College, led to Julia's selection as campus architect.

Perhaps her most outstanding work was William Randolph Hearst's monumental castle, San Simeon. Hearst bought many castles and churches across Europe, had them dismantled, and shipped them to California. Julia Morgan's task was to incorporate all of his whims into one structure. The project took twenty-three years and cost millions. He never allowed her to put on a permanent roof, lest it give the impression that his dream had been completed. More than 600,000 visitors tour San Simeon each year, unaware that a single adult made beauty out of Hearst's chaotic ideas.

Julia Morgan never showed partiality in her work and time; whether she was building a millionaire's guesthouse or one of the many YWCAs she designed, each had her full attention and creativity.

Julia Morgan worked hard and expected her associates to do the same. She opened the door for women in architecture. To this day, a Julia Morgan house commands top resale dollar.

standing it is established."

Proverbs 24:3

Father, help us to invest ourselves in things that will last long after us.

January 27

Charles Dodgson (Lewis Carroll), writer
January 27, 1832–January 14, 1898

Charles Dodgson loved children. They added zest to the Oxford mathematician's life. He published *Elementary Treatise on Determinants* in 1867, *Euclid and His Modern Rivals* in 1879, *Curiosa Mathematica* in 1885, but no one reads those books today.

Had he not had a niece he dearly loved, Alice Liddell, Dodgson's legacy would long ago have been forgotten. The books he wrote for her, *Alice's Adventures in Wonderland* and *Through the Looking Glass,* became classics for children and many adults who are charmed by his rich symbolism, satire, and parody.

"Impress them on your children. Talk about them when you sit at home and when you walk along the road, when you lie down and when you get up."

Deuteronomy 6:7

"What is the use of a book," thought Alice, "without pictures or conversations?"

"I can't explain myself, I'm afraid, sir," said Alice, "because I'm not myself, you see."

"A slow sort of country!" said the Queen. "Now, here, you see, it takes all the running you can do, to keep in the same place. If you want to get somewhere else, you must run at least twice as fast as that."

Charles Dodgson's words have lasted and no doubt will be loved by future generations of children.

Key Thought: "Speak in French when you can't think of the English for a thing—turn out your toes when you walk—and RE-MEMBER WHO YOU ARE."

January 28

William Tudor, author
January 28, 1779–March 9, 1830

Like many other Harvard graduates in 1796, William Tudor entered the business world. He attempted to develop an ice business in the West Indies with his brother, but the endeavor left him unfulfilled. Tudor subsequently ran for the Massachusetts legislature and was elected. The turning point in his career may have been when he was selected to deliver the annual Fourth of July speech in Boston in 1809. Two editions of his speech sold out, and Tudor took up writing full-time.

In 1815, at age thirty-six, Tudor founded *The North American Review;* he was a major contributor to the first four volumes. Tudor helped start the Boston Athenaeum, a private library and art museum for Boston's literary community. Because of his interests in history, he offered a plan to buy Bunker Hill and develop an appropriate historical monument. He was an enthusiastic member of the Massachusetts Historical Society.

Tudor published two books of letters and criticism before his appointment, in 1823, as United States consul in Lima. In 1827, he became chargé d'affaires in Rio de Janeiro. While at his diplomatic post he wrote *Gebel Teir,* an allegory on international politics.

Tudor's health suffered in the climate, and he died at his post of a tropical fever in 1830.

"Do not be anxious about anything, but in everything, by prayer and petition, with thanksgiving, present your requests to God."

Philippians 4:6

Father, remind us that success does not always come early in life.

Simeon Borden, mechanic and engineer
January 29, 1798–October 28, 1856

Simeon Borden dropped out of school when he was thirteen to take care of his family's farm after his father's death. Six years later, his mother died, and Simeon settled the estates of both parents. Once free of the farm, he devoted his attention to metalworking, which had long interested him. Within two years, he was superintendent of a metalworking shop.

In 1830, the state of Massachusetts required Boston and other cities to conduct a trigonometrical study to enhance the accuracy of its maps and boundaries. Borden was hired to construct a base bar, the standard for all measuring, for the measurement process. His base bar was fifty feet long and encased in a metal tube so that the measure would be exact whatever the temperature (metal expands under heat and contracts in the cold). Borden's base bar was the most accurate in the United States and represented a major breakthrough in engineering.

Over the ensuing years, Borden was involved in the mapping, serving as chief surveyor after 1834. Afterwards, Borden worked as an engineer for several railroads. Some of his research was used in a case argued before the United States Supreme Court in 1844 that settled a long-term boundary dispute between Massachusetts and Rhode Island.

In the last years of his life, Simeon Borden often appeared in area courts as an expert witness.

"Then the Lord said, 'Look, I am setting a plumb line among my people Israel; I will spare them no longer.' "

Amos 7:8

Key Point: Standards are vital in the physical world and in the spiritual world. High standards lead to high achievement.

Ella Cara Deloria, linguist
January 30, 1888–February 12, 1971

Ella Deloria was born a Dakota Sioux Indian. Her Indian name was Anpetu Waste Win, or Beautiful Day Woman. Ella's father was an Episcopal priest, so she attended mission school as a child. She later received her bach-

"From these the . . . peoples spread out into their territories by their

elor's degree from Columbia University and began teaching at Haskell Indian School in Lawrence, Kansas, in 1925.

Ella's deep love of the Dakota language and culture attracted the interest of Frank Boas, a leading anthropologist. Boas suggested that she devote herself to studying her people and culture. He provided her a financial stipend, and Deloria quit her teaching post to begin the project. In 1941, she and Boas coauthored *Dakota Grammar*. The next year she compiled *Dakota Texts*, containing the Indian myths and tales she had collected in her research.

Ella's research had lasting significance because it records accurately the native language of the Dakotas. Moreover, it was researched by a woman, which emphasized a feminine cultural perspective.

Ella's scholarship always came second to her concern for her family and her Christian faith. Her research was hampered by constant financial strain. Nevertheless, her thoroughness as a scholar made her contribution to Indian anthropology lasting.

clans within their nations, each with its own language."

Genesis 10:5

Father, Ella Deloria's work reminds us that, although we are from many tribes and cultures, in You we become one people—the people of faith and grace.

January 31

Alice Bennett, physician
January 31, 1851–May 31, 1925

Alice Bennett graduated from medical school in 1876 and began her practice in the slums of Philadelphia. She was appointed to the faculty of the Women's Medical College of Pennsylvania and taught anatomy and maintained a private practice for the next four years. In 1880, she completed a Ph.D. in anatomy at the University of Pennsylvania, the first woman to do so.

In July 1880, Dr. Bennett was appointed superintendent of the women's division of the State Hospital for the Insane, again the first woman to hold such a position. Alice immediately launched a reform program eliminating straitjackets, chains, and cells, methods she thought archaic. Rather, Dr. Bennett developed a bond of respect between patient and attendant. She introduced handicrafts, painting, and music programs—

"When they came to Jesus, they saw the man who had been possessed by the legion of demons, sitting there, dressed and in his right mind; and they were afraid."

Mark 5:15

innovations that were soon copied by other mental hospitals. Dr. Bennett was published widely in medical journals on the treatment of the insane.

In 1900, she returned to private practice, then in 1910 she became affiliated with New York Infirmary for Women and Children, serving as head of the outpatient department and delivering more than two thousand babies during the next fifteen years.

Father, for those who model compassion and mercy, we give You thanks. Help us to make time in our busy schedules to be kind and considerate.

February 1

Lydia Bailey, printer
February 1, 1779–February 21, 1869

Robert Bailey's death in 1808 left his wife and four children in dire financial stress. But after ten years of marriage and working with her husband in the printing business, twenty-nine-year-old Lydia decided to keep the business going. "Impossible," her competitors mumbled. "She won't last six months!"

Poet Philip Freneau, upon learning of Lydia's condition, admired her spunk and asked her to print the third edition of his *Poems* in 1808. Her determination paid off, and she soon gained printing contracts from the city of Philadelphia. Her work was of such high quality that, from 1830 to 1850, Lydia Bailey was the official printer for the city. Her son, Robert, began working with her as soon as he was tall enough to stand at a press.

At age eighty-two, grieving over Robert's untimely death in 1861 and unable to adjust to the new printing technology of steam presses, Lydia retired.

She accomplished a great deal in rearing her family and in training a legion of printers who were outstanding craftsmen. The *Philadelphia North American* praised her as a person who "had enjoyed women's rights to the fullest though living before a formal exposition of that doctrine."

"She sets about her work vigorously; her arms are strong for her tasks."

Proverbs 31:17

Father, the death of a spouse is not our death. Give us the strength to survive our loss.

February 2

Eliza Agnew, missionary pioneer
February 2, 1807–June 14, 1883

When Eliza Agnew was converted on December 28, 1823, she had no idea how the Lord would use her life. Soon after her conversion, Eliza began to entertain the idea of missionary work, but few denominations sent unmarried women to mission fields at that time. Eliza worked in the Sunday school in her church and distributed tracts and religious materials.

After the death of her parents, thirty-two-year-old Eliza applied to the American Board of Commissioners for Foreign Missions in Boston and was appointed to Ceylon. On January 17, 1840, she arrived in Ceylon and began her work in Oodoobille as a teacher in a boarding school. This was to be her home for the next forty-three years, with only one brief furlough.

Out of one thousand students in the school, more than 60 percent became Christians. Eliza stayed in touch with the graduates, often visiting them in their homes. Some scholars believe that Christianity developed significant roots in Ceylon because of her work. Many of Eliza's girls married doctors, lawyers, and other professionals.

A woman known for her devotion to prayer, her watchword was, "I'll tell the Master."

> "I tell you the truth, wherever the gospel is preached throughout the world, what she has done will also be told, in memory of her."
>
> **Mark 14:9**

Key Thought: Sometimes the secret to success is staying in one place long enough to make an impact.

February 3

James Clark McReynolds, Supreme Court justice
February 3, 1862–August 24, 1946

James Clark McReynolds graduated from Vanderbilt University and earned his law degree from the University of Virginia. As assistant United States attorney general from 1903 to 1907, he earned a reputation as a trustbuster. After establishing a private law practice in New York, he became attorney general of the United States in the Wilson administration and vigorously prosecuted violators of the Sherman Antitrust Act.

A legal conservative and strict constructionist,

> "For the authorities are God's servants. . . ."
>
> **Romans 13:6**

39

A legal conservative and strict constructionist, McReynolds was appointed by Wilson to the Supreme Court in 1914. He quickly became known for his opposition to the growth of government power and as an advocate of states' rights. Never in his twenty-six-year tenure did Justice McReynolds write an opinion reversing a lower court.

McReynolds frequently dissented on Supreme Court decisions. From 1937 to 1941, he dissented 119 times; in his tenure on the bench, Justice McReynolds set the record of 310 dissents.

McReynolds spent his last years in quiet retirement, winning national attention when he "adopted" thirty-three British refugee children during World War II.

Only after his death was it learned he had remained single in honor of Miss Will Ella Pearson, whom he had loved and who died in 1885 at the age of twenty-four.

Father, there is a place for dissent. Give us the courage to stand for our convictions once we are assured that our convictions are Yours.

February 4

Dietrich Bonhoeffer, theologian
February 4, 1906–April 23, 1945

World War II was grinding to a halt. Clearly, the Nazis were defeated, but now they were executing their enemies within Germany. On April 23, 1945, at dawn, a young single adult was led from his cell, stripped naked, and tied to a tree. Within moments, with a simple order to the firing squad, a great theologian was dead.

Dietrich Bonhoeffer received his doctoral degree from the University of Berlin at age twenty-one; his dissertation had been a study of the communion of the saints.

Bonhoeffer's theology was rooted in rejection of self and a commitment to others. "Christian brotherhood is not an ideal which we must realize; it is rather a reality created by God in Christ in which we may participate."

But Bonhoeffer had growing questions about Hitler's rise to power. When other Lutheran pastors caved in, he spoke out against the Nazis. In 1933, in a sermon broadcast on Berlin radio, Bonhoeffer flayed the Germans for pandering to a leader who would become an idol and then a "misleader." The broadcast ended before Bonhoeffer's sermon.

"How good and pleasant it is when brothers live together in unity!"

Psalm 133:1

As war with England loomed, friends wanted him to leave Germany. He accepted a professorship at Union Theological Seminary in New York. However, he could not stay. "I shall have no right to participate in the reconstruction of Christian life in Germany after the war if I do not share the trials of this time with my people."

Returning to Germany and avoiding military service, Bonhoeffer became actively involved in the resistance movement. In 1943, he was involved in an attempt to assassinate Hitler and was arrested.

But even prison became a place to minister. Kind guards often helped him smuggle out scraps of paper with notes to friends (which later comprised *Letters and Papers from Prison*). They also left his cell unlocked, so he could move among the cells, ministering to other prisoners. Particularly during the Allied bombing of Berlin, when prisoners screamed and beat their fists against the locked doors, Pastor Bonhoeffer was there: praying, comforting, and in more than one instance, holding prisoners until the bombing stopped.

After the war, his books became best-sellers. Bonhoeffer's words of warning must again be heard: "Cheap grace is grace without discipleship, grace without the cross, grace without Jesus Christ, living and incarnate."

"Thou has granted me many blessings; Now let me also accept what is hard from thy hand. Thou wilt lay on me no more than I can bear. Thou makest all things work together for good for thy children."

Dietrich Bonhoeffer

February 5

Adlai Stevenson, diplomat
February 5, 1900–July 14, 1965

Adlai Stevenson came to politics from a background in newspapers and law. He was elected governor of Illinois as a reform Democrat in 1948. The next year his wife sued him for divorce. Stevenson served his term as a single man in the governor's mansion, often inviting friends to come and spend the weekend with him.

In 1952 and 1956, he was the Democratic candidate for president but was defeated both times in landslides by Dwight Eisenhower. In both races, his divorce became an issue: If he could not govern his household, how could he govern the nation? After his defeats, Stevenson worked closely with Mrs. Eleanor Roosevelt to revitalize the Democratic party.

"A merry heart doeth good like a medicine: but a broken spirit drieth the bones."

Proverbs 17:22 KJV

He believed in active participation in the political process by common men. He reminded his supporters in his concession speech of 1956, "Take heart—there are things more precious than political victory; there is the right to political contest.

"Democracy cannot be saved by supermen, but only by the unswerving devotion and goodness of millions of little men."

In 1961, Stevenson became ambassador to the United Nations, where he served until his death in 1965.

Father, it is so easy to fail to take seriously our responsibilities as citizens. Remind us of the price others have paid so that we may enjoy our freedom.

February 6

Philander Deming, court stenographer
February 6, 1829–February 9, 1915

Americans are guaranteed by the Constitution a right to a speedy, fair trial by a jury of their peers. One of the accompanying rights is to a record of the court proceedings.

Philander Deming helped develop that tradition. As a boy, he taught himself shorthand. After graduation from college and law school, he went to work as a legislative reporter. However, in November 1865, Deming demonstrated the value of verbatim reporting of court proceedings, which soon became an essential ingredient in the appellate process.

In 1865, Deming became the official stenographer of the supreme court for the third judicial district of New York, holding that assignment for seventeen years. His handbook, *The Court Stenographer,* contributed to the development of professional court stenographers.

In the 1870s, Philander Deming published in *Atlantic Magazine* the first of his sketches on people and places in the Adirondacks and Hudson Valley of New York.

Deming was quiet and withdrawn—even his pastor had difficulty having conversations with him—but was an early advocate of walking.

"Be completely humble and gentle; be patient, bearing with one another."

Ephesians 4:2

Father, thank You for the gift of a fair trial and for those such as Philander Deming, who have made that gift a reality for so many people.

Hazel Hall, poet
February 7, 1886–May 11, 1924

Disaster struck twelve-year-old Hazel Hall when she lost the use of her legs. Confined to a wheelchair, Hazel spent much of her time sewing and writing poetry. Although she did not publish until she was thirty, her work was featured in some of the nation's leading periodicals.

Poetry magazine honored her in 1921 with its Young Poet's Award, and that led to the publication of three of her books: *Curtains* (1921); *Walkers* (1923); and *Cry of Time,* which was published posthumously.

Hazel's world, largely confined to her home, provided time for dreams and fantasies that stimulated her writing. She wrote about the bride and the bishop for whom she sewed, and she wrote powerfully about physical surroundings: the walls and windowsills of her room.

Because of her deteriorating health, dark themes such as death, grief, and frustration appeared more frequently in her last writings.

Hazel captured the moods of many single adults. Though trapped by her body, she possessed a free soul.

> **"He gives strength to the weary and increases the power of the weak."**
>
> **Isaiah 40:29**

Father, help us today to rise above our circumstances and limitations. Free our spirits from the emotional fetters that bind.

Jennie Evelyn Hussey, hymn writer
February 8, 1874–1958

Very little is known about Miss Jennie Hussey. She is remembered for only one song, but millions of people can sing that song from memory.

Jennie began writing poetry when she was quite young. Her entire life was spent on the family farm in Concord, New Hampshire, caring for her invalid sister.

Her poem "Lead Me to Calvary" was first published in hymn form in 1921 when it appeared in *New Songs of Praise and Power, No. 3.* It is particularly popular during the Easter season.

> **"I have been crucified with Christ and I no longer live, but Christ lives in me."**
>
> **Galatians 2:20**

King of my life I crown Thee now—
Thine shall the glory be;
Lest I forget Thy thorn-crowned brow,
Lead me to Calvary.

May I be willing, Lord, to bear
Daily the cross for Thee;
Even Thy cup of grief to share—
Thou has borne all for me.

Jennie Hussey's words may have been directly tied to her sister's physical care, which became a "cross" for both of the women.

The chorus is appropriate for many of us in this fast-lane generation:

Lest I forget Gethsemane,
Lest I forget Thine agony,
Lest I forget Thy love for me,
Lead me to Calvary.*

Father, sometimes we construct a "comfortable" Jesus in our lives. Let us not forget that Jesus as a single adult faced Jerusalem and a cross. Lead us daily back to Calvary.

* Copyright © 1921. Renewal 1949 by Hope Publishing Co., Carol Stream, IL. All rights reserved. Used by permission.

February 9

Samuel Jones Tilden, politician
February 9, 1814–August 4, 1886

Samuel Jones Tilden was admitted to the New York bar in 1841. Long a political activist for Martin Van Buren, Tilden became active in the free-soil movement, but because of infighting within the Democratic party, Tilden turned his attention to his law practice. He became quite wealthy and successful in dealing with railroads.

Although he opposed Lincoln and the Civil War, Tilden did encourage the rapid defeat of the South. He also supported Andrew Johnson's liberal Reconstruction policies. As head of the New York Democratic party from 1866 to 1874, he ousted the Boss Tweed machine in New York City and lobbied for legislative remedies to emerging urban problems. He also helped reorganize the state judiciary.

"A heart at peace gives life to the body, but envy rots the bones."

Proverbs 14:30

Nominated for president by the Democrats in 1876, he won the general election. However, the results in Oregon, Louisiana, South Carolina, and Florida were challenged by Republican candidate Rutherford B. Hayes. When an electoral commission was forced to investigate, they ruled Hayes, not Tilden, the winner.

Despite the defeat, Tilden remained active in politics. Samuel Tilden left his considerable estate to establish a free public library in New York City.

Father, defeat is not always a strange word to us. Give us courage to face our defeats without becoming victims.

February 10

Walter Malone, jurist and poet
February 10, 1866–May 18, 1915

Walter Malone made his living as a lawyer and jurist. For some twenty years he was a circuit court judge and jurist in Memphis, Tennessee. He grew up in a large family and sold his first poem at age twelve. Malone's first book of poetry, *Claribel and Other Poems*, was published before he was sixteen.

The poem for which Malone is best remembered is "Opportunity." He wrote it in response to a poem written by a former Kansas senator that suggested that opportunity only knocks on our door once.

"Always be prepared to give an answer to everyone who asks you to give the reason for the hope that you have."

1 Peter 3:15

> They do me wrong who say I come no more,
> When once I knock and fail to find you in;
> For every day I stand outside your door,
> And bid you wake, and rise to fight and win.
> Wail not for precious chances passed away,
> Weep not for golden ages on the wane;
> Each night I burn the records of the day;
> At sunrise every soul is born again.

Malone wrote that poem in less than a half hour and mailed it to *Munsey's Magazine*, a popular periodical of that day. He received ten dollars in payment from the magazine.

Once it was printed in 1905, no one could keep up with the demands for reprints. Businessmen read it to motivate their sales staffs, publishers printed it on calendars. But it was from the lips of the golden orator of that day, William Jennings Bryan, that it gained its popularity.

Father, we thank You for the opportunities that come our way. Help us to treasure each one. Keep us from mourning the past. Point us to the futures You prepare for each one of us.

45

February 11

Alexander Hamilton Stephens, Confederate vice president
February 11, 1812–March 4, 1883

Although Alexander Stephens was born into a poor Georgia family, a mentor recognized his potential and paid the young boy's way through the University of Georgia, where Stephens graduated first in the class of 1832. After a series of jobs, he passed the Georgia bar, and in 1836 he was elected to the legislature. In 1843, Stephens was elected a United States congressman and was a leading force in the Whig party for sixteen years.

Stephens was a unionist in a time when most of his Southern colleagues were leaning toward secession. Although he retained his stance at the Georgia Secessionist Convention in 1861, Stephens finally signed the Declaration of Secession. Later, at the Montgomery convention that created the Confederacy, he argued for a conservative constitution. The first Confederate Congress elected him as Jefferson Davis's vice president.

Davis and Stephens had philosophical differences. Eventually Stephens returned to Georgia and formed an opposition coalition with Governor Joseph Brown. In 1864, he led the Confederate Senate in a futile attempt to stop the war when it became evident that the Confederates could not win.

In 1865, Northern troops arrested Stephens; he served six months in a Boston prison. When he was paroled, he was elected Georgia's new United States senator; however, the Senate would not accept his election as valid. That rejection turned Stephens into a strong opponent of Reconstruction. Eventually Alexander Stephens bought the *Atlanta Southern Sun* and used its editorial page to nettle the Yankees.

"Your faithfulness continues through all generations; you established the earth, and it endures."

Psalm 119:90

Key Thought: Peace of mind is the result of being faithful to our convictions, even if it means going against the tide of public opinion.

February 12

Abram Piatt Andrew, congressman
February 12, 1873–June 3, 1936

Abram Andrew earned his doctorate in economics from Harvard in 1900, after a two-year stint at three European universities. For ten years he taught economics at

"Why then didn't you put my money on deposit, so that

Harvard and had a lasting influence on many students, particularly one named Franklin D. Roosevelt.

While teaching at Harvard, Dr. Andrew edited publications for the National Monetary Commission, which was working to institute banking reforms. He was an aide to Senator Nelson Aldrich on his European study tour of banks in 1908 and became part of a core of economists consulting with the senator on economic reform.

Andrew spent eight months as director of the United States Mint under President Taft and two years as assistant secretary of the treasury. At the outbreak of World War I, he organized the American Field Service, made up of college volunteers serving in Europe before America officially entered the war. In September 1917, Andrew was commissioned a major in the army.

After the war, the much-decorated humanitarian returned to Massachusetts, helped found the American Legion, and ran for Congress. Andrew served from 1923 to 1936, where—as a conservative—he never hesitated to take tough stands. He supported a large navy but repeatedly warned against deficit spending by the federal government. His pleas fell on deaf ears.

Abram Andrew died when he was sixty-three. At his request, the funeral was jointly conducted by a Catholic priest, a Jewish rabbi, and a Baptist minister.

when I came back, I could have collected it with interest?"

Luke 19:23

Father, Abram Andrew invested his life in warning people against debt. What about my debts? Am I a good steward of those resources that You have given me?

February 13

Ehrman Syme Nadal, author
February 13, 1843–July 26, 1922

Ehrman Nadal demonstrated the value of writing as an avocation. He may have begun to write because his father was a writer and minister. He held a number of jobs during his lifetime, usually writing on the side.

For eighteen months, Nadal was a staff secretary at the United States embassy in London. When he returned to the United States, he began writing on civil-service reform. His first editorial, written as a free-lancer, led to a position with the *Saturday Evening Post*.

On June 8, 1877, he was appointed second secretary to the London diplomatic mission and spent the next

"He seldom reflects on the days of his life, because God keeps him occupied with gladness of heart."

Ecclesiastes 5:20

six years in England. Beyond his diplomatic responsibilities, he found time to write essays on life in England. His *Impressions of London Social Life*, published in 1875, is still valued for its candid observations about social life in that time period. A second collection, *Essays at Home and Elsewhere*, also proved popular.

Notes of a Professional Exile, published in 1895, reflected Nadal's interaction with German and English tourists. Later in life, he compiled *A Virginian Voice,* composed of essays published in various publications during a twenty-year period. His study of Henry James was well received in literary circles.

Father, the balanced life is what You want for all of us. Remind us that we can find meaning and make a difference in areas other than our work.

February 14

Marie Marguerite Bouvet, linguist
February 14, 1865–May 27, 1915

After her father lost his fortune in the Civil War and died, Marie Bouvet went to France to live with her paternal grandparents. When she returned to New Orleans, she attended the school where her mother taught.

After her graduation from St. Mary's College, Marie taught French and compiled *Fleurs des Poetes et des Prosateurs Francais* in 1900. Soon, writing became more important to her than teaching. Although her primary audience was children, because of her writing style, many adults enjoyed her books, too. Most of the books were set in foreign countries and were richly filled with local mannerisms and customs.

Sweet William (1890), which describes the heroics of William the Conquerer, is the book best recognized by children's librarians. *Tales of an Old Chateau* (1899) offered children insights into the French Revolution.

Marie made two prolonged visits to Europe to gather historical details and local color to make her writing more realistic.

Marie's French charm won her many friends on both sides of the Atlantic.

"May the God of hope fill you with all joy and peace as you trust in him, so that you may overflow with hope by the power of the Holy Spirit."

Romans 15:13

Key Thought: Whatever our arena of service or our occupation, that place offers single adults an opportunity to overflow with hope.

Susan B. Anthony, reformer
February 15, 1820–March 13, 1906

Susan B. Anthony believed in the equality of the sexes before God because of her Quaker upbringing. She was a quiet woman who left teaching to help manage the family farm. But Susan, who founded the New York State Women's Temperance Society, would emerge as a leader to be reckoned with.

Susan, a natural organizer, teamed up with Elizabeth Cady Stanton in 1868 to create the Working Woman's Association. Their early partnership led to the enactment of laws in New York giving property rights to women, particularly widows.

In 1869, she and Mrs. Stanton founded the National Woman Suffrage Association, the first women's organization devoted to getting the right to vote passed. In 1872, Susan was arrested for voting in the presidential election but refused to pay the fine.

By the turn of the century, Susan B. Anthony was recognized as the foremost woman leader in the country. But at eighty she was tired and turned the reins over to younger leaders. At the last suffrage convention she attended, aware that the Nineteenth Amendment still had a long way to go, she cheered the delegates with this thought, "Failure Is Impossible!"

Twenty years passed before the amendment was ratified.

Susan B. Anthony gave American women the right to vote.

"There is neither Jew nor Greek, slave nor free, male nor female, for you are all one in Christ Jesus."

Galatians 3:28

Father, remind us that big victories don't always come overnight. Remind us that although we may never see the victory, by our work and energy and commitment, others will.

Mary Elizabeth Switzer, federal official
February 16, 1900–October 16, 1971

Deserted by her father and orphaned by her mother's death, Mary Switzer was raised by two aunts and an uncle who encouraged her to make the world different. She attended Radcliffe College on scholarships and

"When you give a banquet, invite the poor, the crippled, the lame, the blind,

49

studied international law. After graduation, she went to work in Washington, D.C.

Eventually, Switzer became director of the Office of Vocational Rehabilitation and an activist in educating the public to the needs of the handicapped. Her vision was to meet "the total vocational needs of the mentally as well as physically handicapped."

Mary challenged federal, state, and local governments and private organizations to accept one goal: to help *all* disabled persons find satisfying work. Through her lobbying, the Vocational Rehabilitation Act of 1954 was passed, providing funds for research, for training specialists, and for building comprehensive rehabilitation centers.

In 1970, when Mary retired as administrator of the Social and Rehabilitation Service of the Department of Health, Education and Welfare, John Gardner, the former secretary, commented, "She made light shine around her." No one in Congress could ever refuse an appropriations request from this single adult. She made the needs of the handicapped hers.

and you will be blessed."

Luke 14:13, 14

Father, it is possible to be so wrapped up in ourselves that we forget single adults who are handicapped. Bring their needs to our attention.

February 17

Uriah Atherton Boyden, engineer and inventor
February 17, 1804–October 17, 1879

Uriah Boyden never completed a formal education. At age twenty-one he began working for his inventor brother, Seth. During the industrial development of New England, he gained experience by working on the survey team for two railroads.

Daringly, at age twenty-nine, without an academic degree or financial backing, he opened an office in Boston, advertising himself as an engineer. Three years later, he began a two-year stint supervising the construction of the Nashua and Lowell Railroad.

Boyden then worked for a manufacturing concern designing hydraulic pumps. In 1844, he invented a turbine waterwheel that won a wide reputation among profit-minded mill owners for its operating efficiency and consistent generation of horsepower. Through a group of inventions, such as the hook-gauge, he be-

"What has been will be again, what has been done will be done again; there is nothing new under the sun."

Ecclesiastes 1:9

came wealthy. Hydraulics was a rapidly expanding component in the industrial development of America, and Boyden was a key player. In almost every mill or power plant in the country, one could find a Boyden invention.

In his retirement, he focused his interests on pure science, particularly the study of water and light. After his death, his estate financed the construction of several observatories. Although lacking a formal education, Uriah Boyden made a significant contribution to America's industrial growth.

Key Point: The lack of a formal education did not keep Uriah Boyden from making his mark. Nor should it keep you from your dream.

February 18

Henry Martyn, translator
February 18, 1781–October 16, 1812

Henry Martyn established himself as a brilliant scholar at Cambridge his first year there; by Christmas, he was ranked number one in his class. His sister influenced him to begin exploring religious issues. Through reading of Scripture, he was converted. "The work is real," he explained, "I can no more doubt it than I can doubt my own existence. . . . I am walking quite another way, though I am incessantly stumbling in that way."

During his fourth year of study, Henry began reading about the exploits of David Brainerd among the Indians. Under shade trees along a river, the young student repeated Brainerd's prayer: "Here I am, Lord. Send me to the ends of the earth; send me to the rough, the savage Pagans of the wilderness. . . ."

Martyn presented himself as a candidate to the Church Missionary Society and began serving with the leader of evangelical England, Charles Simeon, at Holy Trinity Church. In the meantime, he had fallen in love with a woman named Lydia. However, because she had a broken engagement (and due to the integrity of an engagement in those days), she did not feel free to marry Henry until the other man married. At times Henry thought his love for Lydia and his hunger for mission service seemed "a deadly rivalry." Henry could not wait. "If God made me, and wills my happiness, as I do not doubt, then He is providing for my good by separating me from her."

"Should you then seek great things for yourself? Seek them not."

Jeremiah 45:5

51

During the next seven years, Martyn traveled to India, Persia, and Arabia. He translated the New Testament into Arabic, Persian, and Hindustani. After his last translation, Martyn decided to return home to England, despite a serious bout of fever.

On horseback, riding toward Constantinople, Henry grew sicker; he could barely stay in the saddle. He died on October 16, 1812, and was buried in an unmarked grave alongside the road.

One biographer described Martyn's life as "a meteor-like spirit which burned and flamed as it passed across the first 12 years of the nineteenth century."

Key Thought: "May the Lord, in mercy to my soul, save me from setting up an idol of any sort in His room, as I do by preferring a work professedly for Him to communion with Him."

Henry Martyn

February 19

Bertha Munro, college dean
February 19, 1887–January 19, 1983

Bertha Munro was returning to Boston from Washington, D.C., in 1911, when the train on which she was riding derailed and she was trapped in the wreckage. She lived the rest of her life with a weak back and crippled hand, but during those hours of waiting to be rescued, she made a final commitment to her life's work.

In 1916, she graduated with a master's degree from Radcliffe and then taught at Indiana's Taylor University. Three years later she was invited to be a founding faculty member at a small college opening near Boston. Soon Bertha Munro was dean of Eastern Nazarene College. She later wrote, "From 1919 on the story of my life is in one sense the story of Eastern Nazarene College."

Balancing a full teaching load, administrative work, being a friend and counselor, Munro commuted across town to complete her Ph.D. at Harvard. After two years of work on her dissertation, she discovered that her thesis had been duplicated in a book published in England. Rather than abandoning that dissertation and finding a new topic, she decided not to complete her degree; her students and her college needed her.

Munro poured herself into the college and into her students. Her goal was to create a Christian liberal arts college in the shadow of Boston's prestigious academic giants. Bertha Munro did just that.

"I am coming to you now, but I say these things while I am still in the world, so that they may have the full measure of my joy within them."

John 17:13

Father, Miss Munro made a difference. She lived through

52

She is most remembered for what she called the Munro Doctrine:

- Truth cannot contradict truth.
- God will not waste a consecrated life.
- Persons are more than things.
- Not somehow but triumphantly.

personal tragedies and turned them into triumphs. Remind us of the wisdom of her words: "not somehow BUT triumphantly!"

February 20

Angelina Grimké, abolitionist
February 20, 1805–October 26, 1879

Angelina Grimké was only twenty-four years old when the elders expelled her from the church. The expulsion was of Angelina's own doing: She had confronted church leadership and urged them to speak out against slavery. This was 1829, in Charleston, South Carolina.

Polite Southern society forced Angelina to leave Charleston. She joined her sister, an abolitionist speaker, in the North. Angelina challenged her audiences:

"Who knows but that you have come to royal position for such a time as this?"

Esther 4:14

> I know you [women] do not make the laws, but I know that you are the wives and mothers, the sisters and daughters of those who do; and if you really suppose that we can do nothing to overthrow slavery you are greatly mistaken. . . . Let your sentiments be known. . . . Try to persuade your husband, father, brothers and sons that slavery is a crime against God and man.

Revolutionary words in the 1830s.

On February 21, 1838, Angelina became the first woman in American history to address a legislative body. So many men crowded into the Massachusetts statehouse that it was feared the gallery would collapse. The chairman fought to maintain order in the chamber.

> I stand before you as a southerner, exiled from the land of my birth by the sound of the

lash and the piteous cry of the slave. I stand before you a repentant slaveowner. . . . I feel that I owe it to the suffering slave and to the deluded master, to my country and to the world, to do all I can to overturn a system of complicated crimes, built upon the broken hearts and prostrate bodies of my countrymen in chains and cemented by the blood, sweat and tears of my sisters in chains.

The *Boston Gazette* editorially stated that it was obvious why no man had married such a woman.

Miss Grimké opened the door for women to be heard on the issues of the day.

Key Thought: "If my Heavenly Father opens a door . . . it is sinful for any human being to resign his or her conscience to any society or individual."

Angelina Grimké

February 21

Barbara Jordan, member of Congress
February 21, 1936–

Barbara Jordan found herself in the glare of the public spotlight as one of the thirty-eight members of the House Judiciary Committee that weighed the potential impeachment of Richard Nixon. Much of the debate behind the scenes was wordy: What exactly was an impeachable offense? Everyone had an opinion. But when Barbara Jordan spoke, the nation listened. Bruce Morton, of CBS News, labeled her "the best mind on the committee." She always chose her words carefully.

The daughter of a black Houston clergyman, Barbara Jordan used to say, "I always wanted to do something unusual. I never wanted to be run-of-the-mill." For a while, she considered becoming a pharmacist. "But then I thought, whoever heard of an outstanding pharmacist?" She remained undecided until she heard a lawyer, Edith Sampson, speak at her high school career day. The black woman's words captured Barbara's imagination.

Her course was set. By 1959, Jordan had developed a reputation as a spellbinding orator and champion debater, had a law degree from Boston University, and had passed the Texas and Massachusetts bar exams. Her first law office in Houston was at her mother's dining room table.

"The words of the wise are like goads, their collected sayings like firmly embedded nails."

Ecclesiastes 12:11

In 1966, Barbara became the first black woman elected to the Texas State Senate. She ran for Congress in 1971 in Houston's Eighteenth District. She ran on her record: "I can get things done." She won by 66,000 votes.

Jordan did not rule out marriage but preferred to remain single to concentrate on her career. "Politics is almost totally consuming. A good marriage requires that one attend to it and not treat it as another hobby."

Based on her powerful oratory during Democratic national conventions, many assumed Barbara Jordan might be destined for higher office, but she stunned the political world by leaving Congress to teach political science at the University of Texas.

Father, so often we cling to man's standards of success and failure rather than to Yours. We thank You for the example of Barbara Jordan, who never thought defeat to be the final word.

February 22

Walter Washington DeLacy, surveyor
February 22, 1819–May 13, 1892

For bachelor Walter DeLacy, life was one adventure after another. Walter's parents died when he was a child, so he was reared by two single aunts. After four years at Maryland's St. Mary's Catholic College, DeLacy was a candidate for West Point, an appointment that never came through.

Instead, he worked as an engineer for the Illinois Central Railroad, then joined the West Point faculty in 1840 to teach French. In 1846, DeLacy went to Mexico to search for abandoned mines but wound up fighting in the Mexican-American War as a volunteer.

After the war, he worked on survey crews on the thirty-second parallel, surveying from San Antonio to San Diego. In the 1850s, he moved to the Washington Territory and worked on the building of a road between Fort Benton and Walla Walla. In 1860, he went to Montana to look for gold but found more money in trading supplies to miners.

In 1863, DeLacy led a group of miners seeking gold into the Snake River country and discovered Shoshone Lake and the Lower Geyser Basin of Yellowstone. The next year he was hired by the Montana legislature to map the territory. DeLacy produced a map that proved accurate for years to come.

". . . Stand up and praise the Lord your God, who is from everlasting to everlasting. . . ."

Nehemiah 9:5

Key Thought: Some single adults live such adventurous lives, they are never bored. A little adventure will go a long way in enriching your single season.

George Frederick Handel, composer
February 23, 1685–April 14, 1759

George Frederick Handel's name had once been on the lips of the cultural leaders of London, but his last productions had been dismal failures. He was deeply in debt, in risk of being sent to debtor's prison. Against that reality, Handel was asked to write an oratorio for a Dublin charity.

For twenty-three days George wrote. When a servant removed his dinner tray the last night, he noticed tears streaming down the composer's face. On his desk lay the completed work: "The Hallelujah Chorus." Now Handel turned his attention to rehearsing the chorus and orchestra for the first performance. Word spread of the majesty of the music, and the premiere was a packed success. Handel returned to London with applause ringing in his ears, only to find creditors pounding on his door.

Quickly he organized a London concert on March 23, 1743. But from Westminster Abbey to tiny churches, Handel and his *Messiah* were attacked as blasphemous. Imagine dragging the sacred texts into theaters! The concert was boycotted year after year.

Eventually Handel decided to give ownership of the oratorio to the London Foundling Hospital. A benefit performance was arranged in the hospital's chapel, and Londoners ended their boycott.

There was nothing to indicate that first night in Dublin that Handel's music would become the most famous work of music in the world. Ironically, he is remembered not for his oratorios or operas, but for the music he gave away.

"For to us a child is born, to us a son is given, and the government will be on his shoulders. And he will be called Wonderful Counselor, Mighty God, Everlasting Father, Prince of Peace."

Isaiah 9:6

Father, we cling so tightly to our possessions. Make us willing to give up anything to advance Your Kingdom.

February 24
Gladys Aylward, humanitarian
February 24, 1902–January 1, 1970

What can a single adult do with a *no?*

The mission board had said no to Gladys Aylward. "We do not believe you are suited for missionary service," board members told her. Seeking to soften their rejection, the board suggested that Gladys work as a maid for a retired missionary couple.

Gladys said yes to the offer—but only as a way of saving money for purchasing her own fare to China. If the mission board would not send her, she would send herself. By 1932, she had enough to buy a train ticket across Europe to Vladivostok, Russia. She then hitchhiked to Yangcheng, China, where she lived with an elderly Scottish widow.

Feeling restless, she traveled south and established an inn for muleteers, which she called the Inn of the Sixth Happiness. In 1936, to identify with the people she was trying to evangelize, she relinquished her British citizenship.

In 1938, the Japanese invaded China, and Gladys discovered she was considered a threat to the new regime. In 1940, she led one hundred small children from Yangcheng more than one thousand miles to safety.

Although ill, she remained in China another nine years, until the Communists forced her out. After she returned to England, her life was made into the movie, *The Inn of the Sixth Happiness*, which starred Ingrid Bergman.

In 1957, she moved to Taiwan to work with refugees there and to open an orphanage.

> "I am your servant; give me discernment that I may understand your statutes."
>
> **Psalm 119:125**

> *Father, give us the courage to find the opportunity in the no's we encounter.*

February 25
Myra Hess, pianist
February 25, 1890–November 25, 1965

For the past sixteen seasons, Dame Myra Hess had delighted audiences on both sides of the Atlantic. She was one of the largest box-office attractions in the musical world, as well as one of the most consistently acclaimed pianists.

> "When the foundations are being destroyed, what can the righteous do?"
>
> **Psalm 11:3**

However, London, the home of Miss Hess, was nightly being bombed by the Germans. Yet in the depression of the bombing, Myra knew the power of music to lift the spirit, so she started giving noonday concerts five days a week in the cupola of the National Gallery. At the first concert, on October 10, 1939, she explained: "I want to keep this little oasis of peace going in the heart of London, and although we may be a small community, the principle of not being deterred by evil forces is important."

At times, the concerts were held underground; when the National Gallery was hit by a bomb, Myra moved the group across the street. Not one concert was ever canceled.

After one particularly devastating raid, Myra drove to the concert noticing the burning houses and debris. "There will be a small audience tonight," she fretted. Hardly. Five hundred Londoners turned out that evening.

Father, when it seems our worlds, our foundations are being destroyed, give us courage to find the music within and share it.

The concerts continued until 1946, Myra supervising all of them. For her work she was awarded the highest honor an English king can bestow on a British female: Dame Commander.

February 26

Horace Binney Wallace, essayist
February 26, 1817–December 16, 1852

Horace Wallace, after graduation from Princeton, expressed an interest in becoming a physician but dropped out of medical school because he disliked surgery. He next studied chemistry and then turned to law. Although he passed the Pennsylvania bar, he never practiced, choosing instead to write legal and literary commentary.

He began writing in college but published under pen names. Modesty motivated him not to put his name on his only novel, *Stanley, or Recollections of a Man of the World*, in 1838. After a twelve-month stint in Europe studying art and church architecture, he returned to the United States and found himself praised as one of the country's most promising young writers.

"He who gets wisdom loves his own soul; he who cherishes understanding prospers."

Proverbs 19:8

In 1848, his *Napoleon and the Marshals of the Empire* was published, followed the next year by *The Military and Civil Life of George Washington*, both well-received.

The only writings he published under his real name were his legal documents, such as *Select Decisions of American Courts* (1847), revised in 1857 as *American Leading Cases*, which won wide readership in the legal profession.

After his death, Wallace's writing was praised and compared to that of Thomas Jefferson.

Father, life is too precious to waste. Remind us to live each day as if it were our last.

February 27

Alice Hamilton, industrial medicine specialist
February 27, 1869–September 22, 1970

In 1893, Alice Hamilton graduated from the University of Michigan School of Medicine. After studying in Europe, she spent two more years at Johns Hopkins Medical School. In 1897, she moved to Chicago to become Professor of Pathology at Women's Medical School, Northwestern University.

In the evenings she taught the poor. During a typhoid epidemic, she discovered that flies spread the disease, and her work provoked new policies by the Public Health Department. In the neighborhoods around her house, Alice found workers suffering from exposure to poisonous fumes in mills and factories. She soon realized that industrial conditions, particularly vapors and poisons, were harming thousands of workers.

Through the influence of friends, Hamilton won an appointment from the governor of Illinois to a commission studying industrial poisons in factories. Her work led to the first state laws on occupational safety and workers' compensation. Hamilton's study earned her an appointment by the United States Commissioner of Labor to review the lead, mining, and munitions industries. For ten years she labored alone, without staff and with little cooperation within industry, except the support of the workers.

In 1919, Dr. Hamilton became the first woman faculty member at Harvard Medical School and began to develop the field of industrial medicine as a recognized

"The righteous care about justice for the poor, but the wicked have no such concern."

Proverbs 29:7

59

specialty. In 1925, her book *Industrial Poisons in the United States*, the first on the subject, led to increased consciousness by management and labor of hazardous working conditions.

This single adult invested her life making the workplace a better environment. She understood that safe working conditions were a right of the worker.

Father, give us the stamina to embrace unpopular causes to protect lives.

Mary Lyon, college founder
February 28, 1797–March 5, 1849

In the eighteenth century, Americans had strong fears about the education of women; too rigorous study was believed to ruin their health. Mary Lyon, a single adult, spent her life deflating that prejudice. Known for her quick mind and thirst for education, she introduced geography into women's education. One popular jingle said it well: "Geography was too abstruse/Till Mary Lyon taught its use."

Mary Lyon attended Byfield Female Seminary and was influenced by the progressive notions of the Reverend Joseph Emerson, who advocated the establishment of permanent institutions of higher education for women.

After a chain of teaching experiences, some of which were negative, she devised a plan to open a first-class college for women (most schools for women were propriety schools, owned and controlled by men). Mary Lyon launched such a successful fund-raising program that in 1837 Mount Holyoke College opened in South Hadley, Massachusetts. That fall, eighty students began a three-year curriculum based on the program of nearby Amherst College.

Mary Lyon continued to teach until her death in 1849. She not only left a first-class college but also favorably influenced the American consciousness for higher education for women. That development, in turn, opened the door for women to enter the professions of medicine, law, and social work.

Mary Lyon provided a role model of what an educated single woman could be and accomplish.

". . . that our daughters may be as corner stones, polished after the similitude of a palace."

Psalm 144:12 KJV

Father, one woman opened the door for the education of women. Thank You for her courage, her persistence, and her commitment to a dream.

Augusta Christine Savage, sculptor
February 29, 1892–March 26, 1962

Even as a child, Augusta Savage had an artistic bent. She turned the red clay of northern Florida into all kinds of figures, much to her father's disgust. He called them "graven images" and punished her for making them.

Years later, after winning a prize for her sculptures at the Palm Beach county fair, Augusta decided to go to New York to pursue her talents. When she arrived she had $4.60. She was accepted into the tuition-free art program at Cooper Union, and her work attracted attention.

In 1923, Augusta applied for a special program sponsored by the French government. She was rejected because she was black. For the good of other black artists, Augusta determined to expose the discrimination.

Suddenly her work and her name were public; many considered Augusta a heroine. But life was tough; some gallery owners branded her a troublemaker. She married for the third time in 1923, but her husband died four months later. In 1925, she was offered a scholarship to the Academy of Fine Arts in Rome but didn't have money for travel and living expenses. Still, she kept sculpturing, often working in laundries to support her daughter and parents.

In 1929, Augusta finally got her chance to study in Paris. During the Depression, she opened a school of arts and crafts to employ artists under the Federal Arts Project. Several of her students went on to earn national recognition.

Augusta Savage remained modest. She often sacrificed time and energy she might have invested on her own work to help others, many of whom could not pay her. She explained: "I have created nothing really beautiful, really lasting, but if I can inspire one of these youngsters to develop the talent I know they possess, then my monument will be in their work."

Augusta Savage left a legacy in her works of art and in the student artists she helped achieve recognition. What will be *your* legacy?

"See, the Lord has chosen Bezalel son of Uri . . . and he has filled him with the Spirit of God, with skill, ability and knowledge in all kinds of crafts—to make artistic designs for work in gold, silver and bronze, to cut and set stones, to work in wood and to engage in all kinds of artistic craftsmanship . . . [and] the ability to teach others."

Exodus 35:30–34

Father, You have not insulated us from the harshness of life. But You share the harshness with us. We thank You that You not only give us these skills, but also give us the ability to teach our skills to others.

Joseph Wright Taylor, philanthropist
March 1, 1810–January 18, 1880

After Joseph Taylor graduated from the University of Pennsylvania Medical School at age twenty, he assumed his career would be in medicine. But after service as a ship's surgeon and a brief medical practice in India, he returned to the United States to join his brother's leather business in Cincinnati.

After fifteen years of great prosperity, Taylor retired and toured Europe. Eventually he bought an estate in New Jersey and settled down to live the life of a country gentleman, devoted to his unmarried sister. But Taylor had made a great deal of money, which troubled his Quaker conscience. What should he do with it?

For twenty years Taylor was a trustee of Haverford College, a Quaker school for men. During that time, Taylor experienced a growing conviction that Quakers—based on their belief of equality between the sexes—should be providing opportunities in higher education for women. In 1875, he decided to found a women's college.

The philanthropist consulted with the leading educators of his day and twice visited Mount Holyoke, Smith, and Wellesley, looking for ideas. Finally, he purchased land at Bryn Mawr, Pennsylvania, in 1878, and instructed architects to use the administration building at Smith as a model for the first campus structures. Taylor personally supervised the construction, but his overwork contributed to his death before the school opened.

He left his entire fortune to the college. Bryn Mawr continues to be one of the nation's leading colleges for women.

"Moreover, when God gives any man wealth and possessions, and enables him to enjoy them, to accept his lot and be happy in his work—this is a gift from God."

Ecclesiastes 5:19

Father, give us a sensitivity to the wise use of those resources You have given us. Give us wisdom to discern the permanent from the temporary.

March 2

Louis Sanford Schuyler, humanitarian
March 2, 1852–September 17, 1879

In the summer of 1879 Memphis, Tennessee, was a city floundering in death. Thousands of panicked citizens had fled the onslaught of yellow fever. The question in the city each morning was, "Who lives, and who has died?"

Louis Schuyler had just begun his pastorate at Holy Innocent's Episcopal Church in New Jersey when the headlines in the daily papers told of the increasing death toll in Memphis. Louis had just returned from study in England, where he had chosen not to be a monk. When his parish received word that the last Episcopal priests in Memphis were ill and that there was no one to administer the sacraments or to hold services, he immediately volunteered for assignment to Memphis.

Schuyler was discouraged by his bishop, but he knew that God had called him to go to Memphis.

When he arrived, Schuyler was greeted by Dr. W. T. D. Dalzell, who later said of their first conversation, "Louis impressed me . . . that he had come in a spirit of noblest self-devotion, counting the cost, and cheerfully willing to pay it."

Louis visited the homes of the ill, particularly in the portions of the city where the epidemic was striking hardest. He wrote his father:

> I am so very glad that I came, for I can be of good assistance. It was God's will, and He will keep me. Do not worry about me, for I am in God's hands. . . . I shall exercise all prudence. God will only allow what is best for me to happen.

Louis was on the way to a funeral when he learned that Memphis's leading infidel was dying. He jumped from his buggy and raced off on foot to talk to the man. As a result, Louis prayed with the man and led him to Christ.

On September 12, four days after he arrived in Memphis, Dr. Dalzell looked at Louis and said, "You have the fever!" Louis wept because he would have to stop visiting. "I had so hoped that I should be spared long

"The groans of the dying arise from the city, and the souls of the wounded cry out for help."

Job 24:12

Key Thought: A few weeks before the epidemic, Louis wrote out some resolutions. One

63

enough to do some good for the Church, something for the glory of Christ," he said.

Louis's nurse said that he prayed during most of his last hours. At 2:30 A.M. on September 17, Louis died, one of fifty-six clergymen who died in the epidemic. He is buried across from the mass grave of 1,400 other victims.

read: "To go and work in the strength of the Name of the Lord Jesus— forget myself, and do all for God."

March 3

John Maclean, university president
March 3, 1800–August 10, 1886

John Maclean graduated from the College of New Jersey (now Princeton) as the youngest member of the class of 1816. After teaching school for a year, he studied theology and became a tutor at his alma mater. John taught math until his ordination as a Presbyterian minister in 1828. The next year, he began teaching ancient language and literature.

John was a brilliant teacher. His devotion to Princeton led him to found its alumni association (now the second oldest in the nation). In 1829, Maclean was appointed vice president and assigned duties such as fund-raising and faculty recruitment. The college was floundering due to a weak president, poorly paid faculty, declining enrollment, and trustees who favored retrenchment. Maclean inherited these problems in the assignment.

Instead of defeat, Maclean saw opportunity. He raised endowment money, hired new faculty, and reinforced the college calendar. He changed graduation from the traditional September date to June, and he resisted attempts to increase Presbyterian control.

When the president finally retired, Maclean was elected to replace him. Shortly thereafter fire gutted the largest building on campus, then the Civil War began and enrollment declined. But Maclean's strong commitment to the institution and his spirit kept Princeton moving toward the future.

John Maclean was a friend to every Princeton student. Many times he loaned money to needy students. As president he still made time to teach Bible classes. In retirement, Maclean wrote Princeton's history and used the book proceeds to fund scholarship programs for economically deprived students.

"A generous man will himself be blessed."

Proverbs 22:9

Father, any organization is only as strong as the vision of its leadership. Even great institutions have rocky starts. Help us to see the opportunities to participate today.

March 4

Mabel Gillespie, labor leader
March 4, 1867–September 24, 1923

Few people have battled harder for hourly workers than Mabel Gillespie. After two years' study at Radcliffe, she went to work for the Boston Associated Charities and had occasion to learn about the problems of industrial urban society. She first worked with women workers in the Fall River textile strike of 1904. Then Mabel worked for the New York Child Labor Committee and Consumers' League.

In 1907, she conducted an intensive statewide survey of the canning industry in New York by working as a cannery hand twelve to sixteen hours each day. Through the experience, Mabel gained a new perspective on workers' conditions.

In 1909, she became the executive secretary of the Boston Women's Trade Union League and was influential in organizing women workers for unions, particularly in the garment, laundry, textile, and office-cleaning industries. In 1912, she organized telephone operators.

Through her efforts, women were included in the labor movement as equal partners. The governor of Massachusetts appointed her to the first Minimum Wage Commission in the country.

Miss Gillespie, although a strong and persuasive lobbyist, rarely spoke in public. Her effectiveness was based on her contacts and friendships. No one ever accused this woman of being afraid to get her hands dirty; she knew about the spindle and the distaff.

"In her hand she holds the distaff and grasps the spindle with her fingers."

Proverbs 31:19

Father, we believe that You care about our jobs. Thank You for the lives of those who have helped improve our working conditions. Let us be thankful.

March 5

William Segar Archer, congressman
March 5, 1789–March 28, 1855

William Archer launched his political career at the age of twenty-three, when he was elected to the Virginia House of Delegates. Re-elected six times before 1819, he then ran for Congress and served from 1820 to 1835.

"If anyone does not provide for his relatives, and especially for his imme-

Six years later he was elected to the Senate and served until 1847.

William Archer was a strong proponent of statehood for Texas and used his influence as chairman of the Senate Foreign Affairs Committee to promote the idea. He retired from politics and built a large home for himself and his two unmarried sisters.

According to his epitaph, William Archer "stood almost throughout his life to his sisters in the double relation of father and brother."

Archer helped bring Texas into the Union on December 29, 1845, as the twenty-eighth state.

diate family, he has denied the faith and is worse than an unbeliever."

1 Timothy 5:8

Key Thought: Life may offer us only one opportunity to make a lasting difference, so we must be ready at all times.

March 6

Belle Kearney, temperance reformer
March 6, 1863–February 27, 1939

Belle Kearney was the child of a politician-planter in Mississippi. At age eleven she became a Christian and joined the Methodist Church. Early in her life, Belle rebelled against the social restraints placed on women, opening a private school in her bedroom against her father's wishes.

Belle's life was changed when she heard Frances Willard speak on the need for temperance reform. At age twenty-six she decided her days of teaching school were behind her. Soon she joined the Women's Christian Temperance Union; by 1891, she was a national lecturer and organizer. In 1895, she was elected president of the Mississippi State W.C.T.U.

Slowly the skills she gained in speaking out on temperance convinced her to support women's suffrage. From 1906 to 1908, she was president of the Mississippi Women's Suffrage Association.

In 1920, she decided to run for a seat in the Mississippi State Senate. Although women had just gained the right to vote and Mississippi was a conservative state, she made a surprising showing in the primary, gaining 18,285 votes. In 1924, she became the first woman in the South to be elected to a Senate seat. Belle won the respect of her colleagues in the legislature and opened the door for the next generation of women in politics.

"Turn my eyes away from worthless things; preserve my life according to your word."

Psalm 119:37

Father, give us the wisdom to know the difference between good causes and great causes. Then give us the courage to fully invest ourselves in the great ones.

March 7

Mary Hopkins Norton, congresswoman
March 7, 1875–August 2, 1959

When Mary Hopkins's mother died, the seventeen-year-old took charge of her sisters and the household. She and her sisters graduated from the Packard Business College and became secretaries. In 1909, she married Robert Norton, a widower. Their only child died in infancy in late 1910. In her grief, she turned to public service with the strong encouragement of her pastor.

In 1920, Mary became active in Democratic party politics. In 1924, she became the first woman elected to the United States Congress without being preceded by her husband and the first woman ever elected in an eastern state. Many people assumed that she was a widow.

In 1934, Robert Norton died, and Mary again felt a great sense of loss. She poured herself into her congressional career, becoming chairman of the powerful House Labor Committee in 1937. She changed the direction of United States labor laws through her long battle for the Fair Labor Standards Act, which set a minimum wage and maximum hours for nonunion labor. This legislation also helped women workers by eliminating sex-based pay differentials.

Mary Norton became the champion of the working woman and lobbied hard for equal pay for equal work. As early as World War II, she had proposed federal aid for day care.

A staunch Catholic, she opposed the Equal Rights Amendment and birth control. Mary retired from Congress at age seventy-five but continued in federal government as a consultant on women's labor law to the Department of Labor.

> "The Lord tears down the proud man's house but he keeps the widow's boundaries intact."
>
> Proverbs 15:25

Father, thank You for the career of this widow who made working conditions better for so many women.

March 8

Emily Elizabeth Parsons, nurse
March 8, 1824–May 19, 1880

At thirty-eight, Emily Elizabeth Parsons had never been away from home. Blind in one eye, hearing impaired, and living with a limp, she read the stories of the grow-

> "Do not say to your neighbor, 'Come back later; I'll give

ing casualties in the Union army and wondered what she could do to help. When the call came for nurses, Emily volunteered despite her father's strong objections.

Emily began work at Massachusetts General Hospital in Boston and learned quickly. In 1862, she moved to Fort Schuyler in New York, where she worked sixteen-hour days. She cared for fifty men, ordered diets and supplies, and assisted the surgeons on duty. "To have a ward full of sick men under my care is all I ask," Emily wrote to her mother.

When Emily's health faltered, she met Jessie Benton Fremont, the wife of a general, who was recruiting nurses for the army hospital in St. Louis.

After her recovery, Emily joined the staff of Lawson Hospital in St. Louis. She was immediately named senior nurse on the *City of Alton,* a hospital ship. Under her orders, the ship sailed down the Mississippi to a point near Vicksburg, where she supervised the loading of some eight hundred wounded and sick soldiers. "I feel now as if I had really entered into the inner spirit of the times—the feeling which counts danger as nothing," she said.

After a bout with malaria, Emily assumed control of the new Benton Barracks Hospital of 2,500 beds. As an administrator, she relied on her organizational skills, her faith, and her good sense of humor to get her through the long days. Her biographer noted that she won the admiration and praise of surgeons and male attendants, "an achievement few women volunteers of the Civil War could claim."

During the final days of the war, Miss Parsons again battled malaria. Back in Cambridge, recovering, she asked, "I wonder what I shall do with myself when the war is over; I can never sit down and do nothing."

In 1867, Emily established a hospital in Cambridge, Massachusetts. It opened in a rented house, where Emily lived. Eventually Emily Parsons's brainchild became Mount Auburn Hospital.

it tomorrow'—when you now have it with you."

Proverbs 3:28

Key Point: You are never too old to start a dream—or to make a difference.

March 9

Moses Aaron Dropsie, lawyer
March 9, 1821–July 8, 1905

Moses Aaron Dropsie was born to Jewish-Christian parents and, at age fourteen, adopted his father's faith and converted to Judaism. In 1837, he was apprenticed as a watchmaker and completed his training in two years.

At age twenty-seven, Dropsie decided to study law. He studied under a lawyer who eventually became attorney general, Benjamin Brewster. Dropsie passed the bar in 1881 and set about establishing a reputation as a stunning trial lawyer. For a hobby, he collected first-edition law books and began writing on the history of law. He translated *Hand Book of Roman Law* into English and published *The Roman Law of Testaments*.

In Philadelphia, Dropsie was known for his civic spirit. He was a strong advocate of railways, serving as the president of the Lombard and South Street Railroad for twenty years. He chaired the commission that built the first major bridge across the Schuylkill River and was a major contributor to Whig causes and an abolitionist. In 1856, he helped establish the Republican party in Pennsylvania.

Dropsie supported religious education and served as the president of the Hebrew Educational Society of Philadelphia for forty-four years. He was a supporter of Russian Jewry.

He bequeathed his considerable estate to founding what became Dropsie University. Although blind the last fifteen years of his life, Dropsie lived alone and traveled throughout the world by himself.

In a Jewish culture strong on marriage, Dropsie's singleness was a distinction.

"The entire law is summed up in a single command: 'Love your neighbor as yourself.' "

Galatians 5:14

A Jewish bachelor demonstrates the difference that can be made by carefully investing money and energy. Remind us to choose our causes as carefully.

March 10

David Holmes, governor
March 10, 1770–August 20, 1832

David Holmes passed the Virginia bar in the early 1790s and practiced law in Harrisonburg. From 1793 to 1797, he

"My back is filled with searing pain;

was a commonwealth attorney. In 1797, he began the first of six terms in Congress, as a Jeffersonian Republican.

In 1809, President James Madison named Holmes the first governor of the Mississippi Territory, where he served until Mississippi became a state.

The territory demanded a great deal from its governor. Hostile Creek and Choctaw Indians constantly threatened the settlers that Holmes enticed to come to the area. In South Mississippi, Holmes had to constantly be wary of the influence of the Spanish in Florida and the French to the west.

The Creek War and the War of 1812 created great concern for Holmes. However, the number of settlers was growing, and so was the state. In 1816, two large tracts of land in the northern part of the territory were ceded by Indian tribes.

In 1817, the territory was divided, and the western portion became the state of Mississippi. Holmes was elected governor by the citizens and served until January 1820, when he chose not to run again. However, in late summer, Holmes was appointed United States senator, was re-elected, and served until 1825.

In 1826, he again took the oath as governor, but poor health forced him to resign in July. He returned to his family home in Winchester, Virginia. Holmes was an invalid until his death, but "cheerfully endured" his afflictions.

there is no health in my body."

Psalm 38:7

Key Thought: What would Mississippi have been like without the steady guidance of a man like David Holmes?

March 11

Thomas Ewbank, inventor
March 11, 1792–September 16, 1870

Thomas Ewbank left school at the age of fifteen to begin a seven-year apprenticeship as a coppersmith. At age twenty he began to work his craft in London. In his spare time, Thomas constantly read and studied. He soon decided that living in a monarchy limited his potential, so he immigrated to the United States in 1819. Within four years of his arrival, he had obtained his first patents for improved methods in tinning lead.

Ewbank's tin, copper, and lead tinning business in New York prospered and resulted in more patents and comfortable financial security. Ewbank sold his busi-

"Send me, therefore, a man skilled to work in gold and silver, bronze and iron, and in purple, crimson and blue yarn, and experienced in the art of engraving."

2 Chronicles 2:7

ness in 1836 in order to have time to read and travel. In 1842, he published his *A Descriptive Account of Hydraulic and Other Machines for Raising Water,* which became a key resource for engineers and other inventors for decades to come.

On May 4, 1848, Thomas Ewbank became United States Commissioner of Patents and developed a reputation for his essays—designed to arouse scientific curiosity—included in official reports of his office. As commissioner, Ewbank doubled the examining staff and developed more efficient procedures for expediting the patent process.

After he left that post, he wrote and served on a governmental commission evaluating the marble to be used in an addition to the United States Capitol. His work led to new standards in the construction industry.

Father, we thank You for those who can take earth's raw resources and turn them into practical tools to improve society. Keep us sensitive to our responsibility as good stewards.

March 12

Jane A. Delano, nurse
March 12, 1862–April 15, 1919

The words of Psalm 91:5, 6 characterize the life of Jane Delano. A year after her graduation from Bellevue Hospital School of Nursing, she was superintendent of a hospital for yellow fever victims in Jacksonville, Florida. In 1888, she treated typhoid victims in an isolated mining camp in Arizona. In 1891, she assumed the superintendency of the University of Pennsylvania Hospital School of Nursing. Then, at age forty-six, Jane resigned it all to devote two years to caring for her aged mother.

Later, Jane returned to Bellevue as Superintendent of the School of Nursing, where she developed her administrative skills and introduced significant curriculum changes. During this time, Jane worked tirelessly to gain more respect for the profession of nursing. She taught that the patient, not paperwork, should come first.

Jane Delano coauthored the first Red Cross textbook for nurses. In 1911, she began to head the Bureau of Nursing Service of the American Red Cross. In 1914, as war spread across Europe, she enrolled nearly 19,000 army and navy nurses for overseas service.

"Thou shalt not be afraid for the terror by night; nor for the arrow that flieth by day; Nor for the pestilence that walketh in darkness; nor for the destruction that wasteth at noonday."

Psalm 91:5, 6 KJV

Father, terrors, pestilence, and destruction are not a daily personal threat to us. But we never know. Help us to be confident that there

71

Jane became ill in 1919 with a severe ear infection. She rallied, but after several operations, she died in France. Her last words were, "What about my work? I must get back to my work."

is no place that You lead us that Your grace cannot keep us.

March 13

Bertha Everett Mahony, children's book enthusiast
March 13, 1882–May 14, 1969

Bertha Mahony had a passion for books that was passed down from her parents. After graduation from a secretarial college, she went to work in a bookstore in Boston.

As Bertha surveyed children's literature, she became aware of the opportunities for women in bookselling and the need for better books for children. She opened The Bookshop for Boys and Girls in 1916.

To help parents select good books for their children, she published *Books for Boys and Girls—a Suggestive Purchase List,* which matched one thousand titles with book descriptions. She also started Caravan, a mobile bookstore that she drove across New England during the summer months. Bertha believed that, "given a comfortable setting and good books, a child could begin 'to think truly . . . and feel deeply.' "

Bertha's friend Elinor Whitney soon joined her as a working partner, and they expanded the store to include a room for adults with books about children, a storytelling hour, and a series of art exhibits featuring the work of children. The two ladies promoted children's literature together for fifty years.

Bertha's major contribution was founding *Horn Book Magazine,* the first American magazine devoted exclusively to children's literature. The purpose was "to blow the horn for fine books for boys and girls." Long after her death, *The Horn Book* has remained an instrumental influence in children's literature.

Although she lived in a time period when all women were expected to marry and have children, Bertha impacted millions of other people's children. She did marry in 1932, at the age of fifty.

"He settles the barren woman in her home as a happy mother of children."

Psalm 113:9

Father, thank You for the privilege of being involved with children. Remind us that, although we may not have children of our own, we can love the children of others.

72

John Sappington Marmaduke, governor
March 14, 1833–December 28, 1887

When John Marmaduke was eleven years old, his father served one year as governor of Missouri. There was little to indicate that someday his son would be governor, too. After a year at Harvard, John left to attend West Point. He graduated in 1857 and was assigned to the Seventh Regiment and served in the Mormon War, 1858–1860.

When the Civil War erupted, Lieutenant Marmaduke came home to Missouri to talk over the issues with his father. Although the elder Marmaduke was a Unionist, he told his son to make up his own mind. In 1861, Marmaduke went to Richmond, where he joined the Confederate army as a lieutenant.

In late 1861, he was reunited with his former commander during the Mormon Wars, Albert Sidney Johnson. Soon Marmaduke was elevated to brigadier general. He transferred to Arkansas, where he made a name for himself and organized several raids into Missouri. He was promoted to major general in 1864.

After the war, Marmaduke owned an insurance business in St. Louis. In 1871, he became editor of the *St. Louis Journal of Agriculture*. In the early 1880s, he served on the state railroad commission.

Marmaduke was elected governor of Missouri in 1884. Although he only served one year, as had his father, he forced the legislature to pass laws regulating railroads in the state. He also won praise for his decisive action in the first railroad strike that impacted the state.

> "The race is not to the swift or the battle to the strong . . . time and chance happen to them all."
>
> **Ecclesiastes 9:11**

Father, John Marmaduke died young, but he lived excitingly and abundantly. Help us discover that we can live the same way.

Andrew James McCosh, surgeon
March 15, 1858–December 2, 1908

Although one problem of single adults is the tendency for many of them to be workaholics, the problem is not new. As a surgeon, Dr. Andrew James McCosh had few equals. The son of a Princeton president, he graduated from the College of Physicians and Surgeons in New York. After his eighteen-month internship, he spent time studying in Vienna with the renowned surgeon Billroth.

> "The Lord confides in those who fear him; he makes his covenant known to them."
>
> **Psalm 25:14**

He returned to New York in 1883 and spent eleven years with T. Gaillard Thomas, a prominent gynecologist. In 1887, McCosh became attending surgeon at Presbyterian Hospital and served until his death. He also taught surgery in two medical schools during this period.

He did not limit himself to a surgical specialty and published medical papers in a variety of fields. During his tenure at Presbyterian, for instance, he did 1,600 appendicitis operations. McCosh's idea of a vacation was going to Europe and studying their surgical practices.

Not only was Andrew McCosh a talented surgeon, he influenced the next generation of surgeons to be better at their work.

Father, what can we do to influence the next generation in our chosen profession? Give us that insight.

March 16

Samuel Abbott Green, physician
March 16, 1830–December 5, 1918

Dr. Samuel Green began his medical career by studying at Harvard and later at Jefferson Medical School in Philadelphia, graduating in 1854. Because of poor health, he took a long voyage before continuing his studies in Vienna, then returned to Boston and established his practice.

When the Civil War began, Samuel Green was the first doctor to join the army. By the fall of 1861, he had a surgeon's commission. Dr. Green organized the medical ship *Recruit* and commanded the hospital steamer *Cosmopolitan* off the South Carolina coast. In October 1863, he was in Jacksonville and St. Augustine, overseeing medical affairs. He finished his army career as a surgeon in Richmond during the final days of the war.

He returned to Boston and became active—despite a busy practice—in civic affairs. He was the city physician from 1871 to 1882, and then mayor. Green was a trustee of the Boston Public Library for ten years and served as acting librarian from 1877 to 1878. He actively participated in the Massachusetts Historical Society for almost fifty years.

Green died in 1918 and left his estate to Lawrence Academy.

"You will be made rich in every way so that you can be generous on every occasion."

2 Corinthians 9:11

Father, help us be generous not only with our money but with our time, our compassion, and our communication skills.

74

March 17

Anna Wessels Williams, bacteriologist
March 17, 1863–November 20, 1954

The road to a career in medicine began for Anna Williams with her first look through what she called "a teacher's wonderful microscope." Anna decided to be a doctor when her sister lost her baby and almost died. Anna was deeply touched by the inability of physicians to save the baby's life.

Anna applied to the Women's Medical College of New York Infirmary, over her mother's strong objections. However, her mother—who had a long interest in missions—modified her objections when Anna suggested she *might* become a missionary.

In those days, diphtheria was a leading cause of death among children. After obtaining her M.D., Anna went to work in the first municipally operated bacteriology lab in the nation. By 1894, she had isolated a strain of the diphtheria bacillus, eventually called Park-Williams #8 (named for her boss, who happened to be on vacation when the breakthrough came). Williams's discovery led to antitoxin production and to the first successful municipal inoculation program.

Anna also developed a new method to test for rabies and a treatment that eliminated chronic eye infections among poor schoolchildren in New York.

Dr. Williams lived with the knowledge that many of her achievements were credited to her boss, the brilliant bacteriologist, William Hallock Park. However, she gave great encouragement to the cause of women in medicine and proved herself a gifted researcher.

"He has not despised or disdained the suffering of the afflicted one."

Psalm 22:24

Father, mission fields are not always across the sea. Sometimes they are across the street. Give us the willingness to go wherever You send us.

March 18

Grover Cleveland, president
March 18, 1837–June 24, 1908

It was time for a change, argued the Democrats in 1884. The White House had been controlled by the Republicans ever since bachelor James Buchanan departed in

"Surely you desire truth in the inner parts; you teach me

1860. And in the early days of the summer of 1884, the name for change was definitely the young unmarried governor of New York, Grover Cleveland.

Cleveland had grown up in a Presbyterian parsonage; after law school, he became an active worker in the Democratic party in Buffalo. Having served as a district attorney and county sheriff, he was elected as a reform mayor of Buffalo in 1881. The following year, when Democratic officials became deadlocked on a candidate, Cleveland's reputation for independence won him the nomination for governor and the election.

Governor Cleveland became known as "the veto governor" but managed to win the support of conservatives and businessmen. In 1884, in national politics, the Republican party had rejected President Arthur and nominated James G. Blaine; the Democrats, sensing victory, nominated Grover. However, in a spirited fit of mudslinging, Blaine was tarnished by charges of unethical behavior while serving as Speaker of the House.

On July 21, 1884, a Buffalo newspaper published the report that eight years earlier Grover Cleveland had fathered a son out of wedlock.

Seeing the prospect of a sure election disappear down the drain, the Democrats asked Cleveland what they should do in the way of damage control.

"Tell the truth," he answered. He had fathered the child but had cared financially for the child and mother.

Americans were shocked by Cleveland's candor.

Grover Cleveland was elected by a margin of only 23,000 votes, the second bachelor to occupy the Oval Office. He revamped the political patronage system, greatly expanding the civil service; convinced Americans that the protective tariff should be abolished; discouraged the move away from the gold standard; and reminded Americans of the role of conscience in foreign affairs.

Early in his term, due to the press of job seekers, Cleveland demanded, "My God, what is there in this office that any man should ever want to get into it?"

Then, on June 2, 1886, President Cleveland stunned the nation by marrying Frances Folsom, twenty-two-year-old daughter of his former law partner, holding the first presidential wedding in the White House.

wisdom in the inmost place."

Psalm 51:6

Father, remind us to tell the truth the next time we think anything less than the truth would be appropriate or to our advantage.

March 19

Ellen Gates Starr, settlement worker
March 19, 1859–February 10, 1940

Although her father could pay for only one year at Rockford Seminary, Ellen Starr began teaching school after she finished. During this year, Ellen corresponded with her schoolmate, Jane Addams. Both women had great questions about the futility and aimlessness of their singleness. Ellen, in particular, was also on a spiritual pilgrimage, seeking a deeper religious experience.

In early 1889, Ellen and Jane searched Chicago for the right site to open a settlement house, jointly opening Hull House that September. Jane provided the money and management, and Ellen Starr was her biggest booster. At Hull House, Ellen organized art history classes for immigrants and art exhibits; later, she became the first president of the Chicago Public School Art Society. In 1920, she became a Catholic and spent much of her time writing and speaking about Catholic art and worship.

Ellen spent most of her life as an encourager of Jane Addams.

"[Joshua] appointed the priests to their duties and encouraged them in the service of the Lord's temple."

2 Chronicles 35:2

Father, don't let us become too busy with our dreams and our work to encourage others.

March 20

Wilds Preston Richardson, soldier
March 20, 1861–May 20, 1929

Wilds Richardson was determined to have a career in the army. After graduating from West Point Military Academy in 1884, Richardson served in California, in Apache country in the Southwest, and in Nebraska.

In 1897, Lieutenant Richardson was posted to the Alaska Territory, where he stayed for the next two decades. In March 1905, he became president of the United States Alaska Roads Commission and was charged with directing the massive governmental public works program. His tenacity and engineering skills, coupled with his love of the wilderness, often put Richardson at odds with self-serving developers, yet his per-

"Endure hardship with us like a good soldier of Christ Jesus."

2 Timothy 2:3

77

sistence got results; Richardson's policies preserved much of the beauty of the territory. Eventually he built the Richardson Highway, which linked Valdez with Fairbanks—a distance of almost four hundred miles.

By 1914, Richardson made colonel. With the outbreak of World War I, he became commander of the Seventy-eighth Infantry Brigade at Camp Beauregard, Louisiana. In August 1919, he took command of the American troops stationed in Russia. After three difficult years, General Richardson was decorated and returned to the United States to retire from active duty.

Biographers say Richardson was known for his friendliness and was one of the best-loved men in the army. Wilds Richardson had the ability to be a strict disciplinarian and a friend at the same time.

Father, if You lead us into difficult assignments, You will give us the strength to endure triumphantly.

March 21

Antonia Caetana Maury, astronomer
March 21, 1866–January 8, 1952

Antonia Maury read Virgil at the age of nine and attended Vassar at sixteen. After her graduation, she worked in Harvard's observatory, specifically classifying the bright northern stars. Because Antonia was a scientific dreamer, she did not always work comfortably with the director, especially after she discarded his classification system and developed her own. She left Harvard in 1896, pointing out that there were other observatories in which she could work without restrictions.

Forty-six years passed before Antonia received recognition for her contribution to stellar spectroscopy. The American Astronomical Society called her work the cornerstone for much of the emerging field of theoretical astrophysics.

Miss Maury also made significant discoveries about spectroscopic binaries, or double stars. She returned to Harvard in 1918 and studied the orbits of several additional binaries that had been discovered.

Although she loved astronomy, she also worked to preserve the nation's redwood forests, particularly during World War II. She retained a lifelong fascination with the stars, but noted, "But the human brain is greater yet, because it can comprehend it all."

"Then Herod called the Magi secretly and found out from them the exact time the star had appeared."

Matthew 2:7

Father, where would man be today without the scientific progress made by the stargazers across history? Thank You for letting us in on the majesty of Your creation through the minds of such astronomers as Antonia Maury.

John Frederick Kensett, landscape painter
March 22, 1816–December 14, 1872

John Kensett was a young man when he and a group of colleagues went to Europe to study the great artists and paint. John stayed for seven years. In England he painted landscapes while working as an engraver to support himself. "My real life commenced there," he later said. Meanwhile, through the years, he had shipped paintings back to America, so when he returned in the fall of 1847, his reputation was waiting for him.

John Kensett wandered across the Northeast, painting landscapes of the Adirondacks, the White and Catskill Mountains, Long Island, and finally the Eastern seashores. His deep love of nature was evident in his paintings.

He befriended numerous younger artists throughout his career, nurturing the gift of friendship. Even his silences and moodiness were considered friendly.

After his death, his paintings and sketches were sold for a small fortune, many eventually finding their home in the Metropolitan Museum of Art.

"A friend loves at all times, and a brother is born for adversity."

Proverbs 17:17

Key Point: Never be so busy advancing your career that you do not make time for others.

Fannie Farmer, cooking expert
March 23, 1857–January 15, 1915

"A little of this, a pinch of that . . ." was the way Americans cooked, until a single adult named Fannie Farmer changed all that. Born into a poor family, and with a leg paralyzed by a stroke when she was sixteen, Fannie found work as a housekeeper.

When she was thirty, Fannie became a student at the Boston Cooking School. After two years there, she was made assistant principal; with this income, she was able to support her family.

While there, Fannie wrote a book that would make her name a household word in American kitchens: *The Boston Cooking-School Cook Book.* The book was based on a concept Fannie developed when she had

"He will take your daughters to be perfumers and cooks and bakers."

1 Samuel 8:13

worked as a housekeeper. Her employers asked Fannie to explain the directions to a favorite recipe, and Fannie did, using exact measurements. Her cookbook was a major innovation with its clear recipes, specific directions, timing, and measurements. The publisher, however, was so skeptical that he asked her to pay for the book's publication. Since then, her book has gone through eleven revised editions and sold nearly 4 million copies.

Based on the book's success, Miss Farmer founded the Fannie Farmer School of Cookery and lectured not only to cooks but to doctors, nurses, school officials, and others interested in improving American nutrition.

From small farms in the Midwest to the dining halls of Harvard, Miss Farmer's recipes became famous.

Father, food is such a part of our lives, eating, such a pleasant activity. Thank You for the blessing of having enough.

March 24

Edwin Warren Toole, attorney
March 24, 1839–May 17, 1905

Edwin Toole's law study was interrupted by the outbreak of the Civil War. He enlisted in the Confederate army but was wounded at the battle of Pea Ridge and left the military. In 1863, he moved to Denver and then on to what was then the Montana Territory—a good place to start a new life.

When Toole settled in wild-and-wooly Virginia City, the only law was the law of the gun. Despite his limited education, Toole stepped into the vacuum and helped institute a system of law for the mining camps. His practice soon included most of the territory, and his wisdom helped bring a sense of civility into the local towns. Toole settled many disputes that could have resulted in bloodshed.

In 1871, he ran for Congress as a Southern Democrat and lost; thereafter, Toole concentrated on the law. Toole was a master persuader before juries. He relied on "apex" law, which stated that persons owning mineral claims could pursue veins of ore on adjacent land. In *Montana Company* vs. *St. Louis Mining and Milling Company,* the courts upheld Toole's logic and the constitutionality of the principle. The ruling had enormous implications for miners and landowners.

"When you have eaten and are satisfied, praise the Lord your God for the good land he has given you."

Deuteronomy 8:10

His practice was large, his knowledge formidable. With the large income generated from his clients, he invested in real estate and mines.

Toole gave generously to charities and to anyone who asked him for help, living out Deuteronomy 8:18. At times, he even gave his legal services to the poor. One case, for which he received no compensation, he argued all the way to the United States Supreme Court.

Although he had many clients and acquaintances, he had few friends and lived almost as a recluse.

Key Thought: There is a difference between the almighty dollar and the Almighty's dollar. Am I acknowledging God's blessing on my income?

March 25

Luther Rice, missionary
March 25, 1783–September 25, 1836

In the fall of 1808, Luther Rice and a group of his student friends began to pray together regularly, signing a solemn pledge "to effect a mission to the world's teeming in foreign lands." The Brethren, as they were called, desired to go to foreign countries as missionaries. In 1809, they all entered Andover Seminary.

As graduation approached, The Brethren began corresponding with the London Missionary Society about sending out "two or three young unmarried men." Rice was excluded from full consideration because he had not finished seminary, had no money, and had not resolved his love relationship with Rebecca Eaton, to whom he had proposed without telling her about his missionary call.

The American Board of Commissioners for Foreign Missions agreed to send Rice *if* he raised his own money. When Rice learned a ship was sailing for India, he immediately launched a fund-raising effort, literally begging enough money in six days to pay his fare. Luther Rice sailed from Philadelphia on February 18 and reached Calcutta on August 10. During the long voyage, Rice argued theological doctrine with William Johns, an English Baptist. Daily the men debated their traditions, Johns in favor of baptism, Rice against it.

By the time Rice reached India, he had changed. On

"What is man that you are mindful of him, the son of man that you care for him?"

Psalm 8:4

November 1, Luther Rice was baptized. Since baptism would mean a break with the American Board, Rice immediately returned to the United States. Although the American Board was annoyed, Luther found the Baptists receptive.

Rice had planned to return to the mission field but became involved in creating the Baptist Board of Foreign Missions. Until 1817, he rode across America by horseback or buggy, speaking at hundreds of churches. On July 19, 1816, he reported that he had traveled 6,600 miles and collected almost $4,000 for missions the previous year.

In 1820, at Rice's prodding, Baptists approved the idea of opening a school. Henry Clay helped win congressional support for the establishment of the school in the District of Columbia. Rice spent the rest of his life raising money to support Columbian, which eventually became George Washington University.

Key Thought: "I think it is right to plan, act, and labor as if I might have 30 years of service yet before me. . . . but also so to live, plan, act, and labor, as though I might die soon."

Luther Rice

March 26

Bertha Van Hoosen, surgeon
March 26, 1863–June 7, 1952

Faced with the obstacle Bertha Van Hoosen encountered, many women would have given up their dream of attending medical school. Bertha's father refused to pay for her education, but Bertha's life is the story of seizing opportunities that come disguised as problems.

When women were rejected for service as physicians by the military during World War I, Bertha fought the discrimination, but lost. She confessed her ambition was "to be as good a doctor as the best man."

In 1913, Dr. Van Hoosen became the first woman physician to receive a civil-service appointment in Chicago when she was named chief of the gynecological staff at Cook County Hospital.

In 1918, she became the first woman to head a medical division at a coed university when she became head of obstetrics at Loyola University.

In 1930, she established the nation's first "breast milk" bank in Chicago. Dr. Van Hoosen pioneered the use of scopolamine morphine anesthesia in childbirth,

"Charm is deceptive, and beauty is fleeting; but a woman who fears the Lord is to be praised."

Proverbs 31:30

trained over twenty women surgeons, and helped form the American Medical Women's Association.

Bertha Van Hoosen's biography was appropriately called *Petticoat Surgeon*. She performed her last operation at age eighty-eight.

Father, whatever my profession, help me to be as good as I can be.

March 27

George Matheson, hymn writer
March 27, 1842–August 28, 1906

George Matheson lost his eyesight while studying for the ministry; still he was a brilliant student at Glasgow University because his sisters read to him.

George experienced tremendous rejection when his fiancée said to him, "I cannot see my way clear to go through life bound by the chains of marriage to a blind man." His pain was made more acute when his sister married in 1882, reminding him of what he had missed.

On June 6, 1882, Matheson took a pen and in only five minutes wrote the song for which he is most remembered:

> O Love that will not let me go,
> I rest my weary soul in Thee;
> I give Thee back the life I owe,
> That in Thine ocean depths its flow
> May richer, fuller be.
>
> O Joy that seekest me through pain,
> I cannot close my heart to Thee;
> I trace the rainbow through the rain,
> And feel the promise is not vain
> That morn shall tearless be.

"Who shall separate us from the love of Christ? Shall trouble or hardship or persecution or famine or nakedness or danger or sword? . . . No, in all these things we are more than conquerors through him who loved us."

Romans 8:35, 37

Despite his blindness, Matheson pastored the Innellan Church, Argyllshire, England, for eighteen years. Crowds filled the pews week after week, and some who came never realized that Matheson was blind. After hearing him preach, Queen Victoria said, "Your life has been a sorely tried but a very beautiful one."

Father, we thank You that Your love never lets us go, that even if all forsake us, You are there.

March 28

George Martin Kober, physician
March 28, 1850–April 24, 1931

George Kober's father had made a vow: No son of his would serve under any German prince or potentate. So young George immigrated to the United States in 1866 to avoid military duty. Ironically, the sixteen-year-old immediately joined the army and attracted the attention of a surgeon who had him assigned as a hospital steward. Based on his experiences, George decided to become a doctor.

Kober earned his degree from Georgetown University Medical School in 1871 and was appointed an assistant surgeon in the army. He had a successful army career and retired in November 1886. Because of his frugality and wise investments, he retired from medicine in 1893 to pursue teaching and philanthropy. However, in 1901, he was named dean of the medical school at Georgetown University and served until 1928.

Kober loved people and causes. He was a pioneer in the treatment of tuberculosis and designed the Tuberculosis Hospital in Washington. He called attention to the pollution of the Potomac River and cited it as a cause of typhoid. He was also an early advocate of the use of iodine as an antiseptic. A prolific researcher, Kober published over two hundred articles on hygiene and disease prevention. He retained a lifelong interest in the medical corps and in medical education at Georgetown University.

"The noble man makes noble plans, and by noble deeds he stands."

Isaiah 32:8

Father, remind us that we, too, must find arenas in which we can invest ourselves.

March 29

Isabella Thoburn, missionary
March 29, 1840–August 31, 1901

Isabella Thoburn considered becoming a nurse but realized she was not suited for that, so instead she collected supplies and organized relief work.

In 1866, Isabella's brother wrote her from India explaining that the wives of missionaries were so busy

"That in all things he might have the preeminence."

Colossians 1:18 KJV

with their families that they could not always meet the needs of the local women. Moreover, Indian husbands were suspicious of American males who attempted to teach women. There could never be a vigorous growing church in India if the women were not evangelized. Would Isabella like to come and open a school there?

"As soon as possible," she notified her brother. She had not felt called to be a missionary, and no Methodist society had yet sent out a single woman, but the need was there.

When eight women met in Tremont Street Methodist Church in Boston to organize the first women's missionary society in the Methodist Episcopal Church, North, they remembered an appeal for help from the wife of the Methodist bishop of India and voted to send Isabella Thoburn. On November 3, 1888, she sailed for India with Dr. Clara A. Swaim.

When she arrived in India in January, Isabella found three girls' schools open but struggling. On April 18, 1889, she opened her own school with six students and a guard. She had declared that it would be open to all races and classes. Eventually, this school would become known as a place where racial prejudice was forgotten.

That small beginning led to a boarding school, then a high school, and on July 12, 1886, a college for women: Lucknow Woman's College (after her death, Isabella Thoburn College became part of Lucknow University). Although the university had humble beginnings, it trained generations of Indian women for future leadership roles.

A few days before her death, Isabella Thoburn said, "What we want is life, this more abundant life. . . . For myself, I know no other life. I have known no other life for many years. My only desire and constant effort is to enter more deeply into the experiences of its mysteries."

She died of cholera at the age of sixty-one. Her graduates have helped change India.

Key Thought: One would think that the college was the greatest contribution Isabella Thoburn made. When asked what she considered her most important work, she answered without hesitation, "Being kind to the stranger within our gates."

March 30

Harry Bingham, lawyer
March 30, 1821–September 12, 1900

Harry Bingham graduated from Dartmouth College in 1843, taught school, studied law, and passed the bar exam in New Hampshire in 1846. He quickly opened a law office in Littleton and practiced there as the only Democratic attorney in town.

In 1861, Bingham was elected to the state legislature and quickly became a strong party leader. Through persuasion, Bingham was effective among Republican legislators as well. Bingham was re-elected seventeen times. He influenced the appointments to the state judiciary through the three decades he served on the state judiciary committee.

Harry Bingham was twice a candidate for Congress and seven times a candidate for the Senate; he lost all of the elections. He lost confirmation to the state superior court in 1867, as well.

His exceptional legal reputation was based on his attention to detail, his effective presentations to juries, and his accuracy. For thirty years he was the leader of the New Hampshire bar.

"Men listened to me expectantly, waiting in silence for my counsel."

Job 29:21

Father, thank You for Your faithfulness to a chosen profession as exemplified by Harry Bingham. Remind us that You are interested in our chosen professions.

March 31

Robert Ross McBurney, YMCA executive
March 31, 1837–December 27, 1898

Born into a Christian family in Scotland, Robert McBurney came to the United States as an immigrant in 1854. When he was eighteen years old, he found a position in a hat factory and worked there for eleven years.

During this time, McBurney became concerned about the religious needs of men and boys in New York City, becoming a leader in noonday prayer meetings at the North Dutch Church. An organization similar to London's Young Men's Christian Association was founded in New York in 1852 and went through a decade of volunteer leadership until McBurney was hired as secretary in 1862.

McBurney, through friendships, enlisted many prom-

"Thus you will walk in the ways of good men and keep to the paths of the righteous."

Proverbs 2:20

inent city leaders in the work. After attending an international meeting of the YMCA in 1865, McBurney became convinced that more work could be done in New York City. He organized a drive to build a building with game rooms, a gymnasium, a library, and meeting rooms and developed a program around a strong secretary.

From 1887 to 1898, McBurney supervised all the Y work in New York, building branches throughout the metropolitan area. By the turn of the century, more than 5,500 men and boys used the centers daily.

McBurney believed in young men reaching young men; he supported the development of a wide variety of programs to reach more people. He stressed education as well as evangelism and organized leadership classes to train the next generation of YMCA leaders.

Key Thought: The time to influence an organization is often on the ground floor.

April 1

Sophonisba Breckenridge, lawyer and reformer
April 1, 1866–July 30, 1948

Anyone who has studied the life of Sophonisba Breckenridge has come away asking one question: How could one woman accomplish so much? Sophonisba was a teacher, reformer, editor, social activist, and a model of singleness lived to the fullest.

Sophonisba studied law in her father's office and was the first woman to be admitted to the Kentucky bar. She went on to become the first woman to earn a Ph.D. in political science at the University of Chicago, then completed her Doctor of Jurisprudence. For thirty-eight years Sophonisba taught at the University of Chicago, sharing her dream of making life better for the city's poor.

At age forty-one, she began her work as a social activist by joining the Woman's Trade Union League. She also moved into Jane Addam's Hull House. She lobbied for reforms, conducted research on city residents, and inspected tenements for the public health department. Juveniles, children of the poor, and immigrants all won the heart of Miss Breckenridge.

At the University of Chicago, Dr. Breckenridge devel-

"He who opposes the poor shows contempt for their Maker, but whoever is kind to the needy honors God."

Proverbs 14:31

87

oped a professional training program for social workers that balanced intense academic preparation with practical field experience. Her graduates would not occupy ivory towers. The Depression's impact on the city offered an opportunity to put her principles into practice.

She wrote extensively and founded *Social Service Review*. In 1933, President Franklin Roosevelt recognized Dr. Breckenridge's contributions by appointing her a delegate to the Pan American Congress.

Sophonisba Breckenridge was a friend to the poor of the nation.

Father, remind us of our obligations to the poor.

April 2

Hans Christian Andersen, children's writer
April 2, 1805–August 4, 1875

Hans Christian Andersen occupies an immortal place in children's literature; countless generations of children have listened to his stories as they drifted off to sleep. Although Andersen wrote poetry, drama, and novels, he is most remembered for his children's stories. His 168 stories combine wisdom and whimsy and are rich with moral significance. Dissertations have been written on their symbolism.

Stories such as "The Ugly Duckling," "The Emperor's Clothes," "The Tinker Box," and "The Fir Tree" are legendary.

"Teach them to your children and to their children after them."

Deuteronomy 4:9

Key Thought: "His own image . . . was no longer the reflection of a clumsy, dirty, gray bird, ugly and offensive. He himself was a swan! Being born in a duck yard does not matter, if only you are hatched from a swan's egg."

Hans Christian Andersen

April 3

Julian de Lalande Poydras, planter
April 3, 1746–June 23, 1824

After serving in the French navy, being captured by the British in 1760, escaping first to Santo Domingo and then to New Orleans, Poydras became a peddler, traveling the lower Mississippi Valley. He bought his first plantation at Coupee Parish, Louisiana.

Here he established a trading post, then a store, and eventually a cotton gin. When the British fort at Baton Rouge was captured, Poydras celebrated the capture in an epic poem, *La Prise du Morne du Baton Rouge* (1779), which established his literary reputation.

Poydras wanted to return to France, but the Revolution prevented his leaving Louisiana, so he used his trading skills and became prosperous. By the end of 1775, Poydras owned six plantations, prime real estate in New Orleans, and more than five hundred slaves. He gained a reputation for his philanthropy, piety, and high morals.

Poydras's philanthropy lived long after him. In his will he left generous amounts to schools, hospitals, and asylums. He left an endowment to provide dowries for the poor girls of the parishes of Pointe Coupee and West Baton Rouge. As late as 1930, young women in Baton Rouge were benefiting from this bachelor's money as his financial assistance made it possible for many of them to marry.

> "And he let her go for two months. She and the girls went into the hills and wept because she would never marry."
>
> **Judges 11:38**

Father, we thank You for the rich backgrounds of the single adults who made this nation great. Remind us that we are not called to be spectators but participants in our day.

April 4

Dorothea Dix, reformer
April 4, 1802–July 17, 1887

She could smell her students before she could see them. On March 28, 1841, a young Harvard religion student had asked Dorothea Dix to substitute for him at a Sunday school class in the East Cambridge, Massachusetts, jail. To her horror, she discovered the inhumane treatment suffered by those whom society labeled lunatics.

> "When did we see you a stranger and invite you in, or needing clothes and clothe you? When did we see

One cold, naked man was chained like an animal in a small hut.

"He's cold," Dorothea observed.

"Oh, no, ma'am," said the jailer. "He don't feel nothing."

She looked at the jailer as if he were the insane man. "If I'm cold, he's cold! Get him some clothes."

Dorothea went to the jail to teach a Sunday school class; she left to launch a major reform movement. At age thirty-nine, Dorothea began systematically studying every jail in Massachusetts. Eighteen months later she petitioned the state legislature, and her report could not be ignored.

What she did in Massachusetts she also did in New York, Rhode Island, and New Jersey. Her approach was to gather the facts through personal visits, draft an appeal to the legislature outlining the need and a proposed solution, and then, through persistent lobbying, work for passage *and* implementation. On more than one occasion, she shamed a legislature into action.

From 1854 to 1857, she carried her crusade for better care of the mentally ill to Europe. By this time her book, *Remarks on Prisons and Prison Discipline in the United States,* had been widely read and debated.

But war clouds interrupted her campaign. In 1863, she found herself Superintendent of Army Nursing for the Northern army. Although in her sixties, Dorothea carried a grueling schedule. Her high standards for army nurses annoyed many; however, she helped gain public acceptance for women in nursing.

When the war ended, she resumed her campaign for the needs of the mentally ill.

This single adult made a lasting impact on our world. What if she had been too "busy" to accept the invitation to teach Sunday school that day?

you sick or in prison and go to visit you?"

Matthew 25:38, 39

Father, create in us a sensitivity to the opportunities You place in our lives. Keep us on the cutting edge, aware of the danger of making our lives too comfortable.

April 5

Judith A. Resnik, astronaut
April 5, 1949–January 28, 1986

I had never been to a space launch, and since I was vacationing in Florida, I made my way onto the beach and checked my watch as the countdown went off. I will

"Where can I go from your Spirit? Where can I flee

never forget that *Oh, no!* that ricocheted through my mind as I watched the *Challenger* disintegrate.

Aboard was a single adult, mission specialist Dr. Judith A. Resnik.

In 1970, Judy graduated from Carnegie-Mellon University with a bachelor's degree in electrical engineering; by 1977, she had completed her Ph.D. She began work at the National Institute of Health, where one colleague described her as "competent, quick and talented. Everyone knew that she was destined for stardom, in a sense, because she was so good when she was here."

Resnik took a job as senior systems engineer at Xerox and happened to see a poster urging applications for NASA. In 1978, she was accepted into the space program.

Judy made her first space trip on August 30, 1984, on the shuttle *Discovery,* conducting solar-power experiments. She won high praise for her work and competence.

As America's second woman in space and the first Jewish person, Judy only wanted to be "just another astronaut." She insisted that her marriage and divorce be kept private. "If anyone asks," she instructed NASA public relations people, "just tell them I'm single. Period."

Judy once offered this advice to students: "Study what interests you—learn all you can. Don't be afraid to expand into new fields."

During her stint at NASA, Judith Resnik became a positive role model for many young women. In death she became a hero to millions.

from your presence? If I go up to the heavens, you are there."

Psalm 139:7, 8

Father, sometimes making a difference and pursuing our dreams can be costly. Remind us of the fragility of life and the boredom of cowardice.

April 6

Helen Hyde, artist
April 6, 1868–May 13, 1919

Helen Hyde studied art in San Francisco, her hometown. She was particularly intrigued by the children of Chinatown, who became her first models. After initially starting with color sketching, Miss Hyde adopted the Japanese woodblock print method.

"From Zion, perfect in beauty, God shines forth."

Psalm 50:2

Helen also studied in New York, Berlin, Paris, and finally in Holland and England. Later she left for a short trip to Japan that turned into a fifteen-year adventure. As a student, she meticulously mastered the art of woodblock. Her *A Monarch of Japan,* depicting a mother and child, won first prize in a Tokyo exhibit, a stunning achievement for a Westerner.

Hyde also illustrated two books for children: *Moon Babies* and *Jingles from Japan.* She captured women and children in gardens, on bridges, and with umbrellas—all common themes in her work.

After returning to the United States, Helen settled in Chicago. Her art has been exhibited in most American cities and today is found in many American museums, libraries, and galleries.

Helen Hyde blended originality, skill, and a gentle eye into a creativity that enchanted thousands.

Father, You are the inventor of beauty and the giver of artistic genius and creativity. Bless all the single adults who are struggling with their creativity this day.

April 7

William Rufus DeVane King, vice president
April 7, 1786–April 18, 1853

William Rufus King began his political career as a member of the North Carolina legislature and then a member of Congress. After diplomatic service in Russia, he moved to the Alabama Territory and became one of the new state's first senators. He became a friend and supporter of Andrew Jackson. From 1836 to 1841, King was president pro tempore of the Senate and had significant influence due to the poor leadership of the vice president, Richard Johnson.

In April 1844, President John Tyler, afraid that England and France would oppose the annexation of Texas, appointed King ambassador to France. After having influenced the French against such an action, King returned to the United States and ran for the state senate in Alabama. He was defeated in 1846, but two years later he was appointed to fill a vacancy.

Eventually friends maneuvered to get King the vice presidential nomination in 1852. After his election in November, King resigned his Senate seat to go to Cuba and recuperate from his tuberculosis. Congress passed

"I know that there is nothing better for men than to be happy and do good while they live."

Ecclesiastes 3:12

Father, our record doesn't have to be glorious or glamor-

a special act to permit the vice president elect to take the oath outside the United States. To date, he is the only vice president to have done so. He came home to his plantation in Alabama and died.

ous to be effective. Thank You for the example of King's faithfulness.

William Henry Welch, pathologist
April 8, 1850–April 30, 1934

After graduation from Yale medical school, Dr. William Henry Welch studied in Europe for three years, training for his long career as a leader in progressive medical education.

In 1883, Welch became professor of pathology at Johns Hopkins University and researched the formation of thromboses and embolisms. He helped found the University Hospital in 1889 and the medical school in 1893. Acting as both dean and teacher, in 1896 he founded *The Journal of Experimental Medicine* to encourage the publication of medical research.

For thirty-four years he chaired the board of scientific advisers of the Rockefeller Institute of Medical Research, and for twenty-four years he served as the president of the Maryland Board of Public Health. He was a leading consultant on issues of urban public health during this period; many cities followed his recommendations. During World War I, he went on active duty in the army, reaching the rank of brigadier general in 1921.

After 1914, Dr. Welch was involved in the founding of the School of Hygiene and Public Health at Johns Hopkins. He resigned in 1926 to teach the history of medicine and develop the William H. Welch Medical Library.

Welch is best remembered for organizing two graduate schools and selecting exceptional faculty. He helped establish pathology and bacteriology as academic specializations in medical education. Welch's influence was felt far beyond the Johns Hopkins campus. On his eightieth birthday, there were celebrations across the United States and Europe.

"When Joshua was old and well advanced in years, the Lord said to him, 'You are very old, and there are still very large areas of land to be taken over.' "

Joshua 13:1

Father, it's hard to realize the contribution to public health by this single adult. Thank You for his work and tireless effort in creating healthier environments for humans.

April 9

James Topham Brady, lawyer
April 9, 1815–February 9, 1869

James Topham Brady received his legal education by studying law with his father and assisting him in the courtroom. In his first case after passing the bar in 1836, Brady defended a slave accused of murder. Although he lost the case, Brady's skilled defense won him notoriety. Juries could not ignore his summations and courtroom presence.

His career was enhanced by working with Daniel Webster on a particular case. Brady's opening arguments to the jury won Webster's highest praise. For the next twenty years, few major lawsuits in New York City did not involve James Brady. From 1843 to 1845, he was district attorney of New York.

James Brady remained a generalist, intensely interested in both civil and criminal law, and he was as comfortable in an appellate court as in the lower courts. Brady became an expert in the insanity defense. At one point in his career, he won the largest cash judgment ever awarded by a civil court. Out of fifty-two murder trials, Brady lost only one.

Brady ran for governor of New York in 1860, knowing that he could not win but committed to the two-party system and a strong debate on the issues. Another time, he said no to the corrupt Tammany machine that could have guaranteed his election as mayor. Brady also turned down the invitation to become United States attorney general. He remained throughout his life "indifferent to the prizes of political life."

"God gave Solomon wisdom and very great insight, and a breadth of understanding as measureless as the sand on the seashore."

1 Kings 4:29

Key Point: Your yes means nothing until your no means something.

April 10

Margaret Clapp, historian and college president
April 10, 1910–May 3, 1974

Margaret Clapp attended Wellesley intent on studying languages as her father had suggested; however, history and economics won out. She received her B.A. in

"I will lead the blind by ways they have not known,

94

1930 and wanted to do further study, but the economic realities of the Depression forced her into teaching.

Miss Clapp taught at a private girls' school in New York and worked on her master's degree in history at Columbia University during the next seven years. In 1942, she left teaching to pursue a doctorate in history. She completed her Ph.D. in 1946 with a dissertation on John Bigelow, a little-known editor and reformer. After a year as a researcher for the federal government, she published *Forgotten First Citizen: John Bigelow,* which won the 1947 Pulitzer Prize.

Soon afterward, she accepted the presidency of her alma mater, at a time when only five women were presidents of major liberal arts colleges in this country. She was thirty-nine years old.

Wellesley was a challenge, and Dr. Clapp met it head-on. She quipped, "I am not only the president, but the president's wife as well." She tripled the endowment, remodeled many campus buildings, and built three dormitories and a wing to the library. She expanded the faculty, increased salaries 150 percent, and developed an innovative leave program to foster faculty research and publication.

Dr. Clapp believed that Wellesley could train a generation of women who could combine both marriage and careers; she proposed early admission for women and the development of day-care programs. She led Wellesley into the twentieth century.

Margaret Clapp died in 1974 after a long battle with cancer.

> along unfamiliar paths I will guide them."
>
> Isaiah 42:16

Father, thank You for the courageous leadership of women like Margaret Clapp, who never let tradition interfere with vision. Help us to learn from her example.

April 11

Harvey Humphrey Baker, judge
April 11, 1869–April 10, 1915

"Lock 'em up and throw away the key!" was the prevalent mind-set toward juvenile delinquents around the turn of the century. This was not the attitude of Judge Harvey Baker, who took the bench in Boston in 1906. In fact, the appointment of the thirty-six-year-old single adult touched off controversy. What would a bachelor know about disciplining children? Furthermore, Baker

> "A righteous man will be remembered forever."
>
> Psalm 112:6

had grown up in a wealthy family, had a good education, and had been sheltered from the ugly world that many in his courtroom called reality.

Baker took the bench after traveling across the nation visiting courts and institutions for juvenile offenders. He sensed the potential of the judgeship to make a difference in the lives of children who appeared before him.

One biographer described Baker's traits: "fairness, patience, tact, ability to see many conflicting points of view, [and] firmness when necessary." His courtroom was closed to spectators. Often only Judge Baker and the child (occasionally a probation officer) were present. Judge Baker thought of his court as a dispensary and court officers as physicians. His intent was not merely to treat symptoms but to look for solutions that would cure.

Still, Judge Baker thought there was too much emphasis on applying the law and not enough on developing an understanding of the child. Baker longed to create "a clinic for the intensive study of baffling cases." Friends and associates established the Judge Baker Foundation in 1917 to do just that.

The judge was known for his storytelling. Many juveniles who appeared before the judge became model citizens because he showed mercy and compassion.

Father, mercy is often in short supply. Remind us to be merciful.

April 12

Arthur Crawshay Alliston Hall, minister
April 12, 1847–February 26, 1930

Arthur Hall was educated at Oxford and trained in the evangelical school of the Church of England. He was involved in the Society of St. John the Evangelist, which revived monastic life in the English church.

In 1874, Hall became assistant priest at the Church of the Advent in Boston and served there for eight years. His deep voice and strong pulpit manner left an impression on all his hearers. He was a man of influence in Boston.

In 1891, Hall got into a dispute with his superiors in England and, as a result, was ordered to return.

"I will sing of the Lord's great love forever; with my mouth I will make your faithfulness known. . . ."

Psalm 89:1

However, his seventeen years' work in New England had won him many friends. At a special 1893 convocation to fill the vacant position of bishop of Vermont, Arthur Hall was elected. He was allowed to return to the country and was consecrated bishop on February 2, 1894. His service was marked by a new emphasis on pastoral care and church growth.

He was influential in the revision of the lectionary and the prayer book. Bishop Hall developed a reputation as a canonist (a specialist in church law), and he was consulted by bishops from all over the country. Moreover, his deep spiritual life led many to seek him out for spiritual counsel.

He was committed to Christian unity and was active in ecumenical affairs. Arthur Hall was a prolific writer, and his works were widely read, particularly his *Meditations on the Creed* and *Christ's Temptation and Ours.*

Father, thank You for the faithful life of Arthur Hall and his commitment to You and Your kingdom. Help us to commit ourselves to things eternal.

April 13

Frank Murphy, Supreme Court justice
April 13, 1890–July 19, 1949

After graduation from the University of Michigan law school, Frank Murphy was admitted to the bar. He did graduate study in law in England and Ireland before he began work in a prominent Detroit law firm.

In 1919, Murphy was appointed chief assistant attorney general of the eastern district of Michigan. Between 1923 and 1930, he taught law at the University of Detroit, was a local court judge, and ran for mayor.

Elected mayor on the Democratic ticket, Murphy soon found there were more than 100,000 unemployed persons in Detroit. Murphy created the Mayor's Unemployment Committee, which served the jobless, ran emergency lodges for the homeless, and sponsored a variety of programs and resources.

When the state would not provide assistance to the city, Murphy presided over a conference of big-city mayors that influenced the passage of the Emergency Relief and Construction Act, which provided the cities with millions of federal dollars.

In 1932, Murphy became active in Roosevelt's cam-

"What does the Lord require of you? To act justly and to love mercy and to walk humbly with your God."

Micah 6:8

paign, and Roosevelt appointed him the governor general of the Philippines. He was enormously popular with the Filipino people and instituted women's suffrage and judicial reform.

When the Philippines became a commonwealth, Roosevelt convinced Murphy to come home and run for governor.

When Murphy was defeated in his re-election bid in 1938, Roosevelt appointed him attorney general. He prosecuted Kansas City boss Tom Pendergast, launched an investigation into the Huey Long machine in Louisiana, and prosecuted Federal Circuit Judge Martin T. Manion for receiving kickbacks.

In 1940, Frank Murphy took a seat on the United States Supreme Court. There he became a voice for the legally impoverished and was criticized as being more of a crusader than a justice.

Murphy believed that even in wartime the constitutional guarantees of individual freedom had to be honored. He denounced the herding of Japanese on the West Coast into internment camps and argued for the protection of procedural rights of defendants in criminal cases.

Key Point: The life of Justice Frank Murphy was committed to the rights of the defenseless. He was a man who loved justice and mercy.

April 14

Christian Huygens, scientist
April 14, 1629–July 9, 1695

Christian Huygens's parents knew he was a bright child with particular interest in mechanics and mathematics. His father was secretary of state for three princes of Orange in Holland; naturally, Christian would follow suit and study law at the University of Leyden. However, at age seventeen, after he wrote a brilliant mathematical paper, Christian was urged to switch fields.

Soon the scientific community was buzzing with Huygens's papers on the theory of probability and cross section of a cone. Huygens's first contribution to astronomy came when he discovered the nebula of Orion. Later he discovered the rings of Saturn, which he disclosed in a puzzle in 1665, to protect his claim on the

"The highest heavens belong to the Lord, but the earth he has given to man."

Psalm 115:16

find from rival scientists. Huygens also discovered one of Saturn's moons, which he named Titan.

Huygens's research—and that of many other scientists—was hampered by the lack of a precise way to measure time, so Christian developed and perfected the first clock accurately regulated by a pendulum.

Louis XIV invited Christian to France and provided him living accommodations and laboratories. In this period of his life, Huygens devoted himself to improving telescopes and developing in miniature a mechanical sky, the forerunner of today's planetariums. The Huygens Principle is still a relevant concept in the study of light.

Key Thought: The highest heavens may belong to God, but He has placed healthy curiosity about those heavens in the hearts of some men. What would the world of science have lost if Huygens had studied law?

April 15

Corrie ten Boom, evangelist
April 15, 1892–April 15, 1983

Most of the Christian world has heard of the spinster Dutch watchmaker who hid Jews from the Nazis during World War II. However, that was only one interval of her life. In the years before the Nazi nightmare swept Europe into war, Corrie had prayed, "Dear Lord, can You use me in some way?"

During these years, Corrie ten Boom started clubs for young girls and a Christian scouting movement called The Triangle Girls. She was also instrumental in starting programs for the mentally handicapped, most of whom could not attend or comprehend a worship service. Corrie also coached young women in catechism classes, and the ten Booms took in foster children.

After Corrie was miraculously released from Ravensbruck Prison, she prayed, "Lord, I have received my life back from You. Thank You. Will You tell me how to use it?"

One year after her release from prison, Corrie sailed to New York with fifty dollars in her pocket. Over the next decades, the world was her parish.

In 1968, Corrie gained recognition through appearances with Billy Graham, who called her "God's merry saint." Thousands read about Corrie's experiences in her best-selling books such as *A Prisoner and Yet.* When he book *The Hiding Place* was made into a movie, Corrie became the most sought-after woman speaker in the

"The Lord God hath given me the tongue of the learned, that I should know how to speak a word in season to him that is weary."

Isaiah 50:4 (Corrie's translation)

"Father, will You keep us so close to Your heart that even our dreams are peaceful, and that we see things as it were more

99

world. Her message was always the same: "There is no pit so deep that Jesus is not deeper still."

Corrie taught that God had buried our sins in the deepest sea and posted a sign saying, "No fishing allowed."

and more from Your point of view?"

Corrie ten Boom

April 16

Wilbur Wright, aviation pioneer
April 16, 1867–May 30, 1912
Orville Wright, aviation pioneer
May 19, 1871–January 30, 1948

A rubber-band toy helicopter launched a dream in Orville and Wilbur Wright. Watching their toy, the two boys determined that someday they would learn how to fly.

As they grew to young men, the brothers worked on their dream. On December 17, 1903, Orville flew 120 feet in the world's first powered flight. Later that day, Wilbur flew 852 feet in 59 seconds.

Their father wrote, "They are as inseparable as twins. For several years they have read up on aeronautics as a physician would read his books, and they have studied, discussed and experimented together. Natural workmen, they have invented, constructed, and operated their gliders, and finally their 'Wright Flyer,' jointly, all at their own personal expense. About equal credit is due each."

The Wright brothers not only invented the airplane but taught others to fly, helping to usher in a new age in mankind's history.

"Where can I go from your Spirit? Where can I flee from your presence? . . . If I rise on the wings of the dawn, . . . even there your hand will guide me."

Psalm 139:7, 9, 10

Key Point: In Kitty Hawk, North Carolina, a tourist can find this plaque: IN COMMEMORATION OF THE CONQUEST OF THE AIR. BY THE BROTHERS WILBUR AND ORVILLE WRIGHT. CONCEIVED BY GENIUS, ACHIEVED BY DAUNTLESS RESOLUTION AND UNCONQUERABLE FAITH. The dreams of single adults still come true through that combination.

April 17

Mahlon Dickerson, governor and senator
April 17, 1770–October 5, 1853

After graduation from Princeton, Mahlon Dickerson passed the bar and served military duty during the Whiskey Rebellion. He and his brothers moved to Philadelphia, and Mahlon became involved in politics with his 1802 election to the Philadelphia Common Council.

When his father died, Dickerson moved to New Jersey to run the family iron business. As a Democratic businessman, he helped establish the concept of the protective tariff.

From 1811 to 1812, Mahlon served in the state legislature before being elected justice of the state supreme court. In 1815, he became governor of New Jersey and was elected to a second term. Then, in 1817, Dickerson entered the United States Senate and stayed until 1833.

Dickerson had a profound impact on government spending. Convinced that a federal surplus would lead to a centralization of power in the federal government, he lobbied for distribution of the money back to the states, a policy implemented by the Jackson administration.

In 1832, Dickerson was a popular candidate for vice president, but stepped aside for his friend Martin Van Buren. He turned down an appointment as ambassador to Russia to promote the presidential aspirations of Van Buren, then became secretary of the navy and served until 1838.

Eventually Dickerson became disillusioned by the political maneuvering behind the nominations of James Polk and Zachary Taylor and retired from Democratic party politics.

"All the officials and all the people brought their contributions gladly, dropping them into the chest until it was full."

2 Chronicles 24:10

Key Point: Sometimes friends sacrifice their own aspirations in order to help a friend. Mahlon Dickerson might well have been president, but he put friendship ahead of politics.

April 18

William George MacCallum, pathologist
April 18, 1874–February 3, 1944

As a boy, William MacCallum accompanied his physician father on house calls and studied with him in a laboratory in their home. As a young man, he wanted to

"I praise you because I am fearfully and

101

study Greek but gave in to his father and studied medicine at Johns Hopkins, graduating first in the class of 1897.

After graduation he returned to Ontario and conducted experiments in the woodshed behind his father's home. Despite the primitive laboratory, MacCallum made a scientific breakthrough when he discovered that the sex life of avian parasites was involved in transmitting malaria.

In 1902, MacCallum returned to Johns Hopkins as professor of pathology. Two major research contributions soon followed: He discovered that lymphatic vessels systematically functioned like veins and arteries and absorbed red blood cells. Later, William researched the thyroid and parathyroid glands and the body's processing of calcium.

In 1909, Dr. MacCallum became professor of pathology at Columbia University, where he conducted significant research on heart valves and diabetes. His major research led to *Textbook of Pathology* in 1916.

MacCallum also worked to reform the coroner's office, replacing the standard political appointee with a competent pathologist. MacCallum insisted the public would be better served by the move.

He returned again to Johns Hopkins in 1917 to teach pathology and bacteriology. Again he made breakthroughs in the labs, this time in epidemic pneumonia among army personnel in World War I. MacCallum also began reading, writing, and researching the history of medicine, a subject he eventually began teaching.

Despite his brilliance, MacCallum was extremely shy and moody, yet his lifetime career and training of a generation of physicians and scientists led to many medical breakthroughs.

wonderfully made; your works are wonderful, I know that full well."

Psalm 139:14

Father, we are fearfully and wonderfully made. Thank You for researchers like William MacCallum who supply the documentation to the ancient psalmist's claims. Thank You for creating us.

April 19

Samuel Gregory, pioneer in women's medical education
April 19, 1813–March 23, 1872

The first enrollment of women in medical schools prompted riots and walkouts, but many educators such as Samuel Gregory realized that eventually the public would accept and appreciate female physicians.

"And a woman was there who had been subject to bleeding for twelve

Gregory became interested in medical issues as a senior at Yale. He graduated in 1845, and as early as 1847 he was lecturing in favor of medical education for females. For the next twenty-five years, he devoted himself to the idea of establishing a school. He promoted his idea on three assumptions: that women physicians would primarily care for children; that women missionaries could profit from a basic awareness of medicine; and that women could be better nurses through medical training. He believed that female physicians could be particularly helpful in preventive medicine because many women avoided or postponed seeking medical care from male doctors.

On November 1, 1848, the Boston Female Medical School opened with twelve students; Samuel Gregory served as chief executive officer. One of his pamphlets, *Letter to Ladies in Favor of Female Physicians for their Own Sex* (published in 1850), was quite popular. In 1856, the school was empowered to grant the degree of Doctor of Medicine to its graduates.

Two years after Gregory's death, his school was merged with the Boston University School of Medicine and became one of the first coed medical schools in the world. Today almost half of all medical students are female.

> years. She had suffered a great deal under the care of many doctors and had spent all she had."
>
> **Mark 5:25, 26**

> *Father, give us the wisdom to get out of the way of the march of progress. Help us to carefully test our utterances, lest we look back and be embarrassed by our lack of vision.*

April 20

David Brainerd, missionary
April 20, 1718–October 9, 1747

When John Wesley was asked what could be done to revive the work of the Lord, he responded, "Let every Preacher read carefully *The Life of Brainerd*. Let us be followers of him, as he was of Christ . . . in total deadness to the world."

David Brainerd was expelled from Yale University for criticizing the spiritual weakness of a faculty member by saying, "He has no more grace than a chair." Brainerd expected to be readmitted and finish his degree, but Yale authorities said no.

Later Brainerd was appointed a missionary to the Indians. His work to evangelize them was slow, and he

> "And the lord said unto the servant, Go out into the highways and hedges, and compel them to come in, that my house may be filled."
>
> **Luke 14:23 KJV**

attracted the ire of the Dutch who wanted to push the Indians farther west and take their land. Few American colonists were interested in missions to the Indians, so most of Brainerd's financial support came from British sources.

In 1743, after a full apology to the board of Yale, David was readmitted on condition that he spend his senior year in New Haven. But Brainerd was unwilling to give up his work among the Indians, whom he called "my people." On July 21, 1745, Brainerd baptized his first Indian converts. One Indian woman said that Brainerd was the first white man she could trust. He loved the Heavenly Father so much, she said, that he was willing to endure harships to "do my people good."

Brainerd's diaries were edited by Jonathan Edwards and published as *An Account of the Life of the Late Reverend Mr. David Brainerd.* Few books have had such an influence on world missions.

Brainerd wrote: "What are all the storms of this lower world, if Jesus by His Spirit does but come walking on the seas!

"I long to be wholly conformed to God and transformed into His image."

Father, wholly is a tough word. It's easy to think that we want to be conformed to You and transformed into Your image. Are there little areas we are not surrendering to You? Grant us the courage to give them to You.

April 21

Georgia Harkness, theologian
April 21, 1891–August 21, 1974

After six years teaching school, Georgia Harkness knew that God had more for her. When she got an opportunity to pursue a master's degree in theology at Boston University, she said yes. Many denominations had recognized the need for Christian educators and had begun hiring women.

Georgia excelled at Boston and overcame a lot of prejudice and skepticism to complete a Ph.D. in religion. She taught religion and philosophy for fifteen years at Elmira College in Elmira, New York. In 1926, she was ordained as a local deacon and in 1938 as a local elder in the Methodist Church. That was the highest level of ordination allowed for women in Methodism

"A woman should learn in quietness and full submission. I do not permit a woman to teach or have authority over a man."

1 Timothy 2:11, 12

until 1956. Georgia preached often and became an advocate for women's right to full participation in the life of the church.

Harkness had written *Holy Flame,* a devotional book of poetry, and five books on religion and ethics before her father fell seriously ill. On his deathbed, he urged Georgia "to write more books about Jesus Christ." Harkness wrote thirty-eight more books from this commitment.

Harkness reached a turning point in 1949, when she delivered a series of lectures eventually published as *The Gospel and Our World.* In the presentations, she argued that theologians must make the Gospel more relevant to the people in the pews. That theme became increasingly dominant in her writing and fueled the criticism that she had become a "popularizer." Harkness was so committed to the laity that, when she had a chance to be ordained to full clerical membership in 1956, she turned it down to remain a laywoman.

By the time of her death, Georgia Harkness was recognized as one of the ten most influential living Methodists. She opened the door of opportunity for thousands of women to pursue ministerial careers in Methodism and even to advance to the bishopric.

Father, thank You for the life of Georgia Harkness, who opened the door for the recognition of the vital role of the lay servant in the church. Remind me that I am called to serve, and help me to find my place of ministry.

April 22

Ellen Anderson Gholson Glasgow, novelist
April 22, 1873–November 21, 1945

At age seven, Ellen Glasgow decided to become a writer; by seventeen, she had written four hundred pages of a novel, which she eventually destroyed. In 1897, *The Descendant,* her first novel, was published anonymously.

Later she wrote *The Voice of the People,* which chronicled the rise of a poor man to the governorship of Virginia. Her next novel, *The Battle Ground,* focused on Virginia life between 1850 and 1865. *The Deliverance,* pulished in 1904, was her first strong novel. The story revolved around a plantation owner's family who had been displaced by their overseer and had to struggle to reconcile the old ways with the new.

"Remember the former things, those of long ago."

Isaiah 46:9

105

Barren Ground (1925) is considered one of her best novels and also brought her critical acclaim. Her success launched a period of enthusiastic creativity with the publication of *The Romantic Comedians, They Stooped to Folly,* and *The Sheltered Life.*

This Our Life, which portrayed a dark view of the decay of the quality of life in her fictitious town of Queensborough (Richmond), won the Pulitzer Prize for fiction in 1928.

Her biography, *The Woman Within,* published by Ellen's literary executor after her death, "was a remarkably frank picture of a morbidly sensitive woman and committed artist."

Ellen Glasgow was the first Southern voice raised "in loving anger against the falseness and insensitivity of the accepted tradition of the region." In all of her works, she included an individual as protagonist in conflict with society.

Key Thought: To be able to put into words what others can only see in their minds is the act of genius, a gift to be nurtured.

April 23

James Buchanan, president
April 23, 1791–June 1, 1868

"I may sustain the shock of her death, but I feel that happiness has fled from me forever." So wrote twenty-seven-year-old James Buchanan after the death of his ex-fiancée, Anne Coleman.

"Lord, I believe; help thou mine unbelief."

Mark 9:24 KJV

Friends were so concerned about James's depression that they decided to run him for Congress in 1821 to distract him from his grief. He won and served until 1831. In Congress, Buchanan was a strong supporter of the needs of the common people and worked hard for Andrew Jackson. As chairman of the House Judiciary Committee from 1829 to 1831, he fought to defeat an attempt to narrow the Supreme Court's authority in matters of treaties and federal law.

In 1832, Andrew Jackson appointed Buchanan minister to Russia and directed him to develop trading policies with that country. From 1834 to 1845, he was a senator from Pennsylvania. Under the administration of James Polk, he served as secretary of state, then he retired to his estate near Lancaster from 1849 to 1853 before becoming envoy to Great Britain.

In 1856, he was elected president and was the only president to remain a bachelor (Cleveland married while in office). The years of his presidency were turbulent, and Buchanan's most important achievement may have been in keeping the Union together long enough for Lincoln to be elected.

James Buchanan struggled with his faith for decades. As early as 1832, he had written his brother from Russia, "I desire to be a Christian and I think I could withdraw from the vanities and follies of the world without suffering many pangs. . . . My true feeling upon many occasions is; 'Lord, I would believe; help Thou my unbelief.' Yet I am far from being an unbeliever."

While on vacation in 1860, with war clouds growing darker, the president had occasion to spend two hours with William Paxton, pastor of First Presbyterian Church in New York. At the end of the meeting, Buchanan announced that his doubts were settled. However, he feared that making his faith public and joining a church would open him to charges that he was a hypocrite, so he waited until he left the White House to do so.

Key Point: James Buchanan was not a great president, but he kept the country together longer than many expected. Sometimes we cannot work miracles; we merely live one day at a time.

April 24

Arthur Christopher Benson, poet and scholar
April 24, 1862–June 17, 1925

Having the Archbishop of Canterbury as his father opened a lot of doors for A. C. Benson. He was born at Wellington College, where his father was headmaster, and lived his entire life in academic surroundings. After King's College, Cambridge, he taught at Eton and wrote a book on teaching. Ironically, one biographer noted, "he disliked the profession, cared only for a few of his pupils, and found his only happiness in the leisure hours he could give to writing." In 1903, he went to Cambridge and edited the papers of Queen Victoria.

Eventually, he accepted a fellowship at Magdalen College and spent the rest of life there, quickly establishing himself as the cultural leader of Cambridge. During his time there, he wrote nearly one hundred books of poems, essays, and biographies and frequently corresponded with his readers. One American woman left him a large amount of money, which he gave to the college.

"Oh, that you would wonderfully bless me and . . . be with me in all that I do."

1 Chronicles 4:10 TLB

Key Thought: Sometimes it is necessary to do what we dislike to gain the resources to do what we want. Re-

107

One stanza of his poetry has been remembered because it was set to music by Elgar for his "Pomp and Circumstance," traditional graduation music.

member that God is interested in all that we do.

April 25

Paul Oscar Husting, senator
April 25, 1866–October 21, 1917

School ended for Paul Husting when he had to get a job to support his family; however, he eventually found time to study law while working for the Wisconsin secretary of state. From 1902 to 1906, Husting was a district attorney.

After his election to the Wisconsin legislature, he worked closely with Robert La Follette's Progressives to see much of their legislative agenda passed. Husting worked hard to pass a state income tax and to ratify the national income tax amendment; he also vigorously supported the investigation of corruption in government and favored the popular election of senators.

Husting emerged in 1912 as a major Democratic kingmaker in Wisconsin and worked to help Woodrow Wilson win the state in the 1912 presidential election. In 1914, Democrat Husting became the first man in Wisconsin to be directly elected to the United States Senate, taking a traditionally Republican seat.

Many believed he had a great Senate career ahead of him. However, in 1917, in a freak hunting accident, he was shot and killed by his brother.

"Have no fear of sudden disaster or of the ruin that overtakes the wicked, for the Lord will be your confidence and will keep your foot from being snared."

Proverbs 3:25, 26

Father, we know death is the final agenda for all of us. Protect us from an untimely death that catches us unprepared to meet You.

April 26

Alice Cary, poet
April 26, 1820–February 12, 1871

Life became considerably more difficult for Alice Cary after her mother died in 1835; her father's new wife strongly disapproved of Alice's reading and mocked her desire to write verse. Finally, Alice's father built a new house for his wife and moved there, leaving Alice and Phoebe and three other children from the first marriage in his original home.

"Better to live in a desert than with a quarrelsome and ill-tempered wife."

Proverbs 21:19

Alice's first poem, "Child of Sorrow," was printed by the *Sentinel* when she was fifteen. Though her work was primarily published in Western papers and magazines, Easterners began to recognize it. The Washington, D.C., newspaper *National Era* began regularly printing poetry by Alice, which attracted favorable comments from noted writers such as John Greenleaf Whittier, Edgar Allan Poe, and Horace Greeley. In fact, Poe called "Pictures of Memory" one of the most musically perfect lyrics in the English language. With such praise, Alice could overlook her stepmother's biting criticism.

The first book of poetry that Alice and her sister published earned them one hundred dollars. After a tour of the East and a prolonged visit with Whittier, Alice decided to move to New York City. She had been disappointed in an engagement with an Ohio businessman and had misunderstood the intentions of Rufus Griswold, her literary agent, who eventually married another woman. Although she and her sister relied on their poetry to support them, they lived well.

Alice also wrote short stories and novels based on her farm years back in Ohio. The themes of hard work, cultural deprivation, and the frustration of women's limitations in a male-dominated world were common in all her work.

Key Thought: Life is not always fair. Sometimes we must take the pains in life and carefully sift them for the hint of opportunity.

April 27

Charles Townsend Copeland, college professor
April 27, 1860–July 24, 1952

The influence of a teacher can be lifelong. Laura Burns, an English teacher, had that kind of effect on young Charles Copeland. After his Harvard graduation and as long as she lived, Miss Burns was Charles's mentor.

At age thirty-three Copeland began teaching English at Harvard, spending the next seventeen years as a lowly instructor. Slowly, he climbed the academic ladder but did not make full professor until age sixty-five. His love was a course called English 12; one biographer dubbed it a living monument to Copeland's teaching. His students included many of the greats of twentieth-century American literature: T. S. Eliot, Oliver La Farge,

"Commission Joshua, and encourage and strengthen him, for he will lead this people across and will cause them to inherit the land you will see."

Deuteronomy 3:28

John Dos Passos, Malcolm Cowley, Lawrence Spivak, Robert Sherwood, and Rachel Field. Copeland became a mentor to many of these students. He encouraged every student in English 12, including the mediocre ones, to write "out of life." Because of his energy, the class enrollment sometimes reached 250 students.

Copeland lived on campus and organized Monday evening gatherings with a guest of honor for selected students. His guests included many of the greats: Ernest Hemingway, Robert Frost, Felix Frankfurter, and others.

Copeland's books included *Edwin Booth* (1901), *Letters of Thomas Carlyle* (1899), *Representative Biographies of English Men of Letters* (1904), and the highly praised *Copeland Reader* (1927).

On Copeland's seventieth birthday, 300 Harvard grads gathered in New York City to celebrate his lifelong contribution to their lives. Charles Copeland never stopped encouraging and strengthening his students and friends, and his belief in them sparked many to great creativity.

Father, remind us today that we, too, can find and make opportunities to encourage and strengthen others.

April 28

Palmer Cox, author
April 28, 1840–July 24, 1924

Palmer Cox, born in Canada, came to San Francisco in 1863 and worked on the railroad and as a ship's carpenter. As an avocation, Cox wrote and submitted humorous verse and cartoons to several California newspapers. In 1875, his pictures illustrating *Squibs of California or Everyday Life Illustrated* received tremendous public attention.

Palmer Cox moved to New York and joined the staff of a weekly comic paper, *Wild Oats,* which went bankrupt five years later. However, the three major stories he had published during this period led to a job with *St. Nicholas Magazine.* His stories and illustrations attracted the attention of many children who became his fans. Cox created a series called "Brownies," based on the folklore of the Grampian Mountains. He had learned the stories as a child and simply adapted them to American children. The Brownie stories contained no crime

"I tell you the truth, anyone who will not receive the kingdom of God like a little child will never enter it."

Luke 18:17

or pain—only laughter. Two generations of children enjoyed his Brownies. Cox drew more than a million sketches for the thirteen books.

Palmer Cox died a wealthy man for having contributed moments of joy to many children, and although many critics rebuked his work, Cox's real reward came in the delighted laughter of children who saw his work.

Key Thought: A single adult does not have to be a parent to make a difference in the lives of children.

April 29

Henry Malcolm Sargent, conductor and composer
April 29, 1895–October 3, 1967

Malcolm Sargent used his gift of personality, his musical genius, and his love of showmanship to spread the love of music around the world. After the death of his beloved daughter, Pamela, in 1944, and the demise of his marriage in 1946, Sargent poured himself into his musical career.

He was knighted in 1947 and in 1950 followed Sir Adrian Boult as conductor of the prestigious British Broadcasting Corporation Symphony Orchestra. He also directed the BBC Chorus and the Royal Choral Society. He conducted the Promenade Concerts and served as guest conductor for numerous orchestras around the world. From Perth to Johannesburg, he pressed the cause of British music and won the hearts of audiences and critics.

His most glittering performance came in May 1951, when he conducted *Rule Britannia* with a choir made up of singers from seven great London choruses and the members of five London orchestras. At the conclusion of the performance, the king, the queen, and the British prime minister gave Sargent a standing ovation. King George sent for Sargent.

"I have never been moved by any music as much as your arrangement of 'Rule Britannia.' Do remember this—whenever I come to another of your concerts . . . I will command you to perform it again."

Sargent thought a moment, then tactfully replied, "That is very kind of you, sir, but it may be difficult if we have been performing Bach's *B Minor Mass* or the *St. Matthew Passion*."

"Where, O death, is your victory? Where, O death, is your sting? . . . But thanks be to God! He gives us the victory through our Lord Jesus Christ."

1 Corinthians 15:55, 57

111

The king immediately replied, "It won't be difficult. I shan't be there."

In 1966, Sir Malcolm developed cancer but made a courageous effort to keep conducting. He startled friends by saying that death was something he looked forward to greatly. "I have loved life so much, so I know I will love death still more."

Few single adults have died as triumphantly. On his deathbed, Sargent whispered to the Archbishop of Canterbury, "I always had faith. Now I have knowledge."

Father, death is on all of our schedules but on few of our agendas. Help us to so live our lives that we will see death as passing from life to life. Give us safe passage into Your presence.

April 30

Joseph Kinnicutt Angell, legal writer
April 30, 1794–May 1, 1857

Joseph Angell was a member of a family that traced its roots back to Thomas Angell, who came to the Rhode Island colony in 1631. After graduation from law school, Angell went to England to make a legal claim on an estate of one of Thomas Angell's brothers. He lost on a technicality and turned the loss into a lifetime lesson on details.

Joseph Angell returned to the United States in 1822 and devoted himself to legal writing and research. Although the topics sound pedantic, they were quite useful to attorneys in Angell's day: *The Common Law in Relation to Watercourses* (1824) and *The Right of Property in Tide Waters* (1826). Both were valued in the legal community. One prominent judge declared that no intelligent attorney could practice without being acquainted with Angell's work.

Angell's *The Law of Private Corporations* (1832) became a standard legal reference work. Because of new decisions by the courts, Angell continually revised his books. He became reporter for the Rhode Island Supreme Court in 1847—the first such appointment.

At the time of Angell's death, he was working on *The Law of the Highways,* which was completed after his death by Thomas Durfee. His obituary is worth reading:

"Hate evil, love good; maintain justice in the courts."

Amos 5:15

He died as he lived, without an enemy; distinguished through life by the simplicity of his character, by his kindly feelings toward all around him, by his attachment to his friends, by his freedom from prejudice, and by the total absence of all malevolence of spirit.

Key Thought: We write our own obituaries daily. Let us conduct our lives in a manner that speaks well of us.

May 1

May Massee, children's publisher
May 1, 1881–December 24, 1966

One of the delights of adulthood is rediscovering those books we loved as children. Stories that are timeless still warm our hearts. Few people have influenced children's literature as much as May Massee. She began her career as a librarian in White Water, Wisconsin, but eventually accepted a position at the Buffalo, New York, public library, where she oversaw the children's room and spent five years reorganizing it.

In 1913, she moved to Chicago to become editor of *The Booklist,* published by the American Library Association. When Doubleday decided to create a children's department, May was invited to head it. She believed "pioneering is more fun than anything else" and stayed for eleven years.

In 1933, she founded the Viking Press children's book division, where she worked as director for twenty-seven years. There May shaped the direction of all children's books published in the United States. She did this by taking risks. She published such books as *The Story of a Baby,* focusing on a baby's growth from conception to birth. She published books with minorities as heroes. She published books about children in other lands, particularly Russia, Albania, Norway, and Hungary.

Massee published books "that would bring the joy of living of all the world's children to our children." Her genius, many claimed, was in discovering what a writer or artist brought to his work and bringing it to fulfillment.

In 1959, she was the first woman to be awarded the American Institute of Graphic Art's medal "for production of beautiful books."

"Train a child in the way he should go, and when he is old he will not turn from it."

Proverbs 22:6

Father, it's not difficult to find our niche. But it can be difficult to make waves, to keep our commitment to excellence. Challenge us with our potential and discovering the potential in others.

113

May 2
Lorenz Milton Hart, musical lyricist
May 2, 1895–November 22, 1943

Two years studying journalism at Columbia prepared Hart more for a career in newspapers than in writing musicals with Richard Rodgers.

But Lorenz Hart began working with Rodgers in 1918. Their first Broadway success was *The Garrick Gaieties* in 1925, which was a small, intimate revue as opposed to the big productions then popular on Broadway. Rodgers and Hart believed audiences had been bored by musicals and sought to brighten the lyrics and music.

There was a dark side to Hart's music. This is particularly evident in *I Married an Angel*, which portrayed a depression-ridden urban world of unmarried adults in lonely, loveless rooms. But Hart could be sentimental, as in "My Funny Valentine," a tribute to a homely lover.

Hart did not embrace the patriotic trends of wartime. Rodgers wanted to do *Oklahoma!* but the project did not interest Lorenz Hart. Because Hart had become an alcoholic, spending most of his time barhopping in Manhattan, Rodgers turned to Oscar Hammerstein II. *Oklahoma!* was a smash. Rodgers and Hart reunited for *A Connecticut Yankee;* however, Hart disappeared on opening night and was found two days later dying of pneumonia.

Lorenz Hart revolutionized the musical by creating authentic conversation rather than the stilted poetics of previous years. He gave Broadway "sharp, tasteful lyrics finely coordinated with rhythm and melody and with the plot, mood and action of the play."

> "You strum away on your harps like David and improvise on musical instruments."
>
> **Amos 6:5**

> *Father, how much more could Hart have contributed to the world of musical theater if he could have dealt with his alcoholism? Give us courage to face the demons in our lives now.*

May 3
Golda Meir, premier of Israel
May 3, 1898–December 8, 1978

Golda Meir was born in Kiev, the Ukraine. Although her parents initially objected to her desire to become a schoolteacher, she graduated from Milwaukee Teachers' Training College in 1917. Golda was an active participant in the Zionism movement.

She married Morris Myerson in December 1917. After meeting David Ben Gurion (the future prime minister of

> "Deborah, a prophetess, the wife of Lappidoth, was leading Israel at that time."
>
> **Judges 4:4**

114

Israel), Golda became convinced that her future was in Israel. She and her husband moved to Palestine in 1921; in 1923, the couple moved to Tel Aviv, where Golda worked for the Office of Public Works. In 1928, she became secretary of the Women's Labor Council. The next year Mrs. Meir became active in the World Zionism movement and traveled throughout the world for the cause of Jewish organizations.

In 1951, Golda was widowed and poured herself into her work as minister of labor in Ben Gurion's government. In 1956, she became foreign minister. Ben Gurion called her "the only man in my Cabinet" when she supported swift retaliation against Arab attacks. In 1965, she led negotiations to reestablish diplomatic relations with West Germany. From 1953 to 1966, Meir led the Israeli delegations to the United Nations.

In 1965, she resigned her government post. However, after the Six Day War shifted the balance of power in the Middle East, Golda came out of retirement to become the fourth premier of Israel, a modern Deborah. As premier, she demonstrated toughness in dealing with issues inside and outside Israel, but she also developed a reputation as a strong international stateswoman.

Golda Meir led Israel with this conviction: "If we have to have a choice between being dead and pitied, and being alive with a bad image, we'd rather be alive and have the bad image." Meir served until 1974.

Key Thought: "We only want that which is given naturally to all peoples of the world, to be masters of our own fate, only of our fate, not of others, and in cooperation and friendship with others."

Golda Meir

May 4

Paul Leopold Rosenfeld, music and art critic
May 4, 1890–July 21, 1946

As a little boy, Paul Rosenfeld faced a great deal of pressure: His family encountered a great deal of anti-Semitism, and his mother died when he was ten years old. Paul went to live with his grandfather and at thirteen was placed in Riverview Military Academy.

Rosenfeld later attended Yale and the Columbia University School of Journalism. After graduation, he worked for a while as a reporter for the *New York Press* but quit. Some time in Europe, he thought, would help him settle his priorities.

"Also, if two lie down together, they will keep warm. But how can one keep warm alone?"

Ecclesiastes 4:11

115

When he returned from the continent, Paul joined a circle of intellectuals that included noted photographer Alfred Stieglitz, novelist Waldo Frank, and musician Leo Ornstein. Rosenfeld's first literary essays began appearing in 1916. After World War I service, he became music critic for the *Dial* and published his first book, *Musical Portraits.*

Soon, Rosenfeld's name was found in *Vanity Fair, The Nation,* as well as *Modern Music.* The volume of his writing was staggering. His best book was *Port of New York,* in which Rosenfeld presented "portraits" of fourteen modern Americans such as Georgia O'Keeffe, William Coles Williams, Sherwood Anderson, and his friend Stieglitz. Many of Rosenfeld's friends changed the cultural map of America, and Rosenfeld was part of the process.

In the 1920s, artists, writers, and composers gathered nightly in Rosenfeld's salon. Many young artists got their cultural introduction to New York, as well as a boost for their careers, from this single adult. He also used his publication, *American Caravan,* to publish the work of young writers.

Father, on the days we doubt our own creativity, remind us of the encouragement of Rosenfeld to so many. Can I encourage some artist, painter, poet, sculptor, or musician today?

May 5

John Campbell Loudoun, British commander in America
May 5, 1705–April 27, 1782

Few British commanders in chief in North America were loved; the fourth Earl of Loudoun was no exception.

John Loudoun's task was clear when he was appointed by the king in January 1756. He was ordered to combine all the British soldiers scattered across the colonies into an efficient fighting force. Moreover, Loudoun was to unify the thirteen colonies in the war effort against the French and Indians.

Despite his brilliance as a tactician and his military record, Loudoun found the American turf different from anything he had experienced. To compound his problems, the colonists were obstinate, particularly with his strict definitions of loyalty and authority.

After major defeats, John Campbell Loudoun was recalled to England in December 1757. In the following years, he managed to reestablish himself as a military leader and was eventually promoted to general in 1770.

". . . Do not let me be put to shame, nor let my enemies triumph over me."

Psalm 25:2

Key Point: Sometimes you have to know when to say "enough!" with or without an exclamation mark.

May 6

Maximilien de Robespierre, French statesman
May 6, 1758–July 28, 1794

Maximilien de Robespierre had a rough childhood; his mother died when he was young, and his father abandoned him soon after. He was raised by his maternal grandparents and graduated from law school in Paris in 1781. In 1788, he published his first political tract criticizing the government. When the Estates General met in Versailles in May 1789, Robespierre represented his province.

Maximilien played a critical role as a spokesman for the left in the new National Assembly that replaced the Estates General. He gained considerable influence; in every debate, he would be heard. Soon he developed a reputation as the chief advocate of political democracy.

On August 10, 1792, after having been involved with a plot to arrest the royal family, Robespierre was elected to the Commune of Paris. In September, he was elected to the National Convention, the new ruling body in France. He quickly became the chief prosecutor against the king, demanding his execution.

In a bloodless revolution in June 1793, Robespierre took charge. Under his leadership, the infamous Reign of Terror began and thousands of his political enemies died; indeed, many of his former friends also found themselves on the guillotine.

On June 4, 1794, the convention elected Robespierre its president, but he quickly lost the support of the committees, his followers, and the common people. On July 26, Robespierre came to the convention demanding another purge. The convention refused and ordered him arrested.

On July 28, Robespierre stood where he had condemned so many others. He was guillotined and his body thrown into a common grave.

"The wicked draw the sword and bend the bow to bring down the poor and needy. . . . But their swords will pierce their own hearts."

Psalm 37:14, 15

Father, remind us that the capacity to do evil lies in all of us. Guard our quest for power.

May 7

Gail Loughlin, lawyer
May 7, 1868–March 13, 1952

Gail Loughlin's career revolved around a vow she made as a twelve-year-old: "to study law and dedicate my entire life to the freeing of women and establishing their proper place in this 'man's world.'" No doubt some people smiled and thought *how noble,* or said, "We'll see." But Gail never doubted her destiny.

In 1899, Loughlin passed the New York bar and went to work for the United States Industrial Commission. She investigated the condition of domestic servants, particularly black and immigrant women, working for low wages under poor conditions.

From 1902 to 1906, Gail crisscrossed the United States as an agent for the National American Woman Suffrage Association. In 1914, she opened a law practice in San Francisco. Soon after, she founded the California division of the National League for Women's Services, which fought for the passage of legislation permitting women to serve on juries in California. In 1919, Gail was elected the first president of the National Federation of Business and Professional Women, an organization with the goal of eliminating all consideration of sex in occupation, economic opportunity, or remuneration.

Gail lobbied effectively for the National Women's Party. When she discovered that President Calvin Coolidge was vacationing in South Dakota, she organized a 200-car caravan to carry women from California to his vacation site to demand support on women's issues.

In 1924, a group of women in Maine invited Loughlin to move to the state and run for the legislature; Gail did and was elected in 1929. After three terms, she ran for the Maine Senate, was elected, and served until 1941.

Her most memorable legislative accomplishment was the law that prevented women from being committed to mental hospitals solely on their husband's wishes—a common ploy to avoid divorce or to harass a wife. She also traveled extensively, offering legal services to women who had been convicted by all-male juries.

"The Lord is with me; I will not be afraid."

Psalm 118:6

Father, You are a God of justice, and there is no shortage of injustice in the world. Give us courage to be Your servants in righting the wrongs.

May 8

Edward Gibbon, historian
May 8, 1737–January 16, 1794

Few students who have passed a Western civilization or history class fail to recognize the name of Edward Gibbon. His classic history of Rome, *The Decline and Fall of the Roman Empire,* has been read and footnoted by millions.

Gibbon fell in love with a student in Switzerland, but his father would not allow him to marry and live there; the girl's father would not allow her to move to England. Gibbon later noted, "I sighed as a lover; I obeyed as a son."

Gibbon first considered writing the history of the Roman Empire in October 1764, but he didn't publish the first volume of *Decline and Fall* until 1776. Although he angered many with his criticism of the early church and was charged with plagiarism, the book sold well. Volumes two and three were published in 1781 and Gibbon, who had lost his Parliament seat in 1780, regained it.

In September 1783, he moved to Switzerland and shared a home with fellow writer, George Deyverdun. There he wrote the fifth and sixth volumes of *Decline and Fall,* which were published on Gibbon's fifty-first birthday.

He made six attempts to write his memoirs but was devastated by his friend Deyverdun's death in 1789 and returned to England in 1793.

His contribution to history was history—well-written, well-researched.

". . . what he wrote was upright and true."

Ecclesiastes 12:10

Father, You gave many the ability to take complex ideas and explain them in simple terms. Thank You for that gift and for the life and work of Edward Gibbon.

May 9

Belle Boyd, spy and actress
May 9, 1844–June 11, 1900

Even as a child, Belle Boyd was known to be strong willed. After graduation from the fashionable Mount Washington Female College in Baltimore, she was pre-

"Joshua spared Rahab the prostitute, with her family and

sented to Washington society but returned to live with her parents in the South.

When Federal troops occupied Martinsburg, Virginia, Belle began work as a free-lance spy. In spite of shooting a Union soldier who invaded her home, she became quite popular with Union officers. From them, she obtained military information that she passed on to the Confederates. When Union officers discovered her activities, Belle was only reprimanded.

Soon her amateur days were over. By 1861, when she was just seventeen years old, Belle acted as a courier for Generals Beauregard and Jackson. Some scholars believe that she was also involved in blockade-running and smuggling.

Captured again, Belle was released by Union officers. In one of her most daring escapades, Belle passed information that saved strategic bridges and allowed General Jackson's troops to move closer to Washington, D.C. The action won Belle notoriety in the North and South.

In 1863, after two more arrests, she was banished to the South. After a severe bout with typhoid fever, under the guise of sailing to England for reasons of health, the nineteen-year-old smuggled out secret Confederate documents. Her ship was captured by Union officers. Belle was banished to Canada and notified that she would be executed if she returned to the country.

In the process, Belle became engaged to the Union naval officer who had captured her, and she destroyed the papers she was carrying. That ended her career as a spy. She married Samuel Hardinge in London, but he died soon after his return to the United States.

She married again in 1869 and was divorced in 1884. Belle went on stage as a lecturer and carried credentials proving she was "the genuine Belle Boyd."

all who belonged to her, because she hid the men Joshua had sent as spies."

Joshua 6:25

Father, give us courage to act on our convictions, to be participants in life and not just spectators.

May 10

Robert Emmet Bledsoe Baylor, judge and college founder
May 10, 1793–December 30, 1873

As a member of the Kentucky legislature, R. E. B. Baylor and another man fell in love with the same woman, and both men agreed to leave the state. Baylor went to

"The prophets prophesy lies, the priests rule by

Alabama, was elected to the state legislature, and later to Congress.

His life was tragically scarred when his fiancée died. The couple had been riding one day when the girl's horse threw her, and she was killed. Baylor blamed himself for her death.

Soon after, he moved to Texas to rebuild his life there. When Texas entered the Union, he became a federal district judge and served until the Civil War.

His general practice was to ride into a town on a weekend, preach on Sunday, and begin holding court on Monday. Often he used the courtroom as a church.

Judge Baylor was always interested in education, and in 1845 he drew the charter for the first Baptist college in Texas. He made the largest cash contribution to its endowment and served as chairman of the board of trustees. Eventually the college was named for him—against his protests—and moved to its present site in Waco. Baylor University is a legacy to his vision.

"The world here I believe gives me some little credit for trying to do good. . . . I should have preferred to have passed away to the land hereafter in silence, for such a poor sinner as I am deserves not to have any notice taken of him."

their own author-ity, and my people love it this way. But what will you do in the end?"

Jeremiah 5:31

Father, give us the humility of Your servant, R. E. B. Baylor. Make us more aware of our opportunities to be an instrument in Your hands.

May 11

Ethel Bernice Weed, reformer
May 11, 1906–June 6, 1975

The war was over; the emperor's country lay devastated by the atomic bomb. But while others thought of going home, Ethel Weed's work was just beginning. She entered Tokyo with the first convoy of Americans, ready to assume her new responsibility as Women's Information Officer with the Occupation Forces. MacArthur wanted an immediate democratization of Japanese women in the new postwar society. Quickly, Ethel Weed recruited Japanese women who had been active in the prewar suffrage movement in Japan.

On MacArthur's orders, Japanese women were granted the vote in December 1945. Some predicted that only 10 percent would go to the polls. Weed's work

"Give her the reward she has earned, and let her works bring her praise at the city gate."

Proverbs 31:31

surprised everyone: 67 percent of eligible women voters voted! Moreover, thirty-nine women were elected to the new Japanese Parliament.

Next Ethel turned to organizing the Japanese League of Women Voters and the Women's Democratic Club. Her political reform won her an army commendation medal in 1946. She helped rewrite the Japanese civil code to give women more choice in marriage, property ownership, divorce, and inheritance. Some protested the enormity of her changes, but MacArthur defended Miss Weed's vision.

Weed finished her duties in April 1952, having set in motion policies that gave Japanese women a new sense of dignity.

As a personal note, on the day I wrote this devotional, forty-four years had passed since Weed's arrival in Japan. Today's headlines carried the sensational story of Takako Doi, leader of the Japan Socialist Party, which had, under her dynamic leadership, snatched away the ruling party's majority in the upper house of Parliament. Suddenly, it is theoretically possible that in a year or so, a woman could become prime minister of Japan.

It may not hapen, but it *could.* That would bring a smile to the face of Ethel Weed, who gave Japanese women the vote.

Father, thank You for tasks that seem so large we can accomplish them only by relying on You. Give us the courage to take the first step.

May 12

Florence Nightingale, nurse
May 12, 1820–August 13, 1910

Before Florence Nightingale, nurses were thought to be no more than prostitutes or drunks—questionable women with questionable motives. Imagine the response when Florence told her wealthy parents she intended to become a nurse! "My mind is absorbed with the idea of the sufferings of man. All the people I see are eaten up with care or poverty or disease."

The more Florence committed herself to her goal, the more estranged she became from her family. In 1849, she refused to marry Richard Monckton Milnes, "the

"Peter said to Jesus, 'Lord, it is good for us to be here.' "

Matthew 17:4

man I adored," because, "to be nailed to a continuation and exaggeration of my present life . . . would be intolerable."

Florence went to Kaiserwerth, Germany, to a school established for the training of nurses. Although the facilities were crude and the training elemental, Nightingale found what she called "a better life for women."

She returned to London to head The Institution for the Care of Sick Gentle-Women in Distressed Circumstances. By 1854, the Crimean War matched England, France, and Turkey against Russia. The dispatches from the front were disturbing: "No sufficient preparations have been made for the proper care of the wounded."

On October 21, 1854, Miss Nightingale and her party of thirty-eight female nurses sailed for the front. She was unprepared for what she found: The wounded lay in little more than sewers of filth. Not only were there battle casualties, but typhus, dysentery, and cholera, plus a shortage of medicine and water and poor food. Florence encountered uncaring, negligent officers who began to take bets on when she would give up and go home.

In the infamous Barracks Hospital, hope focused on Florence Nightingale. One soldier wrote in a letter home, "We could kiss her shadow." She spent long hours on the wards but found time to write reports to the War Office, some of which were published in the *London Times*. As a result, a royal commission was appointed to inspect the hospitals in war zones.

In 1856, Florence went home to England, having raised the reputation of nurses and instituted new high standards of sanitation and efficiency in nursing and in the army.

After Florence Nightingale's death, the nation wanted to have her funeral in Westminster Abbey, but her will would not allow that. A cemetery in East Wellow, Hampshire, contains her simple tombstone: F. N. Born 1820. Died 1910.

Key Thought: "Life is a splendid gift. . . . But to live your life you must discipline it. You must not fritter it away."

Florence Nightingale

Percy Stickney Grant, clergyman
May 13, 1860–February 13, 1927

A desire to be helpful led Harvard student Percy Grant to study for the ministry. Coming from a long line of New Englanders, Grant came to adulthood with a strong sense of tradition. Though he had been a Baptist Sunday school teacher, he was disenchanted with Baptist theology. As a result, he joined the Episcopal Church and jointly studied at Harvard graduate school and Episcopal Theological Seminary. In 1886, Grant began pastoring in Fall River, Massachusetts. He developed a significant ministry among the town's mill workers, and one biographer observed, "All Fall River was his church."

Grant was called to the Church of the Ascension in New York City, which was in socioeconomic transition, many of its wealthy members having moved uptown. Preaching to empty pews for several Sundays led Grant to consider some innovations: He would reach out to the whole city of New York. Pews, formerly rented, were made free. The vesper services were given musical formats, and the church building was used by a variety of groups. Attendance increased dramatically as large crowds gathered to hear Grant's spirited preaching.

Grant called for more compassionate attitudes on divorce and became involved in a wide variety of social issues: labor, free speech, deportation, and socialism. The church branded him a social and ecclesiastical heretic, but the crowds came to make up their own minds.

Eventually, Grant resigned his pastorate in an ecclesiastical power struggle after he announced his engagement to a twice-divorced woman. His bishop forbade any clergyman in the diocese to perform the ceremony, and Grant used the pulpit to offer a heated response to his bishop.

He retired to his farm and died three years later, unmarried.

" 'Everything is permissible for me'—but not everything is beneficial."

1 Corinthians 6:12

Father, life sometimes requires tough decisions of us. If such should be in our path today, give us courage to choose wisely.

Bryan Jeffery Leech, composer
May 14, 1931–

Bryan Jeffery Leech calls himself "the Apostle to the Late Bloomer" because, by his own admission, his composing didn't catch fire until he was forty. Since then, he has been making up for lost time.

Leech has written ten hymn texts and five hymn tunes that are included in contemporary hymnals. He also wrote two ballads, a musical play, *Ebenezer,* and a musical adaptation of Charles Dickens's *A Christmas Carol.*

He served on the commission that developed *The Covenant Hymnal* in 1973 and assisted in the preparation of *Hymns for the Family of God.*

Why was his success delayed so long? Most writers, Bryan contends, are afraid to change. They want too much, too soon. Some lyricists are repetitive because they are not into the Word. Some have a moment of success, or what he calls, "too much too soon," and then burn out.

The lyricist's writing is produced by a sensitivity that comes through experience. Bryan says that during the years before he published, he was experiencing a spiritual stockpiling that has led to his creativity today.

One favorite Leech hymn is "We Are God's People," set to Brahms:

> We are a Temple, the Spirit's dwelling place.
> Formed in great weakness, a cup to hold
> God's grace.
> We die alone, for on its own Each ember
> loses fire;
> Yet joined in one the flame burns on
> To give warmth and light, and to inspire.*

"So is my word that goes out from my mouth: It will not return to me empty, but will accomplish what I desire and achieve the purpose for which I sent it."

Isaiah 55:11

Father, for the gift of music we thank You, and for those talented musicians who write music to thrill our hearts, to encourage us, to remind us of the great grace given to us.

* © Copyright 1976 by Fred Bock Music Company. All rights reserved. Used by permission.

Mary Eugenia Charles, prime minister
May 15, 1919–

The president of the United States listened carefully to the woman who had telephoned him. Most Americans couldn't even identify her nation of Dominica on a map, but that October 1983, Miss Charles asked Ronald Reagan to send troops into Grenada to overthrow the leftist military government there.

Eugenia Charles is the granddaughter of a former slave. She attended the University of Toronto and received her law degree from the London School of Economics and Political Science. She had planned to practice in England, but her parents persuaded her to return home, and she opened her law practice in 1949 as the first woman lawyer in Dominica.

Her career in politics began with letters to the editor protesting injustices within her country. When repressive laws limited freedom of speech, Miss Charles and others organized the Freedom Fighters and toured the island, speaking out for their rights. The Freedom Fighters became the Dominica Freedom party, and Eugenia became party leader. She entered the national assembly in 1970 and was a member of the team that negotiated Dominica's independence from Great Britain.

On May 29, 1979, when government troops opened fire on protesters, Eugenia led the outcry that resulted in the prime minister's resignation. A year later, Eugenia's party won the general election and she took office as prime minister. Eugenia declared her government to be "liberal, democratic, and anti-Communist." She immediately cracked down on drug dealers, tax-dodging businessmen, and corrupt bureaucrats.

She survived two coup attempts, one by American mercenaries hired by drug dealers, and kept her government pro-Western despite overtures from the Soviet Union, Cuba, and Libya.

In her years in office, the unemployment rate has declined from 23 percent to 13 percent, the inflation rate has dropped to 2.2 percent, and economic growth is flourishing.

Although there was great international debate about the invasion of Grenada, Miss Charles's call to Reagan was not unlike the message to Paul, "Come help us."

"During the night Paul had a vision of a man of Macedonia standing and begging him, 'Come over to Macedonia and help us.' "

Acts 16:9

Key Point: "I think people like decision. They like to know where you're going, not wavering."

Mary Eugenia Charles

May 16

Amy Loveman, editor
May 16, 1881–December 11, 1955

After graduation from Barnard College in 1901, twenty-year-old Amy Loveman began editing encyclopedias for her uncle. With another uncle, she helped compile a book marking the fiftieth anniversary of *The Nation.* In 1915, Amy worked for the *New York Evening Post,* and beginning in 1920 she acted as an editor of the *Post's Literary Review.* Amy founded the *Saturday Review of Literature* in 1924, where she wrote reviews, edited copy, ran the office, and demonstrated what Norman Cousins called a rare "combination of incisiveness and kindness."

As a critic, Loveman valued portraits of the human character and condition. She thought that too much modern fiction was focused on states of mind and emotions, rather than on conduct, so readers could not love or cherish the characters.

Loveman also influenced the books that Americans read. She headed the reading department of the Book of the Month Club from its inception in 1926 and eventually became a member of its editorial board. Every month she read at least twenty manuscripts to make recommendations for selection as the book of the month. Even from her hospital bed, battling the final stages of cancer, she continued to read manuscripts.

One biographer noted, "Amy Loveman is best remembered" not for the literary careers she helped launch or redirect but "for her ability to bring out the best in others."

"Therefore, as God's chosen people, holy and dearly loved, clothe yourselves with compassion, kindness, humility, gentleness and patience."

Colossians 3:12

Father, am I so engrossed in my occupation that I am failing to bring out the best in others?

May 17

Elias Nelson Conway, governor
May 17, 1812–February 28, 1892

Politics has a way of challenging the reputations of those who enter that arena, but there are men and women who have been successful politicians without

"A good name is more desirable than great riches;

soiling their reputations. Elias Nelson Conway was one of them. He not only refused to sling mud at other candidates, he refused to campaign. "The people know me. Let them decide."

As a young man, Conway followed three of his brothers to the territory of Arkansas. In 1835, President Andrew Jackson appointed him auditor of the territory. When Arkansas achieved statehood, Conway continued in the auditor's post for another fourteen years. He supervised the distribution of public lands, some of which had been designated for veterans but were never claimed. Conway instituted a new plan to provide land for the needy, which became the model for the Federal Homestead Act of 1862, providing land for so many homesteaders.

In 1852, Conway ran for governor and was elected. His record was impeccable. Conway started by cleaning up a state banking scandal, then devoted himself to building roads, railroads, and levees to prevent flooding. He also established a school for the blind. After eight years as governor, he retired from public life.

Although he was not a member of a church, Elias Conway had high morals. His success was due to his character rather than his politics.

to be esteemed is better than silver or gold."

Proverbs 22:1

Father, in those moments when there is so much temptation—to sell out, to compromise, to play politics in our own spheres—give us the courage to guard a good name.

May 18

Marie Josepha Mergler, physician
May 18, 1851–May 17, 1901

Marie Mergler came to the United States from Germany when she was two years old. As a seventeen-year-old, she graduated from Cook County Normal School. After four years of teaching, she entered the Woman's Medical College of Chicago and graduated with honors in 1870. Although she passed the intern boards at Cook County Hospital, she was denied acceptance into the program because she was female.

Marie studied an additional year in Zurich and then returned to Chicago and opened a practice, specializing in pathology and clinical medicine. During the same period, she taught at her alma mater, becoming profes-

"The Lord watches over you—the Lord is your shade at your right hand; the sun will not harm you by day, nor the moon by night."

Psalm 121:5, 6

sor of gynecology in 1890. After the college's merger with Northwestern University in 1899, Dr. Mergler became dean.

In 1882, Cook County Hospital appointed her as an attending physician, the second woman to occupy such a position. She moved to Women's Hospital in 1886, Wesley Memorial Hospital in 1890, and became head physician and surgeon at Women and Children's Hospital in 1897. In 1895, she joined the faculty of the Post Graduate Medical School of Northwestern University. Marie developed a solid reputation because of her success in abdominal surgery. She wrote one medical textbook, *A Guide to the Study of Gynecology* (1891), and contributed to others.

In her will, she remembered Women's Hospital and established a scholarship for medical students at the University of Chicago.

Key Thought: Marie Mergler never accepted the culturally imposed barriers to her success in medicine. Barriers can only stand if we do not challenge them.

May 19

Johns Hopkins, merchant and philanthropist
May 19, 1795–December 24, 1873

When Johns's parents, who were Quakers, decided they had to free their slaves, their sons had to go to work, so Johns Hopkins began his career at the age of twelve. When he was seventeen, Johns started working for his uncle, who ran a wholesale grocery business. The uncle left Johns in charge when he went to fight in the War of 1812, and the business prospered.

Within a few years, uncle and nephew had a falling-out. Johns had fallen in love with his cousin Elizabeth, but his uncle forbade their marriage (neither of them would ever marry). Because of financial strain in 1819, many customers wanted to pay their debts in whiskey, but the uncle would not consent to "sell souls into perdition" by trading in whiskey.

So Johns, in a bold move, set himself up in the wholesale grocery business (on his uncle's $10,000). During the first year he sold $200,000 worth of food. Johns was a young man with a bright future.

When he had a chance to buy shares in the fledgling Baltimore and Ohio Railroad, Johns invested heavily;

"You may say to yourself, 'My power and the strength of my hands have produced this wealth for me.' But remember the Lord your God, for it is he who gives you the ability to produce wealth, and so confirms his covenant, which he swore to your forefathers, as it is today."

Deuteronomy 8:17, 18

his years of driving wagons across mountains had convinced him railroads had a future. Soon he was the company's third-largest stockholder.

After making provisions for the financial security of his family, Johns structured a will that would have long-lasting significance. Aware of the unpreparedness of the medical community during the cholera and yellow fever epidemics, Johns had dreamed of a great hospital and university.

In 1870, he signed his will, leaving $7 million for that purpose, specifically directing that the medical needs of the black community be addressed. Today the Johns Hopkins University is a lasting reminder of the rewards of persistence and hard work.

Father, help us always to remember that You are the source of our financial security. You give us the strength and stamina to produce our wealth.

May 20

George Washington Tryon, scientist
May 20, 1838–February 5, 1888

George Tryon's fascination with science began as a small boy, when he began to collect shells of mollusks. A gifted child, before he could fully understand taxonomy, he had devised an intricate organization system for his own collection. He was more than just another boy with a hobby.

In 1859, although only twenty-one, Tryon was elected a member of the Academy of Natural Sciences of Philadelphia. He helped raise funds for a new facility to house its growing collection of specimens, to which Tryon donated his own collection of 10,000 species. By the time of his death, the academy could boast of possessing one of the largest and most complete collections of Mollusca in the world. Tryon was curator between 1869 and 1876, and a conservator from 1875 until 1888.

Tryon wrote more than seventy scientific papers on land, fresh-water, and marine mollusks. He also edited *The American Journal of Conchology* from 1865 to 1872. His major scientific magnum opus was *Manual of Conchology, Structural and Systematic, with Illustrations of the Species,* composed of more than twelve volumes that surveyed all the living species of Mollusca known in that day.

"He described plant life, from the cedar of Lebanon to the hyssop that grows out of walls. He also taught about animals and birds, reptiles and fish."

1 Kings 4:33

130

Tryon was also a music connoisseur who edited and published librettos of more than fifty operas; he also actively encouraged amateurs to sing and influenced the popular musical tastes of his day.

This Quaker single adult made an incredible contribution to science and popular music.

Father, for all creatures, great and small, we give You thanks.

May 21

Hiram B. Pierce, physician
May 21, 1845–September 17, 1878

Memphis was a dying town; more than 25,000 people had fled the city at the outbreak of the dreaded yellow fever. The Howard Medical Association sent a request across the nation for physicians to come and help Memphis. Many of the city's physicians were either dead or dying.

Memphis was a long way from Cincinnati, where Dr. Hiram B. Pierce practiced medicine. Pierce had graduated from Ohio State Medical School in 1866, done a year of advanced study at Bellevue Medical College in New York, and spent three years of additional medical study at the University of Vienna.

The Cincinnati Medical Society called for three of its members to volunteer for a brief stint in Memphis. Pierce, a member of a prominent wealthy family, volunteered. Officers of the society and friends accompanied the doctors to the railroad station. Just before boarding the train, Dr. Pierce was handed a note from his father, disinheriting him if he went to Memphis.

Two weeks later, banner headlines in the *Cincinnati Enquirer* announced DR. PIERCE IS DEAD! Dr. Pierce's eulogy said, "Young, brilliant and brave, he fell a martyr to the profession of his own choice."

A colleague, Dr. Augustus Kuekne, who was present in Memphis, said that Hiram Pierce's motivation to go had been his "true sense of duty as a physician and his belief in Christ."

Over 7,500 died in Memphis in September 1878. Hiram B. Pierce was one of forty-five physicians who gave their lives.

"Greater love has no one than this, that he lay down his life for his friends."

John 15:13

Father, to ask us to give up our life for a friend is one thing, but for strangers? We thank You for the example of Your servant, Hiram B. Pierce. Remind us of his sacrifice.

131

Mary Cassatt, artist
May 22, 1845–June 14, 1926

Mary Cassatt received no parental encouragement for her desire to study art. Although she graduated from the Pennsylvania Academy of the Fine Arts, she soon departed to study in Europe on her own.

In 1874, Edgar Degas, a famous artist, saw her work on exhibit in Paris and declared, "I will not admit that a woman can draw like that!" Soon Mary was an active member of a group of Impressionists that included Paul Gauguin and Camille Pissarro. In the next five years, she gained her reputation in Europe but remained unknown in America.

In her spare time, Mary Cassatt was involved in purchasing paintings for two American collectors and was instrumental in introducing Degas and other Impressionists to America in the late 1870s. Most of this art is in the Metropolitan Museum in New York City.

Cassatt worked in oils, pastels, and aquatints. Her mural on modern women was part of the Women's Building at the Columbian Exposition in 1893. Critics and art historians agree that Miss Cassatt's best works were portraits and small groupings. Mother and child was a particularly common theme in her work.

She was America's most distinguished woman painter.

> "The Lord is near to all who call on him, to all who call on him in truth."
>
> **Psalm 145:18**

Father, thank You for the gift of art.

Mabel Walker Willebrandt, assistant attorney general
May 23, 1889–April 6, 1963

In a time when few women studied law, many people thought Mabel Willebrandt was chasing fantasies. She persisted in her legal studies and became a model of commitment and excellence. Within six years of passing the bar, Mabel was the assistant attorney general of the United States and called by many "the first lady in law."

Soon after she began her practice, Mabel helped establish the public defender's office in Los Angeles. As

> "He who works his land will have abundant food, but the one who chases fantasies will have his fill of poverty."
>
> **Proverbs 28:19**

assistant public defender, Mabel handled the cases of 2,000 women. In 1918, she addressed the California Legislature on the need for a property law for married women.

Mabel Willebrandt was an avid prohibitionist and used her position in the attorney general's office to investigate the appointments of United States marshals, many of whom she dismissed as "brokendown politicians, fond of drink and low company." In 1924 to 1925, Willebrandt's office prosecuted 48,734 cases and won more than 39,000 convictions. Her aggressiveness earned her the nickname, Prohibition Portia.

One of Mabel's most significant decisions was to recommend a young attorney, John Edgar Hoover, to head the newly created Federal Bureau of Investigation. Moreover, she rallied ministers to support his nomination "because the enforcement of prohibition must be in the hands of those who believe in it."

John Sinclair quipped, "If Mabel had worn trousers she could have been elected President."

Father, it's one thing to achieve and another to help others achieve. Remind us that we win when we help others achieve.

May 24

Morris Longstreth Keen, inventor
May 24, 1820–November 2, 1883

How dependent we are on paper, even in the computer age. Without Morris Keen, many of the paper products we take for granted might not be available today.

Keen began his industrial career in the flat-iron-making business, working his way up from an apprentice to a successful inventor and manufacturer.

However, Keen's real love was always the development of new ideas and technology, rather than the day-to-day routine of manufacturing. Eventually he turned his interests to the new field of paper manufacturing. Many men had attempted to make wood pulp out of the soft woods, but Keen was especially intrigued by a breakthrough developed in a British firm.

Based on their work, which is still in use today, Keen turned his attention to experiments on the design of

"I have much to write to you, but I do not want to use paper and ink."

2 John 12

Father, we thank You for those who have gone before us and have developed the materials we take for granted. Remind us that our faithful-

wood-pulp boilers. Using the American patent on the British process, he secured his first paper-making patent on September 13, 1859, for a boiler to make paper pulp out of poplar wood. In the years that followed, Morris Keen won other patents on processes that improved the manufacturing of paper in this country.

ness today could lead to the discovery of resources that will be useful for tomorrow's dreamer.

May 25

Diane Bish, organist
May 25, 1941–

Diane Bish began playing the piano at age five, but as soon as her legs were long enough for her feet to touch the pedals, she switched to the organ. That change marked the beginning of an outstanding career. As a student of one of the finest organ teachers in the country, Mildred Andrews, Diane won numerous competitions and awards. After graduation from the University of Oklahoma, she was a Fulbright scholar at the Amsterdam Conservatorium. She spent another year on a grant from the French government studying organ in Paris.

Eventually Diane was invited to become organist at Coral Ridge Presbyterian Church in Fort Lauderdale. She accepted and moved with the congregation into its new sanctuary, where she began playing the imposing, 117-rank Ruffatti organ that was built to her specifications. To utilize the potential of this instrument, Diane began composing. Her four major organ works are *Festival Te Deum,* for organ and orchestra; *Passion Symphony; Symphony of Psalms,* for organ, choir, and orchestra; and *Morning Has Broken.* She has written seven books of organ compositions and numerous solo pieces.

Diane is an exciting performer who has helped the organ come alive for millions.

"Too many organists play to other organists. They play very dryly. The organ can be the most drab of instruments because it is completely mechanical. You can't bring a lot of emotion out of it unless you have an awful lot inside you."

What makes Diane Bish different from thousands of other organists? "I love to hear music," she said, "but it's not an end in itself. We acknowledge God and the eternal value of souls in the music we produce."

"Sing to him a new song; play skillfully, and shout for joy."

Psalm 33:3

Key Point: "I see my work as a means of acknowledging that God is the giver of every gift."

Diane Bish

May 26

Julia Catherine Stimson, nurse and administrator
May 26, 1881–September 20, 1948

Julia Stimson wanted to be a doctor after her graduation from Vassar, but her uncle convinced her to study nursing instead. Soon after she graduated from the New York Hospital Training School for Nurses in 1908, Julia accepted a post as superintendent of nursing at Harlem Hospital. In 1909, she published *A Nurse's Handbook of Drugs and Solutions.*

During the Ohio Valley flood of 1913, Julia went to work for the Red Cross. In May 1917, she went overseas as a nurse attached to the British Expeditionary Forces, directing a large battlefield hospital. In April 1918, she became chief of all Red Cross nurses in France.

When the war ended, as director of nursing services for the American army, she directed the orderly return to civilian life of ten thousand nurses. In January 1919, she became dean of the Army School of Nursing and served until its closing in 1933.

Julia worked hard to increase the status of nurses in the military. She became the first woman to hold the rank of major in the United States Army. From 1938 to 1944, she served as president of the American Nurses Association and directed the first census of American nurses. In August 1948, she was promoted to colonel.

Julia was a quiet woman and an avid violinist. After her left hand was injured in an automobile accident, she devised a new fingering system to accommodate her physical limitations.

"As you go, preach this message: 'The kingdom of heaven is near.' Heal the sick, raise the dead, cleanse those who have leprosy. . . . Freely you have received, freely give."

Matthew 10:7, 8

Father, where would we be today without nurses to care for us? Thank You for the leadership of Julia Stimson.

May 27

Rachel Carson, environmentalist
May 27, 1907–April 14, 1964

Words have power. Rachel Carson demonstrated that by her well-chosen words on the environment, and her words led to action.

"Let heaven and earth praise him, the seas and all

135

Rachel grew up in rural Springdale, Pennsylvania, encouraged by her mother to read and to enjoy nature. Although she wanted to be a writer, a college course in biology caused her to switch majors from English to zoology.

Rachel began her formal study of the sea at Wood's Hole Marine Biological Laboratory. In 1932, she earned her M.A. at Johns Hopkins and spent the next seven years teaching at the University of Massachusetts. In 1935, she was one of the first women hired by the United States Bureau of Fisheries. Soon articles written by Miss Carson were appearing in the *Baltimore Sun*.

In 1951, the literary world was taken by storm with the publication of *The Sea Around Us*, which for an astonishing eighty-eight weeks remained on the best-seller list and was translated into thirty-two languages. The book blended science and poetry to awaken its readers to environmental issues.

In the early sixties, the widespread use of DDT and other toxic chemicals captured Rachel's attention. She debunked the manufacturer's claims that the poison's effects could be limited, contending that its cumulative effect would have catastrophic results on animals (particularly birds and fish) and humans. Her book *Silent Spring* (1966) ignited a violent protest from chemical makers, but the president's scientific advisory committee backed her.

Rachel Carson reminds us that one person can call a nation to task through the power of the printed page.

> that move in them."
>
> **Psalm 69:34**

> *Father, this is Your world, and we are at times rather reckless stewards. Forgive us for our carelessness and greed.*

May 28

William Pitt, prime minister
May 28, 1759–January 23, 1806

As a boy, he grew up in the shadows of William Pitt the Elder, first earl of Chatham, who had directed England to victory over France in the Seven Years War. Under the influence of his father, young William Pitt entered Cambridge at the age of fourteen. At age twenty-one, he ran for Parliament and lost; however, soon thereafter he was elected from another district.

Pitt challenged Prime Minister North's policies on the American colonies and championed the reform movement. In 1782, Pitt became Chancellor of the Exchequer

> "But as for you, be strong and do not give up, for your work will be rewarded."
>
> **2 Chronicles 15:7**

and negotiated the peace settlement with the Americans.

In 1783, at twenty-four, Pitt became prime minister of England, the youngest in British history. Pitt helped restore the standing of King George III.

After the elections of 1784, Pitt led nine years of reform. He was the first significant politician to embrace the economic theories of Adam Smith. He reduced the war-swollen national debt, negotiated a commercial treaty with France, and overhauled taxes. Moreover, William Pitt made sure that the American revolt did not spread throughout the British empire.

However, his attempts to outlaw slavery failed. After the death of French single-adult Robespierre, England went to war with France. Pitt, fearing that the French would try to invade England through Ireland, convinced the Irish Parliament to vote itself out of existence. As a result, William Pitt created the United Kingdom of Great Britain and Ireland in 1801 and set in motion the struggle for Irish independence that continues to this day.

Key Point: One single adult gave his life to making and keeping England a major world power.

May 29

Joel Benton, journalist
May 29, 1832–September 15, 1911

Joel Benton launched his career in journalism at nineteen when he began editing the *Amenia Times,* a Connecticut weekly newspaper. Five years later, after developing close friendships with many of New England's greatest writers, he gave up the newspaper to farm and lecture. Benton also spent a lot of time organizing lecture series for his hometown and was himself in constant demand on the lecture circuit.

Benton's writing was noted for its keen observation, pleasant use of humor, and stunning word play. Some critics, however, contended that his writing was influenced more by sentiment than emotion.

His books included *Emerson the Poet* (1883), *Greeley on Lincoln* (1893), *The Life of P. T. Barnum* (1902), and his memoirs, *The Twilight Club* (1907).

"He who began a good work in you will carry it on to completion until the day of Christ Jesus."

Philippians 1:6

Father, some of us are so busy doing good things we don't have time to do great things. If we need to change careers, give us that kind of courage, so we do not go through this great experiment called life dragging our feet.

Theodore Emanuel Schmauk, clergyman
May 30, 1860–March 23, 1920

In his entire ministerial career, Theodore Schmauk pastored only one church. However, his influence was felt far beyond his parish and throughout the Christian world. After graduating from the University of Pennsylvania and Lutheran Theological Seminary in 1883, he served as associate pastor under his father in Lebanon, Pennsylvania. When the elder Schmauk died, the son succeeded him in that pulpit. Some families lived a lifetime with only the father and son as their pastors.

Pastor Schmauk edited significant Lutheran periodicals: *Lutheran Sunday School Lessons* and *General Conference Graded Series,* beginning in 1896; *The Lutheran Church Review,* from 1895; and *The Lutheran,* the official magazine of the denomination, from 1889. He also found time to write many booklets on practical issues. Schmauk did not hesitate to critique the work of other editors, especially those with liberal overtones.

He was elected president of his denomination's general council in 1903 and committed the denomination to the fundamental conviction of uncompromising confessionalism. He took pride in the fact that the general council was totally accepting of both the "confessions" and "the history of the church."

However, times change, and despite his best efforts, Schmauk could not prevent a split in 1919, when almost half the membership formed a new synod.

"Whether you turn to the right or to the left, your ears will hear a voice behind you, saying, 'This is the way; walk in it.' "

Isaiah 30:21

Father, a lifetime spent with one congregation— that's a long time. Remind us to wisely choose what we give our lives to in a day of abundant and competing choices.

Emily P. Bissell, humanitarian
May 31, 1861–March 8, 1948

"I need your help, Emily." Dr. Joseph Wales looked intently at his cousin. "We have hundreds dying with tuberculosis."

"But I'm not a nurse," Emily protested.

"We have to have help with the tuberculosis shack. That's the only place people can turn for help. We need three hundred dollars."

"She opens her arms to the poor and extends her hands to the needy."

Proverbs 31:20

"Let me see what I can do."

For days after that conversation, the plight of the poor tuberculosis patients housed in makeshift shacks on the hillsides troubled Emily Bissell. Although she had been born into a prominent Delaware family, Emily's interest in the needs of others had been strong ever since a Sunday school teacher took her along on visits to the needy.

As Emily considered the problem, she remembered an article she had read about the Danish government's annual sales of Christmas stamps as a way of raising money. Since Christmas was coming, surely the idea would work here. The American Red Cross gave her permission to use their seal, and friends financed the printing of the first 50,000 stamps.

On December 7, 1907, at a table in the lobby of the Wilmington post office, Emily Bissell began selling Christmas seals for a penny each. The first year raised $3,000. The next year, with the help of the American Red Cross, the national campaign netted almost $135,000.

In just a few years, Christmas seals were a tradition, and in a few decades, because of the funds raised for research and treatment, tuberculosis was no longer a killer.

Father, it is not always apparent where an idea will lead, but ideas are too precious to waste. Give us an idea that will make a difference.

June 1

John Van Druten, playwright
June 1, 1901–December 19, 1957

As a boy, John Van Druten spent a lot of time alone, reading books, writing, building a toy stage, and relying on a vivid imagination to pass his time. He wrote his first play, *Mary, Queen of Scots,* as a seven-year-old.

His father demanded that John prepare himself for a career more stable than writing, so John studied law. After his father died, John still felt obligated to pursue his father's plans for his life. He passed the bar in 1923 and began teaching at the University of Wales.

Meanwhile, he wrote, firmly following the advice of poet J. C. Squire to write about what he had experienced, not what he had read. Soon his work was being regularly published in London's *Mercury* and other

"He is like a tree planted by streams of water, which yields its fruit in season and whose leaf does not wither. Whatever he does prospers."

Psalm 1:3

magazines. He vowed that he would either have a play published in a year or abandon writing. *The Return Half* was produced under the deadline by the Royal Academy of Dramatic Art. Its positive reviews encouraged Van Druten to keep writing.

His *Young Woodley* was banned in England because of its unfavorable treatment of English public schools but opened to raves in New York and was voted one of the ten best plays of 1925–1926.

In 1938, John Van Druten moved to the United States, becoming a citizen in 1944.

His greatest play may have been *I Remember Mama*, based on Kathryn Forbes's *Momma's Bank Account*. His last major production was Rodgers and Hammerstein's *The King and I.*

Father, for those who have the gift of dramatic arts, we give You thanks.

June 2

John Randolph, orator and statesman
June 2, 1773–May 24, 1833

John Randolph's educational record was quite eclectic: He studied at Princeton, College of William and Mary, and Columbia. But Randolph thought all his teachers were inferior, so through extensive reading, he educated himself.

Randolph developed into a brilliant orator. He won his first seat in Congress in 1799. In 1801, at twenty-eight, he became chairman of the House Ways and Means Committee, a key position in controlling the pace at which legislation is introduced into Congress.

Randolph was a brilliant parliamentary strategist and speaker. He swaggered in Congress, often carrying a whip in his hand. After his reputation was damaged by his poor handling of the impeachment proceedings against Justice Samuel Chase, Randolph increasingly distanced himself from the Jefferson administration.

Congress changed with the arrival of Henry Clay and John Calhoun. Randolph was no longer the leading orator. Because of his opposition to the War of 1812, he was unseated in 1813.

Randolph fought a duel with Henry Clay in the Virginia countryside on April 8, 1826. He was defeated by

"He who guards his mouth and his tongue keeps himself from calamity."

Proverbs 21:23

John Tyler in the Senate race of 1827 but returned to the House, where he led opposition to John Quincy Adams, whom he bitterly disliked. With the inauguration of Andrew Jackson, Randolph became the majority leader of the House.

In 1833, Randolph's health failed. He became mentally ill and died in Philadelphia. He was buried with his face to the West so that he might "keep an eye on" his enemy, Henry Clay.

Key Thought: A tongue can be used for helping or for harming. John Randolph chose to use his tongue as a sword. How are you using your tongue?

June 3

Irwin Russell, poet
June 3, 1853–December 23, 1879

Irwin Russell read at the age of four and comprehended Milton's poetry by age six. He graduated from St. Louis University as a teenager and, after studying law with Judge Baldwin, by special act of the Mississippi legislature, passed the bar at age nineteen.

Russell's first poem, "A Chinese Tale," was published when he was sixteen. By his twenty-fifth birthday, his work had been published in the nation's leading magazines. Russell mastered the Negro dialect and incorporated it into his writing as early as 1876 in "Uncle Cap Interviewed."

During the yellow fever epidemic of 1878, although many fled, Irwin stayed with his physician father. They struggled for months, without relief. Dora Donald, the love of Irwin's life, died in that epidemic. When the epidemic finally ended, Russell went to New York for a change of pace. However, although graciously accepted as a peer by the city's leading writers, he didn't stay. Soon after his arrival, Russell's father died and Russell's depression deepened. He turned to alcohol, which had hampered his productivity throughout his life.

August 1879 found him in New Orleans, living in a cheap boardinghouse, writing for the *New Orleans Times*. Just a few days before Irwin Russell's death, his last piece, ironically entitled "The Cemetery," was published.

"My soul is overwhelmed with sorrow to the point of death."

Matthew 26:38

Key Point: Grief either becomes a weapon for destruction or an implement for healing. It is our choice.

Frank Nathan Daniel Buchman, religious leader
June 4, 1878–August 7, 1961

After graduation from Muhlenberg College and seminary study, Frank Buchman began pastoring a Lutheran congregation in Overbrook, Pennsylvania, and organized the Luther Hospice in Philadelphia in 1905. In 1908, he traveled to Europe, and through a spiritual awakening, he found a new direction for his life.

As a result of that spiritual nourishment, Buchman began conducting evangelistic campaigns on college campuses, in wartime prisoner camps, and in the Far East, converting a large number of young students.

Buchman emphasized four key ingredients in spiritual awakening: absolute love, honesty, purity, and unselfishness. He taught that through prayer, Bible study, and the guidance of the Holy Spirit, one could know the will of God and experience a vital walk with Christ. Out of that commitment, one could make a difference in the world.

In 1921, Buchman went to Oxford and organized a group of students into the First Century Christian Fellowship, or Oxford Group Movement. This group used private conversation, group confessions, and silent meditation to spark religious renewal and commitment. Buchman especially evangelized the aristocrats, people who could use their resources to spread the Gospel.

When war clouds crossed Europe, Buchman declared that God would use the occasion to prevent war through a spiritual and moral "re-armament."

Frank Buchman spent his entire life leading seminars, writing, and discipling leaders. To the critics of his movement, Buchman said that Moral Re-Armament "can win all men because its standards are universally valid. It is not a religion nor a substitute for religion. It is not a sect. It has four mighty pillars on which human living must be based. Every man must accept these ideas if he is honest with himself."

This single adult gave his life to discipling individuals who went on to assume leadership posts in the world. His dying words echoed his lifelong compassion.

"You will keep in perfect peace him whose mind is steadfast, because he trusts in you."

Isaiah 26:3

Key Point: "I want Britain to be governed by men governed by God. I want to see the world governed by men governed by God. Why not let God run the whole world?"

Frank Buchman

June 5

Adam Smith, economist
June 5, 1723–July 17, 1790

Adam Smith's father died two months before Adam was born, so he grew up in a single-parent home. Adam was kidnapped during his early childhood but returned to his mother unharmed. At age fourteen he enrolled at the University of Glasgow.

In 1748, Smith moved to Edinburgh and developed a friendship with noted philosopher David Hume. Three years later, he returned to Glasgow as professor of moral philosophy, and in 1759 his *Theory of Moral Sentiments* was published.

From 1764 to 1766, Smith was a traveling tutor for the Duke of Buccleuch and his brother; two years on the continent expanded his worldview. Smith began working on his great treatise, *An Inquiry Into the Nature and Causes of the Wealth of Nations.* The work was influenced by his interaction with many of Europe's best thinkers, whom he had met in his travels.

When one of his students was killed, Adam Smith returned to his mother's home in Kirkcaldy, where he worked on the *Wealth of Nations* manuscript, which was published in 1776.

Adam Smith argued that a nation's wealth can be judged by its consumable goods. He believed free trade is essential for the maximum development of wealth and objected to government interference with entrepreneurial spirits. The capitalist, Smith believed, benefited society while satisfying his own needs.

From his deathbed, Smith demanded that most of his manuscripts be destroyed.

> "For the love of money is a root of all kinds of evil."
> 1 Timothy 6:10

Father, You own the cattle on the thousand hills. Help us to keep money in perspective in our lives. Deliver us from the love of money, which is the root of all evil.

June 6

Charles Lee Hoagland, physician
June 6, 1907–August 2, 1946

When Charles Lee Hoagland volunteered to do some typing for a guest in a hotel where he worked as a busboy, he didn't dream he was opening the door to his

> "Do you not know that your body is a temple of the Holy

future. The hotel guest, Alfred L. McCawley, an influential member of the Missouri legislature, was so impressed with Charles that he hired him and eventually adopted him.

Hoagland graduated from Washington University Medical School in 1935. In 1939, he became a professor in the school of medicine there. Soon after, he began a research career at the hospital of the Institute for Medical Research. Most of his research was on the cowpox virus. Hoagland's work demonstrated that this virus was a complex biological entity and not easily traceable.

During World War II, Hoagland joined an intensive navy research program studying and treating sailors suffering from hepatitis. He led a team of researchers in designing a test to evaluate liver damage and to devise strategies for convalescence. Soon Hoagland's reputation spread, and leading medical schools throughout the nation offered posts to the young physician.

However, he had so overworked himself that in June 1946 he was hospitalized with malignant hypertension. Two months later he died in the hospital where he had treated so many navy personnel.

Spirit, who is in you, whom you have received from God? You are not your own; you were bought at a price. Therefore honor God with your body."

1 Corinthians 6:19, 20

Key Thought: Our body is the temple of the Holy Spirit, and single adults must care for that body and that temple. Overwork, even for a noble cause, is hard for the body to forgive.

June 7

Susan Elizabeth Blow, kindergarten developer
June 7, 1843–March 26, 1916

Susan Blow grew up with Presbyterian parents and early acknowledged the religious elements of her personality. She was educated in St. Louis and New York, and in her twenties toured Europe, where she was exposed to the teaching of Friedrich Froebel, who founded the kindergarten movement in Europe.

When she returned to St. Louis, Susan Blow decided to open a kindergarten. William Harris, a philosopher who headed the St. Louis school system, assisted her in its formation. In 1873, Susan opened the first public kindergarten in a suburb of St. Louis; the next year she added a training school for teachers.

Susan translated Froebel's *Mother Play* and used many of his songs and games in her school. However, because of her strong personality and rigidly doctrinaire views

"Her children arise and call her blessed."

Proverbs 31:28

144

she was challenged by some of her teaching students. She resigned in 1884 and eventually moved to Boston.

In 1895, she began to lecture again and to teach the Bible, Shakespeare, Dante, and Goethe. She also wrote a series of books on Froebel's teaching methods and taught at Teachers' College, Columbia University.

She was a strong conservative voice in the kindergarten movement and attacked many progressive leaders in her last book, *Educational Issues in the Kindergarten.*

Key Thought: Find a need and meet it.

June 8

Thomas Green, Confederate general
June 8, 1814–April 14, 1864

Thomas Green wanted more adventure than Tennessee could offer in the 1830s, so he joined the Revolutionary Army of Texas in 1835. Green liked Texas and decided to stay and make a life there. From 1839 to 1840, he fought Indians in East Texas and served in the Texas Congress. For the next twenty years, Green was clerk of the Texas Supreme Court.

Having been a volunteer in the Mexican War, Green volunteered for the Confederate Army at the outbreak of the Civil War. He was given the rank of colonel and assigned a regiment made up of volunteers from New Mexico and Arizona. He fought in every battle on Texas soil.

In January 1863, Green and his troops helped recapture Galveston, and in a few months Green was promoted to brigadier general. In 1864, he fought in the Red River campaign in Louisiana and was commanding a cavalry division when he was shot. He died five days later.

"And the peace of God, which transcends all understanding, will guard your hearts and your minds in Christ Jesus."

Philippians 4:7

Key Thought: The courage of one's conviction sometimes takes him to battlefields that are not his choosing. In such moments, we discover either heroes or cowards.

June 9

Sylvanus Thayer, military educator
June 9, 1785–September 7, 1872

The United States Military Academy at West Point is one of the finest military institutions in the world, a

"For I myself am a man under author-

reputation gained through the superintendency of Sylvanus Thayer, who served from 1817 until 1833.

Previous to Thayer's appointment, the academy was a playground for the sons of the wealthy and privileged; casualness and a lack of discipline prevailed. But Thayer believed that the first responsibility of the academy was to prepare trained officers for the military and preference should not be given to faculty or governmental employees' favorites. Thayer devised a merit roll so each cadet could be ranked in his class. A cadet was graded on all his activities at the academy, not just his academic performance.

Thayer instituted a series of demerits for infractions of the rules. He created a discipline system and ordered that all cadets be treated uniformly, regardless of social class. He ordered that all students live on their government stipend. Finally, he instituted a policy that all graduates had to serve in the army to partially repay the cost of their education.

Thayer never married. His biographer said that the academy was his only love.

Thayer modeled character and self-discipline as he developed a program to produce "gentlemen soldiers." His life became the standard of excellence. Military historians have called him "the father of the military academy."

ity, with soldiers under me. I tell this one, 'Go,' and he goes; and that one, 'Come,' and he comes. I say to my servant, 'Do this,' and he does it."

Matthew 8:9

Father, our lives are closely watched by others. Help us to be examples, not hindrances.

June 10

Henry M. Stanley, explorer
June 10, 1841–May 10, 1904

"Dr. Livingstone I presume?" is one of the most famous phrases in Western civilization. What else could Henry Stanley say after his eight-month trek across Africa in search of the missionary?

Stanley was born John Rowlands but was abandoned by his mother soon after his father's death. After nine cruel years in an orphanage, he ran away. Eventually, he made his way from Wales to New Orleans on a ship he described as "a floating hell." At age eighteen, he was befriended by a merchant named Henry Stanley, whose name he adopted.

"The Lord will fulfill his purpose for me; your love, O Lord, endures forever—do not abandon the works of your hands."

Psalm 138:8

After his benefactor's death, Henry joined the Confederate army and was captured at Shiloh. After months of imprisonment, he was released on his promise to serve in the Union army. However, he was found physically unfit to serve, although he did later serve a brief stint in the Union navy. He moved to San Francisco after the war and began his career as a writer.

In 1866, Stanley was captured by bandits in Asia Minor and later by Comanche Indians. He was known to take almost any risk in order to get a story; no challenge seemed too great.

When missions executives became convinced that Livingstone had died in Africa, James Gordon Bennett, owner of the *New York Herald,* sent Stanley on an expedition to find him—or what was left of his body.

It was a major journalism event when Stanley found Livingstone alive.

After the missionary's death, Stanley returned to Africa on an expedition to measure the major lakes of the continent. From 1879 to 1884, he explored the Congo Basin, discovered the Congo River, and established twenty-one trading posts. Stanley's work and writing stimulated Europeans to colonize Africa.

In one discouraging moment in the jungles of Africa, Stanley was constrained to confess that without God's help, "I was powerless. I vowed a vow in the forest solitude that I would confess him before men."

Stanley was a strong believer in prayer. "Prayer made me stronger morally and mentally than my nonpraying companions. It gave me confidence. Without prayer, I doubt that I would have endured the flourishing of spears."

Stanley married at the age of forty-nine.

Key Point: "Those whose faith in God is strong feel the same sense of security in the deepest wilds."

Henry Stanley

June 11

Jeanette Rankin, congresswoman
June 11, 1880–May 18, 1973

Jeanette Rankin worked hard to get her seat in the House of Representatives. She was the first woman elected to a seat in Congress. At the time of her election, women could vote in only six states. Rankin, a representative from Montana, was not popular in Congress.

"I am a man of peace; but when I speak, they are for war."

Psalm 120:7

147

During her time in office, Jeanette introduced legislation to help women, lobbied for the passage of a federal suffrage amendment, and championed the causes of laborers. However, when the time came to cast her vote on the declaration of war in 1917, with tears in her eyes, she said, "I want to stand by my country, but I cannot vote for war." It wouldn't matter that forty-nine other members voted no; Rankin's patriotism was questioned. In 1918, when she ran for the United States Senate, she was defeated.

After her defeat, she continued to work for the causes close to her heart: peace and women's issues. Then, in 1940, running as an antiwar candidate, she was elected to Congress. On December 8, 1941, Jeanette Rankin cast the only vote against the declaration of war against Germany and Japan. She was defeated for re-election in 1942, returned to private life, and worked on peace issues.

In January 1968, at eighty-seven, Rankin led five thousand women on a march on Washington, protesting the war in Vietnam. She explained why she insisted on tackling the tough issues:

"You take people as far as they will go—not as far as you would like them to go."

Father, convictions are hard to come by and even harder to live by. Help us to be faithful whatever the price.

June 12

Carolyn Conant Van Blarcom, nurse
June 12, 1879–March 20, 1960

Carolyn Van Blarcom's father abandoned her family when she was a child. She contracted rheumatic fever and rheumatoid arthritis when she was six, and her mother died when Carolyn was fourteen.

Perhaps because Carolyn had been so ill during her childhood, she enrolled in the nursing program at Johns Hopkins Hospital. Despite her disability, Carolyn was asked to join the faculty after graduation because of her outstanding academic performance. She taught obstetrics and served as assistant superintendent of nurses.

Eventually Carolyn was appointed to head the New York State Committee to Prevent Blindness. She used the post to orchestrate research into the causes of blindness and to increase public awareness of the issue.

"Or why was I not hidden in the ground like a stillborn child, like an infant who never saw the light of day?"

Job 3:16

Carolyn discovered that the leading cause of preventable blindness among newborns was *ophthalmia neonatorum,* which could be eliminated with the use of silver nitrate. However, most babies were delivered by midwives who were unaware of the treatment. Van Blarcom organized a study of midwifery in fourteen countries, which resulted in her epic book, *The Midwife in England* (1913). In it, she charged that the United States was the only nation in the civilized world "which did not protect its mothers and infants by providing for the training and licensing of midwives."

Van Blarcom became a crusader for reform and was the first nurse to become a licensed midwife. All across the country, this single adult preached her message of better care for children. Her *Obstetrical Nursing* (1922) became a standard text in many nursing schools. Carolyn Van Blarcom retired early because of her health.

Father, out of pain comes hope. Help us to appreciate our good health.

June 13

Christine Herrick, household specialist
June 13, 1859–December 2, 1944

Life doesn't always work out as we planned. Christine Terhune Herrick had a good husband, nice home, and two sons. Her life was comfortable. But then her husband died, and Christine was forced to find a way to support herself. She had no college degree, but she did know how to write and do housework, so she combined the two.

In 1888, her first book, *Housekeeping Made Easy,* established her reputation. She enhanced her success by writing in leading periodicals such as *Ladies' Home Journal* and *Good Housekeeping,* always demanding and receiving top pay for her work.

Christine, like many other single parents, wanted the best for her sons. For her, that meant private school and several trips to Europe.

Christine believed that women's interests should be wide; after all, they could end up single parents and fully responsible for their children's futures. However, she disagreed with many of the militant suffragists.

"Commit to the Lord whatever you do, and your plans will succeed."

Proverbs 16:3

149

She battled with her weight all her life, a struggle that led to *Lose Weight and Be Well*, a book she published anonymously.

Through her cookbooks, Christine was an early advocate of using natural gas for cooking. She wrote such best-sellers as *The Cottage Kitchen, The National Cook Book*, and *The Helping Hand Cook Book*. She was editor in chief for the five-volume *Library of Modern Cooking and Household Recipes*.

Key Point: Sometimes life takes unexpected turns. God's grace provides us the resource to meet every challenge.

June 14

Margaret Bourke-White, photographer
June 14, 1904–August 27, 1971

Margaret Bourke's father was a designer in the printing profession, and her mother worked to develop publications for the blind. At Columbia University, Margaret's interests turned to photography. She married a fellow student but was divorced a year later and began working as a photographer to pay her school bills.

In 1929, publisher Henry Luce asked Margaret to shoot the cover for the first issue of *Fortune* magazine. Afterwards, she joined the staff and went to Russia, where she shot her first book, *Eyes on Russia*.

Margaret became one of the first photographers for *Life* magazine, gaining a national reputation for her photographs of the Dust Bowl and the Depression. She collaborated with writer Erskine Caldwell (whom she married and divorced after three years) on *Have You Seen Their Faces?* a book on the rural poor.

No assignment was too dangerous for Margaret. In 1941, she covered the German attack on Moscow and became the first army air force woman war photographer. In the closing days of World War II, she traveled in Germany with General Patton. She was the first person to photograph the Nazi camps, her pictures prompting a worldwide outcry. Few people who have seen her pictures of Buchenwald can forget them.

Parkinson's disease cut short Margaret Bourke-White's brilliant career, but her pictures are legends and her techniques are the object of study.

"He looks for a skilled craftsman to set up an idol that will not topple."

Isaiah 40:20

Father, how our lives have been blessed by the art of photography. Thank You for those who have talent in this area.

150

June 15

Paul Gilson, composer
June 15, 1865–April 3, 1942

Music has always been an important ingredient in man's humanity. It is born in the hearts and minds of composers. David told the Levites to appoint their brothers as musicians; the Levites had to recognize musical talent.

So it was with the brilliant Belgian musical theorist François Gavaert, who took a personal interest in a young student by the name of Paul Gilson. At Gavaert's urging, Gilson entered the Brussels Conservatory, and three years later won great praise throughout Belgium for his cantata, *Sinai.* That success was followed by the premiere of his symphonic music, *La Mer.* By December 1892, Gilson's music was being performed in the United States.

Gilson also wrote for the ballet and for opera. His works were characterized by strong rhythmic vitality and highly colorful orchestration.

But Gilson also made a strong impression on younger Belgian composers. Young, talented musicians wanted to be around him, for he always encouraged them, whatever their style or interests. Paul Gilson invested his life in music and musicians.

"David told the leaders of the Levites to appoint their brothers as singers to sing joyful songs, accompanied by musical instruments: lyres, harps and cymbals."

1 Chronicles 15:16

Father, help us to encourage the next generation. Keep us from being so preoccupied with our schedules that we do not have time to encourage others.

June 16

Evelyn Ramsey, doctor and linguist
June 16, 1923–June 25, 1989

Evelyn Ramsey looked at the body on the operating table in Papua, New Guinea, and said, "Oh, dear." Although she was not a surgeon by training, she was the only doctor within miles. Dr. Ramsey prayed, "Lord, You made this man in Your image and You know where everything fits. Help me and show me how to put him all back together."

The great adventure began when Evelyn Ramsey felt called to be a missionary and said to God, "You make it

"And it was very good."

Genesis 1:31

151

possible, and I will do it." She attended medical school at Tufts University, surviving on horsemeat sandwiches and bathing with discarded pieces of soap she found on the shower room floor.

Dr. Ramsey served as a medical missionary in Swaziland, Africa, from 1956 to 1968. Then she learned that a doctor was desperately needed in Kuddjip, Papua. Many males and married physicians had turned the job down, so Dr. Ramsey again prayed her covenant: "You make it possible, and I will do it." In 1969, she served a brief tour in New Guinea and then returned in 1970.

Immediately, Evelyn Ramsey was confronted with the problem of languages—an estimated 750 distinct languages in Papua alone, in addition to all the dialects. How could a doctor understand any patient?

How could Evelyn balance a medical practice with linguistics work in a Third World language? Dr. Ramsey's answer came in the summer of 1980, when she developed phlebitis. She created herself a new life-style: half a day at the hospital and half a day at home (with her feet up), working on her translations.

In May 1989, Dr. Ramsey was diagnosed as having inoperable brain cancer. Six weeks later, while friends who gathered around her hospital bed sang "How Great Thou Art," this missionary-physician-linguist and courageous single adult died.

Key Thought: The Ramsey Covenant: "You make it possible, and I will do it" is not limited only to Evelyn Ramsey. The God who calls, enables.

June 17

Charles Frohman, theater manager
June 17, 1860–May 7, 1915

Charles Frohman grew up in a family interested in the theater. His father had aspirations of acting and produced small plays in their hometown. Because he wanted his children educated in New York City, he moved the family to New York and opened a small store in the theater district. Some of the city's most famous actors were customers and encouraged young Charles to pursue a career in the theater.

Charles began selling souvenir copies of *The Black Crook,* a New York hit, when he was eight. Then he

"Trust in the Lord forever, for the Lord, the Lord, is the Rock eternal."

Isaiah 26:4

worked as a ticket seller and gained valuable experience as an advance man for a traveling production company.

At twenty-three, Charles Frohman became an independent manager and opened a booking office in New York. He brought *Shenandoah* to Broadway and founded the Empire Stock Company, which became a theater star factory.

By his early thirties, this single adult had a solid reputation as a star maker. One detractor labeled him "the Napoleon of the theater." Frohman gave many playwrights their start and was a constant encourager of new ideas. He never used a contract; his word was his bond.

Frohman produced a string of plays that invigorated the American theater. After a great new play, *The Hyphen,* opened in New York, Frohman sailed to Europe on the *Lusitania*. On May 7, 1915, the ship was torpedoed by German U-boats. Frohman's dying words were preserved by survivors: "Why fear death? It is the most beautiful adventure of life."

Key Thought: If we have lived to the fullest, we can see even death as an adventure. The key to such a philosophy is a commitment to Jesus.

June 18

Elizabeth Cecilia Clephane, hymn writer
June 18, 1830–February 19, 1869

Elizabeth Clephane's father was an English sheriff. After his death, the family went to live in the little village of Melrose, Abbotsford, where Elizabeth stayed the rest of her life. Because of her generosity and compassion, she was nicknamed Sunbeam, particularly by the poor and neglected whom she befriended. Miss Clephane, a member of the Church of Scotland, wrote eight hymns for *The Family Treasury,* which was published after her death.

One hymn was destined to become well-known. It happened when the great evangelist Dwight L. Moody, who was conducting services in England, turned to his singer, Ira D. Sankey, at the end of a service and said, "Sing something." Sankey had torn Miss Clephane's poem out of a newspaper earlier that day. He walked to the organ, sat down, and spontaneously composed a tune for "The Ninety and Nine."

"If a man owns a hundred sheep, and one of them wanders away, will he not leave the ninety-nine on the hills and go to look for the one that wandered off?"

Matthew 18:12

153

Frederick C. Maker took her poem "Beneath the Cross of Jesus" and turned it into one of the great hymns of the Christian faith.

Beneath the Cross of Jesus I gladly take my stand:
The shadow of a mighty rock within a weary land,
A home within the wilderness, a rest upon the
way,
From the burning of the noontide heat
And the burden of the day.

Thousands have made the third verse their commitment:

I take, O Cross, thy shadow for my abiding place;
I ask no other sunshine than the sunshine of His
face,
Content to let the world go by, to know no gain or
loss
My sinful self my only shame, my glory all the
Cross.

Father, it's easy to sing hymns and never hear the words. Is Thy shadow my abiding place? Whatever comes into my life, let me see the sunshine of Your face.

June 19

Samuel Macauley Jackson, church historian
June 19, 1851–August 2, 1912

Samuel Jackson was a graduate of City College of New York and Union Theological Seminary. He studied with the great church historians Henry Boynton Smith and Philip Schaff, who encouraged him to do further work at Leipzig and Berlin and to travel in the Middle East. Jackson was ordained in 1876 but pastored only four years.

Over the next five years, he was involved in social outreach work in New York City. Then, in 1886, Jackson became affiliated with the Charity Organization Society, remaining active there until his death. When he became convinced that poverty and crime were linked, Jackson became involved in prison reform. Through his generosity, literature on prisons was gathered and distributed and public opinion influenced. Jackson edited nine

"And God is able to make all grace abound to you, so that in all things at all times, having all that you need, you will abound in every good work."

2 Corinthians 9:8

154

volumes of the popular *Handbooks for Practice Workers in Church and Philanthropy* and taught in the Amity School for Christian workers.

Jackson was also interested in missions, at one point compiling and publishing a bibliography of five thousand titles. He served as president of the Board of China's Canton Christian College and built the president's home.

However, much of his energy was linked to his former professor and friend, Philip Schaff. Jackson collaborated with Schaff on *A Religious Encyclopedia: Or Dictionary of Biblical, Historical, Doctrinal, and Practical Theology.* Jackson was editor in chief of the ambitious *New Schaff-Herzog Encyclopedia of Religious Knowledge,* some thirteen volumes, but still found time to teach church history at New York University from 1895 to 1912. He was a strong leader and benefactor of the American Society of Church Historians.

He also subsidized the publication of books on Zwingli, particularly the useful *Selected Works of Huldreich Zwingli,* and a translation of six volumes of his writings. The two remaining books on Zwingli's *Works* were published a decade after Jackson's death.

Much of his vast library of Reformation literature was donated to Union Seminary.

Father, today remind us that we, too, can make a difference, through our vocation or our avocation. Interest us in projects larger than ourselves.

June 20

Peter Faneuil, merchant
June 20, 1700–March 3, 1743

Some men are remembered by their companies, some by schools or hospitals they founded. Peter Faneuil is remembered for a Boston landmark, Faneuil Hall, often called the Cradle of Liberty because so many mass meetings took place there before the American Revolution. Its grasshopper weather vane is the most noted steeple in Boston.

After his father's death, Peter went to work for his widowed and childless merchant uncle in Boston. His uncle Andrew had some strong ideas and wanted his nephews to remain bachelors. Andrew had originally

"A good name is more desirable than great riches; to be esteemed is better than silver or gold."

Proverbs 22:1

chosen Peter's brother Benjamin as his heir; however, when Ben married, Andrew disowned him and lavished his attention on Peter.

Andrew died in February 1738, and Peter inherited one of the largest fortunes of Boston. His own businesses continued to prosper, and he named one of his fastest ships *The Jolly Bachelor.*

Faneuil dreamed of a city market and common meeting hall and envisioned a public building that could accommodate both. Bostonians were not so sure; but when Peter offered to donate the building to the city, a public referendum was held, and the measure to build was passed by a slim seven votes.

Today that hall is one of America's major tourist attractions—a memorial to a single adult's vision.

Father, give us the courage to commit ourselves to things that last.

June 21

Egbert Benson, patriot and jurist
June 21, 1746–August 24, 1833

Egbert Benson graduated from King's College (now Columbia) and passed the bar in 1769. Despite his busy law practice, Benson promoted the patriot cause and was particularly influential in creating the government of New York State after the American Revolution. He served in several state posts, including attorney general from 1777 to 1787.

He was a delegate to the Congress of the Confederation from 1781 to 1784, lobbying extensively for New York's ratification of the Constitution.

Egbert served in the first and second congresses as a representative from New York. In the early days of the republic, he advocated a strong executive branch. In 1794, he took a seat on the New York Superior Court, where he was highly regarded for his judicial reforms and philosophy. Benson resigned in 1801, when he was appointed chief judge of the United States Second Circuit Court. However, his appointment was a "midnight appointment" by President John Adams while Congress was not in session. When the law allowing such appointments was repealed, Judge Benson resigned.

"God did not give us a spirit of timidity, but a spirit of power, of love and of self-discipline."

2 Timothy 1:7

Father, we thank You for patriots like Egbert Benson, who dared embrace the concept of liberty, who risked their lives to found this nation and gave their lives to guide its first years. Grant us the wisdom to appreciate our heritage and to be good citi-

156

Egbert Benson served briefly in the seventh Congress. He loved history and helped establish the New York Historical Society, which he served as president after his retirement from the bench.

June 22

William M. Scholl, foot specialist
June 22, 1882–March 29, 1968

Who has not heard of Dr. Scholl's foot products? Billy Scholl began his life's work after being the family cobbler on his father's Indiana farm. Chicago and its bright lights beckoned the boy, who thought he could make a fortune selling shoes in the city.

In Chicago, Billy Scholl quickly discovered that many people had foot problems that were caused or at least aggravated by the shoes they wore. At age twenty-two, he designed and patented his first arch support. He often traveled from shoe store to shoe store, selling his goods. Scholl always began his sales pitch by pulling the skeleton of a human foot from his salesman's kit.

Scholl was industrious. After selling all day, he attended medical classes at night until he received his M.D. from Illinois Medical College in 1904.

In 1912, he founded the Illinois College of Chiropody and Orthopedics and watched it develop into the Illinois College of Podiatric Medicine. Meanwhile, Scholl, Inc., expanded from a sales volume of $815 to 1904 to a quarter of a billion dollars in annual sales in 1976, with five manufacturing plants, three distribution centers, and eighteen overseas companies.

Dr. William Scholl remained untouched by his success, continuing to serve enthusiastically as president until a month before his death at age eighty-five. The bachelor lived most of those years in a single room at the Illinois Athletic Club.

Scholl claimed "never to have forgotten a foot."

"He will not let your foot slip—he who watches over you will not slumber."

Psalm 121:3

Key Thought: Find a new arena and make a difference.

157

June 23

Bronson Murray Cutting, senator
June 23, 1888–May 6, 1935

Tuberculosis ended the Harvard education of Bronson Cutting. He spent the winter of 1909 to 1910 in Southern California recovering and then decided to make his permanent home in the West. In July 1910, Cutting moved to Sante Fe, New Mexico, and in just two years became publisher of three newspapers. He exerted a powerful editorial influence on the territory as it moved toward statehood.

Cutting helped establish the New Mexico Progressive Republican League. However, in 1912, he affiliated with the new Progressive Party.

During World War I he was a military attaché at the American Embassy in London. After he returned to New Mexico, his attempts to run for political office on the Republican platform were negated by old-line Republican loyalists. Meanwhile, Cutting had built new political ties with the Mexican community and with the American Legion, which he had served as state commander.

In 1927, Cutting was appointed to fill a vacancy in the United States Senate; the following year he won the seat by election. A strong liberal, he lambasted Hoover's attempts to deal with the emerging Depression.

Although a Republican, he often crossed party lines to support Franklin D. Roosevelt's New Deal legislation when it was beneficial to New Mexico.

"But it is the spirit in a man, the breath of the Almighty, that gives him understanding. It is not only the old who are wise."

Job 32:8, 9

Father, we thank You for the example of persistence and adaptability modeled by Bronson Cutting. Give us courage to find our new territories, too.

June 24

Henry Chapman Mercer, archaeologist
June 24, 1856–March 9, 1930

After graduating from Harvard and passing the Pennsylvania bar, Henry Mercer's interest in law diminished quickly. At the same time his curiosity about archaeology increased. In 1885, Mercer published a monograph on *The Lenape Stone* and was made an honorary member of

"If you make an altar of stones for me, do not build it with dressed stones, for you will

158

the United States Archeological Commission. In 1893, Mercer became editor of *The American Naturalist* and the following year became curator of American and prehistoric archaeology at the University of Pennsylvania.

During this time, Mercer was actively involved in digs in Mexico and across the United States. In Mexico's Yucatan he established dates for several sites; in the United States his exploration of caves led to the identification of the remains of several extinct animals: tapir, mylodon, peccary, and sloth. Chapman's work in exploring bones along American river valleys was important in establishing migration routes.

Eventually Mercer hired a group of men scattered throughout the world to search for ancient tools used by agricultural societies. This led to the publication of *Ancient Carpenter's Tools* in 1929. Mercer's work helped many Bible scholars understand how such edifices as Herod's temple could have been built.

Mercer became so skilled he could examine the nails, hardware, screws, and timbers in a building and determine its age.

At his death, Henry Mercer's will turned his sixty-six-room mansion into a museum.

defile it if you use a tool on it."

Exodus 20:25

Key Thought: Life is too short to be spent working in a profession that is of no personal interest.

June 25

Gerald Fowke, archaeologist
June 25, 1855–March 5, 1933

After several years of teaching school in the South, Gerald Fowke enrolled at Ohio State University in 1881 to study geology and math. After his training there, the world became his laboratory. Fowke studied in Siberia and Vancouver Island, British Columbia, looking for evidence of an Asiatic migration to America. He also compiled a comprehensive archaeological history of Ohio. From Ohio to the Ozarks, Fowke studied caves, quarries, and mines.

Fowke published sixty scientific papers and two major books: *Archaeological History of Ohio* (1902) and *Evolution of the Ohio River* (1933), both the results of his exhaustive field research.

Friends reported that Fowke possessed "an uncompromising insistence on facts and truth." However, he

"Stand at the crossroads and look; ask for the ancient paths."

Jeremiah 6:16

Father, are we too busy focusing on today to see the an-

159

did not always possess tact. In fact, his "unsparing criticism of anyone and anything falling short of his high ideals often made him temporarily unpopular."

It is estimated that Gerald Fowke walked more than 100,000 miles in his life and was better acquainted with the topography of the Ohio River Valley than any other man in American history.

cient paths? Remind us that there is much to be learned from the past that will make our present more enriching.

June 26
Joseph Bartlett Eastman, reformer
June 26, 1882–March 15, 1944

After graduation from Amherst, Joseph Eastman worked at South End Settlement House in Boston. He attracted the attention of Louis Brandeis and Edward Filene, who were key leaders in an organization called the Public Franchise League, chartered to watchdog the municipal utilities.

For ten years Eastman studied proposed mergers of railroads, exposed stock frauds, testified on legislation related to utilities, monitored rate increases, and drafted guidelines for the Massachusetts Legislature. In 1913, due to Joseph Eastman's lobbying, the Massachusetts State Public Service Commission was established; two years later, Eastman became a member. Based on his work there, in 1919 Joseph was sworn in as one of the youngest men ever to serve on the Interstate Commerce Commission. He held the post for twenty-six years, although the commission was noted for the short tenure of its members. His longevity gave him considerable clout; his competency and consistency led to reappointments by presidents of both parties.

Supreme Court Justice Harlan Stone said of Eastman, "When our court gets a case which involves a decision and an order of the Interstate Commerce Commission, we always thumb through it first to see what Joe Eastman has said in his opinion."

In 1941, Roosevelt appointed Eastman the Director of Defense Transportation. His work was effective as the nation prepared for war.

After his funeral, the *Washington Post* praised Eastman's years of public service: "Here was a man who dignified the title, 'bureaucrat.'"

"Now Daniel so distinguished himself among the administrators and satraps by his exceptional qualities that the king planned to set him over the whole kingdom."

Daniel 6:3

Key Thought: My task as a single adult is to dignify the titles in my life: man or woman; Christian; single adult; friend.

160

June 27

Varina Anne Jefferson Davis, patriot
June 27, 1864–September 18, 1898

Anne Davis, born during the declining days of the Confederacy to President and Mrs. Jefferson Davis, showed a remarkable interest in books. At age twelve she could recite long passages of Shakespeare. Her parents placed her in a European boarding school to help her recover from the emotional wounds of the Civil War. When she returned, Miss Davis became her father's companion and traveled extensively with him across the South.

Governor Gordon of Georgia called her the "Daughter of the Confederacy" and Winnie—as she was called by the family—liked the title. Soon she found herself idolized and cherished by veterans' groups and became a living symbol of "the Lost Cause" of a generation of Southern men who were sure that the old days had been better.

After her father's death, she relied on writing to support herself and her mother, particularly after they moved to New York City. Her books included a biography of Robert Emmet (1888) and two novels, *A Romance of Summer Seas* and *The Veiled Doctor*.

She was buried in the old Confederate capital of Richmond. Tragically, Miss Davis was never known for her own contributions, but only as the daughter of Jefferson Davis.

"Do not say, 'Why were the old days better than these?' For it is not wise to ask such questions."

Ecclesiastes 7:10

Father, how tragic to be a symbol of a lost cause and live our lives in the past. Keep us pointed toward our futures.

June 28

Oley Speaks, composer
June 28, 1874–August 27, 1948

Oley Speaks's mind was on music. He sang in church choirs, wrote music, and was described in the *Columbus Dispatch* as "a musician to his fingertips."

As a young man, Speaks traveled to New York City to audition for a position as soloist at the Church of the Divine Paternity, winning the position over seventy-five other people. For the next four years, Speaks took pri-

"Blessed is the man who does not walk in the counsel of the wicked."

Psalm 1:1

161

vate voice lessons from noted singers and studied composition with Max Spicker and Will Macfarlane. Around 1906, Speaks returned to Columbus but found his old hometown too culturally confining. He returned to New York and spent the next forty years writing some two hundred fifty songs.

Speaks's fame rests on three songs: "On the Road to Mandalay," which sold more than 1 million copies, and "Morning" and "Sylvia," which each sold half a million copies. He also contributed the compositions for the hymns "Hark! Hark My Soul," "Let Not Your Heart Be Troubled," and "The Perfect Prayer."

Speaks wrote music to be sung in church and around a piano in a parlor. His songs appeal to the listener's emotions. Oley Speaks's biographer says he wrote not for classical tastes, but as a good old Methodist Republican from Ohio.

Key Point: I may not be able to sing well, but I can always sing a good song.

June 29

Ida Maude Cannon, social worker
June 29, 1877–July 8, 1960

Ida Maude Cannon graduated from the nurses' training program at St. Paul Hospital in 1898; her first job was to found and supervise a hospital for "the feeble minded." At a later time, when she was temporarily suffering from blindness, Ida took sociology courses at the University of Wisconsin and heard reformer Jane Addams speak about reform in tenements and factories, an experience that had a life-changing impact on her.

As a visiting nurse in St. Paul, Ida had occasion to observe the relationship between poverty and illness. She moved to Cambridge to attend Simmons School of Social Work, then began to work as a volunteer in the social service program at Massachusetts General Hospital, the first of its kind in America. In 1907, she joined the staff and in 1908 became head of social service, a post she held for the next thirty-seven years.

Ida's work was to see that the whole person was treated, so the patient was not dehumanized. Cannon called the medical community to deal with reality. How,

"All they asked was that we should continue to remember the poor, the very thing I was eager to do."

Galatians 2:10

she argued, could a patient follow doctor's orders for complete bed rest when he was the sole support of his family?

Ida Cannon made a significant contribution to the recognition of medical social work, her *Social Work in Hospitals* becoming a standard text for many years. She was a leader in forming the American Association of Hospital Social Workers and helped develop the curriculum used at Boston School of Social Work.

Father, thank You for those single adults who see a need and fill it.

June 30

Louise Pound, scholar
June 30, 1872–June 28, 1958

Louise Pound found Lincoln, Nebraska, to be an intellectual oasis in her childhood. "It may have been mudflats on the outside," she once wrote, "but it was Boston on the inside."

Louise Pound graduated with a degree in music from the University of Nebraska in 1892; two years later she began teaching there while working on her master's degree. She also cycled and coached the women's basketball team.

After taking time to earn her Ph.D. at Heidelberg, Louise resumed teaching in Nebraska. She would stay at the university for the next forty-five years, rising to full professor in 1912. During her early tenure, Louise was ranked nationally as a woman golfer and figure skater. In the summer she could be found teaching at such institutions as Berkeley, Yale, Chicago, Stanford, or Columbia. She pioneered in the teaching of American literature (at that time most universities offered only English literature).

Louise also made time, despite a heavy teaching load, to do research, particularly on ballads. She argued convincingly against the notion of a cooperative origin of ballads. Rather, she insisted, they were the products of individual minds. She helped establish the study of folklore and American speech as academic disciplines rather than intellectual hobbies. The noted author H. L. Mencken wrote that Miss Pound's "early work put the study of current American English on its legs."

"With many similar parables Jesus spoke the word to them, as much as they could understand. He did not say anything to them without using a parable."

Mark 4:33, 34

163

To further her research, she founded and edited the journal *American Speech* (1925–1933).

In 1955, at age eighty-two, Dr. Pound was elected the first woman president of the Modern Language Association and to the Nebraska Sports Hall of Fame. She took both honors in stride: "First woman again—life has its humors."

Outside the classroom and beyond the athletic field, Louise Pound was a powerful advocate of educational opportunity for women. After a long academic career, she died of a heart attack.

Key Thought: A former student, B. A. Botkin, said after her death: "She was a great teacher because she was a great person."

July 1

Irna Phillips, radio and television writer
July 1, 1901–December 22, 1973

Irna Phillips grew up in a one-parent family; her father died when she was eight. She remembered her childhood this way: "[I was] a plain, sickly, silent child, with hand-me-down clothes and no friends." As a result, Irna turned to books and the world of pretend. She told people she wanted to be an actress, but a tough drama professor at the University of Illinois told her, "You have neither the looks nor the stature to achieve professional success." Defeated, Irna taught school for ten years after her graduation from Northwestern University.

During that time, Irna worked as a volunteer at WGN Radio in Chicago. In 1930, the station asked her to write and perform in a family drama. "Painted Dreams"— considered by many to be the first soap opera—aired ten minutes daily and kept a large audience listening for the struggles of Mother Monahan, a widow, acted by Irna Phillips.

When the network tried to buy the show, WGN balked and Irna quit. However, Miss Phillips sold the network a new idea called "Today's Children." In six years, it became radio's number-one daily serial. After her mother's death, Irna quit to turn her attention to two new ideas: "The Road of Life" and "The Guiding Light."

Irna wrote to the instincts of her audience: self-preservation, romance, and family. By 1943, with five soaps running daily, Irna's income was $250,000 a year. *Time* labeled her "America's highest paid aerial litera-teuse."

". . . we spend our years as a tale that is told."

Psalm 90:9 KJV

Irna was wounded in several personal relationships, especially by one man who broke up with her when he discovered she could not have children. So, at age forty-two, she adopted a boy and, eighteen months later, a girl.

The invention of television destroyed the careers of many soap-opera writers, but Irna thrived in the new medium. She developed many innovations, including the tease ending, organ music to build moods, and "cross over" (the appearance of a major character in one series as a minor character in another). Irna's heroines were long-suffering, and their lives focused on their marriage and motherhood. She was a loud opponent of feminism, which she declared would weaken the commitment to the home. "Guiding Light" and "Days of Our Lives" were her masterpieces.

In her last years, Irna Phillips denounced the new trends in TV soaps, particularly rape, illegitimacy, and adultery. She attributed her success to her limited vocabulary and the inspiration of her mother.

Key Point: Sometimes we cannot see the end result of one of our creations.

July 2

Charles Arthur Conant, journalist
July 2, 1861–July 5, 1915

Charles Conant established his reputation as an economist through reporting on financial issues for the *Boston Post, New York Journal of Commerce,* the *Springfield Republican,* and other newspapers. In 1893, he ran as the Democratic candidate for a seat in Congress as a staunch advocate of sound currency rather than silver-based currency. He gained the confidence of leading bankers in the United States and Europe.

In 1901, President McKinley appointed Conant to study the monetary system of the Philippines, then under United States control as a result of the Spanish-American War. For a long time, silver pesos in the Philippines were called "conants," and paper currency featured his photo.

In 1903, Conant was an adviser to the Mexican government as it changed from a silver-based to a gold-based economy. He also served on the Commission on

"A man can do nothing better than to eat and drink and find satisfaction in his work."

Ecclesiastes 2:24

165

International Exchange, which was designed to foster cooperation between gold-standard nations and those with silver-based currency.

A prolific author, Conant edited the foreign banking section of *Banker's Magazine* for years. *A History of Modern Banks of Issue* (1896), his most popular book, went through five editions. Six other books on money and his biography of Alexander Hamilton were widely read and quoted in the financial world.

Although he had a strong personality, Charles Arthur Conant was modest and witty.

Father, money is not the answer to all of our problems, but it is a necessity. As You supply our financial needs, make us aware of others' needs.

July 3

Charles Schuchert, paleontologist
July 3, 1858–November 20, 1942

Formal education was a luxury for this single adult's immigrant family. At age twelve, Charles was sent to a training school to learn bookkeeping and soon found himself working long hours for his father. However, in his limited free time, he took drawing classes and pursued his interest in fossils. Schuchert quickly learned to prepare and describe specimens and also mastered lithography, developing a network to exchange data and samples with other fossil collectors.

The Schuchert family factory burned in 1877. His father's heavy drinking forced Charles to assume responsibility for the family and for the business. Some time later, a second fire totally wiped out the business and Charles was pressured into working for a competitor. Finally, he quit and took a position at the Cincinnati Society of Natural History, working for the director. In his new role, Schuchert collected fossil brachiopods and exchanged specimens with other geologists. His thoroughness won admiration (and a job) from James Hall, director of the New York Geological Survey. Unfortunately, Hall published some of Schuchert's research without crediting him, so Charles moved on, although he considered his time in New York a learning experience.

Without ever attending college, Charles Schuchert joined the Peabody Museum at Yale as a preparator, and

"In the beginning God created the heavens and the earth. Now the earth was formless and empty, darkness was over the surface of the deep, and the Spirit of God was hovering over the waters."

Genesis 1:1, 2

a year later joined the United States Geological Survey as assistant curator of invertebrate paleontology. That position offered him some incredible opportunities for research, including an expedition to Greenland.

In 1903, Schuchert became the curator of geological collections at Yale and was appointed professor of historical geology. He chaired the geology department, headed the graduate school, and directed the museum, still finding time to be a "foster father" to a large number of graduate students.

Schuchert wrote 234 papers. His *Textbook on Historical Geology* went through four editions and was used by almost all undergraduates studying geology between the two world wars.

Father, we are thankful that You are a seeking God, not to add us to your "collection," but because You desire fellowship with us today.

July 4

Morris Joseph Asch, laryngologist
July 4, 1833–October 5, 1902

After Joseph Asch graduated from Jefferson Medical College in 1855, he became an assistant to prominent surgeon Dr. Samuel Gross. When the Civil War began, Asch volunteered and was quickly appointed an assistant surgeon in the Union army. As casualties intensified, he served as surgeon in chief and medical inspector of the Army of the Potomac. Dr. Asch survived the battles at Chancellorsville, Gettysburg, and Appomattox Court House.

Asch's career was tied to the rise of General Phillip Sheridan, under whom he served from 1865 to 1873. He offered decisive leadership in New Orleans during the cholera epidemic in 1866 and the yellow fever epidemic of 1867. After his own bout with yellow fever, Asch joined Sheridan at Fort Leavenworth and was recognized for his compassionate treatment of wounded soldiers. He retired from the military in 1873.

Asch moved to New York and specialized in the new field of laryngology, helping found the American Laryngological Association. Despite his busy practice, he devoted time to research, perfecting a major surgical procedure—the "Asch operation"—to repair the nasal septum.

"Their throats are open graves; their tongues practice deceit."

Romans 3:13

Father, our bodies are the temple of the Holy Spirit. Thank You for the magnificence of Your creation and for those who

167

In his last years, Joseph Asch surrounded himself with young doctors. He believed he could help their careers and that they would keep his perspective fresh.

know best how to do necessary temple maintenance.

July 5

Cecil Rhodes, African colonist
July 5, 1853–March 26, 1902

Africa is a strange place to send an Englishman in ill health, but that's exactly what the Rhodes family did for their son, Cecil. Rather than attending university, Cecil went to Natal to run his brother's cotton plantation.

In 1871, Cecil gave up farming to become a diamond prospector. In 1873, although modestly successful in the Kimberley diamond fields, Rhodes returned to England and entered Oriel College, Oxford. However, he was soon told he had only six months to live, so he immediately returned to Africa. Again, he recovered.

Influenced by Edward Gibbon's *History of the Decline and Fall of the Roman Empire,* Rhodes became convinced that the problems of Rome were present in the British Empire. His solution was to expand the empire. First he poured himself into a new business enterprise with Charles Rudd. They formed the De Beers Mining Company and began to raise diamond prices. The company would become a major force in the diamond industry for the next century.

In 1880, he won a seat in the Cape Colony, South African legislature. Then, in a strategic move, on July 13, 1889, he received a charter from the British South Africa Company to develop a vast area of land eventually called Rhodesia. This was a step toward his dream of bringing all Africa—from the Cape to Cairo—under British rule.

By 1887, Rhodes consolidated his diamond holdings and bought out his competitors, which launched his dream of building a railroad into the interior. Then, in 1890, he became prime minister of the Cape, where he served for six years.

His lasting contribution was the creation of his Rhodes scholarships to Oxford. He gave 6 million pounds to a trust. The interest from the trust would

"Command those who are rich in this present world not to be arrogant nor to put their hope in wealth, which is so uncertain, but to put their hope in God, who richly provides us with everything for our enjoyment."

1 Timothy 6:17

Father, dreams can become nightmares for those who are not included. It is hard to understand Cecil Rhodes. He did much good

bring two students from every state and territory in America, three students from each of the British colonies, and fifteen students from Germany to Oxford for a graduate education. In only a few years, "Rhodes scholar" became an incredible entry on an academic résumé.

In 1909, four states federated to form the Union of South Africa, a belated fulfillment of Rhodes's dream. Tragically, Rhodes did not want blacks to participate in the governing of Africa. Legislation he sponsored in 1894 helped create apartheid.

through educating so many of the world's brightest people but denied the basic human rights of so many of the world's poorest. Teach us to balance our dreams.

July 6

John Paul Jones, naval hero
July 6, 1747–July 18, 1792

John Paul signed up for his first voyage when he was twelve years old, working as an apprentice on the *Friendship,* bound for Virginia from England.

By age twenty-two, John Paul was commander of the merchantman *John.* While sailing his ship to the West Indies, he was charged with murder after a mutiny in which a man was killed when "he rushed upon the sword in my hand." After the incident, John was advised to go back to America incognito. He did so and added Jones to his name.

At the time the American Revolution broke out, Jones was a drifter living on the generosity of strangers. He went to Philadelphia and developed a friendship with leading members of the Continental Congress. On December 7, 1775, he was commissioned a navy lieutenant, and in his first battle he helped capture the British ship *Providence.* He became the ship's commander when it was recommissioned an American vessel of war.

Jones began developing his reputation as an outstanding naval officer and strategist. From December 1777 to February 1781, he won a string of naval victories over often superior British warships. In 1787, Congress awarded Jones a gold star for his outstanding service, but before the medal could be received, Jones entered the Russian navy as a rear admiral. In June 1790, he returned to Paris, where he retired.

In 1913, Jones's remains were conveyed by ship to

"Be strong and courageous. Do not be afraid or discouraged because of the king of Assyria and the vast army with him, for there is a greater power with us than with him."

2 Chronicles 32:7

Father, it's always too early to quit. Give us the courage to pay the price

169

Annapolis and placed in the chapel of the United States Naval Academy. He is best remembered for one sentence in response to a British commander's request for surrender: "I have not yet begun to fight!"

and to go the distance to become what You want us to be.

July 7

Nettie M. Stevens, geneticist
July 7, 1861–May 4, 1912

Nettie Stevens spent the first years of her career as a librarian in Vermont. At age thirty-five, she moved to Stanford University to study physiology. Miss Stevens spent her summers at a research lab in Pacific Grove, California, becoming interested in research. An article she published on the life cycle of the *Boceria,* a protozoan parasite of sea cucumbers, sparked her academic reputation.

After completion of her masters degree in 1900, she moved east to attend Bryn Mawr, interrupting her degree program there to study with German biologist Theodore Boveri. Miss Stevens completed her Ph.D. in 1902.

Dr. Stevens's ultimate contribution would be a scientific breakthrough that proved gender was determined by a particular chromosome. Using the beetle *Tenebrio molitor,* she demonstrated that an X-carrying sperm produced a female, while a Y-carrying sperm produced a male. Several years passed before Stevens's theory was accepted as fact.

Nettie Stevens was noted for her precise research and her cautious interpretation of the results. She used her enthusiasm for biology to improve her effectiveness in the classroom as well as in the laboratory.

"My frame was not hidden from you when I was made in the secret place. . . . your eyes saw my unformed body."

Psalm 139:15, 16

Father, we thank You for letting us in on the great secrets and mysteries of Your creation. Remind us that we are created in Your image.

July 8

Ralph Ingersoll Lockwood, lawyer
July 8, 1798–April 12, 1858

After passing the New York bar, Ralph Lockwood moved to New York City and, combining aggressiveness with a brilliant legal mind, built a successful practice. At age

"Wisdom, like an inheritance, is a good thing and

twenty-seven, he published an intense analysis of the National Bankruptcy Act passed by Congress, focusing on the implications of bankruptcy in a democracy.

Ralph Lockwood was instrumental in legal reform and legal education. He did not have a high reverence for the courts and never hesitated to question the decisions handed down through the judicial pipeline. As a respected legal scholar, he prepared an American edition of *A Treatise on the Law of Husband and Wife* (1850), a key legal text of the period.

Lockwood was a true Renaissance man. Because of his strong French scholarship, he became legal counsel for a large number of French citizens living in New York City. He also wrote, under the pen name of Rosine Laval, two novels, *Rosine Laval* (1833) and *The Insurgents* (1835). The first he wrote while away from New York during an outbreak of cholera; the second, after a nervous breakdown.

In his preface to *The Insurgents,* Lockwood observed that, while he had always threatened to fall in love and marry, he had never gotten around to it.

benefits those who see the sun."

Ecclesiastes 7:11

Key Thought: How many other blessings do we miss because we never get around to them? This moment should not be neglected. Use it.

July 9

Charles Hayden, financier
July 9, 1870–January 8, 1937

After studying mining and economics at M.I.T., Charles Hayden knew how to make money. After a year's apprenticeship as a mining stockbroker, he borrowed $20,000 and set up his own firm of Hayden, Stone and Company. Although he and his partner had seats on the Boston Stock Exchange, they still counted pennies; once they hesitated to invest twenty-five dollars for a list of potential prospects.

Hayden was a brilliant thinker, knowing how to integrate incredible mounds of data on men, business trends, and financial status. His wisdom was legendary; at the time of his death, he sat on fifty-eight corporate boards.

Hayden was not unlike Dickens's Scrooge; he hated low productivity, distractions, and lazy workers. Visi-

"Watch out! Be on your guard against all kinds of greed; a man's life does not consist in the abundance of his possessions."

Luke 12:15

171

tors were given only a few minutes of his time; board and committee meetings were held simultaneously to expedite efficiency.

When asked why he had remained a bachelor, he said, "I married the firm of Hayden, Stone and Company, and you are all my big family."

Hayden's will established the Charles Hayden Foundation, which donated more than $50 million to charities interested in the needs of boys. He also gave generously to the Red Cross and his alma mater, M.I.T.

Father, give us courage to balance all the areas of our lives. Remind us that there is more to life than what we can accumulate.

July 10

Ima Hogg, philanthropist
July 10, 1882–August 19, 1975

With the last name of Hogg tied to the first name of Ima, this young Texan was forced to develop a tremendous sense of self-esteem. Biographers note two legends that circulated through Texas about Ima: first, that she had a twin named Ura; and second, that her puritanical father had named her to protect her virtue.

Ima Hogg's father was a powerful reform Texas politician who eventually became state governor. Ima traveled with him, often filling in for her mother, who was ill. In 1906, Ima's father died and she and her brothers inherited a great deal of money. Many years later, when Ima's single brother, William, died, he left his money to the University of Texas with the stipulation that Ima be consulted on its use. Ima decided to establish university mental health services across Texas. She also founded one of the nation's first child psychiatry centers, The Houston Child Guidance Center.

Ima's great love was music. She helped found the Houston Symphony and was active in its fund-raising programs. She disliked the public eye and devoted her attention to philanthropy. She also encouraged the preservation of historic buildings and sites.

At age ninety-three, Ima Hogg planned a visit to London. When asked why she was going, she answered, "to hear the greatest music in the world one last time." She died in London.

". . . for God loveth a cheerful giver."

2 Corinthians 9:7 KJV

Key Point: Ima Hogg lived with an impatience for obstacles or excuses—two temptations for today's single adults. Her life reminds us to cheerfully give of ourselves and our wealth.

172

Annie Walker Armstrong, Baptist women's leader
July 11, 1850–December 20, 1938

Although Annie Armstrong did not become a Christian until she was nineteen, her influence continues to this day in Southern Baptist circles. Annie was a member of the Eutaw Place Baptist Church in Baltimore and taught the infants' class there for thirty years. She is remembered for her commitment to missionary work around the world.

Although it is not known when her interest in missions began, Annie was deeply moved upon hearing a missionary describe the needs of American Indians. She immediately formed a home mission society in her church, which eventually led to the formation of the Baptist Home Mission Society of Maryland in May of 1882. Annie was elected the society's president.

Six years later, in Richmond, Virginia, the Women's Missionary Union of the Southern Baptist Convention was founded, with Annie as a key leader in the move. She lobbied persistently to frame a constitution that would make the organization an auxilliary to the denomination rather than an independent body. Annie wanted the group to support the Foreign Mission Board rather than send missionaries on its own. Her tenacity prevailed, and she was elected the first corresponding secretary. For the next eighteen years, the Women's Missionary Union was Annie's life.

Annie's greatest contribution came as a result of a letter from missionary Lottie Moon in April 1888. Lottie asked Annie for financial help and for two missionaries to help her work in China. When the Foreign Mission Board said it would take $2,000 to equip and pay the salaries of two missionaries, Annie proposed that an offering be taken to raise the money. The offering raised $3,315.26 and, as a result, three missionaries went to China. In 1918, at Annie's suggestion, the annual campaign was renamed the Lottie Moon Offering.

Annie resigned in 1906 but remained interested in missions. In the 1930s, the Southern Baptists renamed their Home Missions Offering after Annie.

In 1938, shortly before her death, Annie Armstrong sent greetings to the Women's Missionary Union on its

"And the Lord said unto Moses, Wherefore criest thou unto me? speak unto the children of Israel, that they go forward."

Exodus 14:15 KJV

fiftieth anniversary. "My message for the Union in its 50th year is that I hope it may grow every year stronger and stronger . . . go forward."

Key Thought: Go forward.

July 12

Benjamin Altman, merchant and philanthropist
July 12, 1840–October 7, 1913

Benjamin Altman's training as a salesman began in his boyhood, when he worked in his immigrant father's store in New York. After working in a string of New York–area dry-goods stores, Benjamin opened his own shop in 1865. For the next forty years, this hard-driving single adult built his business. B. Altman was one of the first New York department stores to move to Fifth Avenue.

Altman took a personal interest in his employees. He was an innovator in providing lunch hours, rest breaks, and medical care for workers.

Over the years Altman gave much of his attention to art. In the 1880s, he began a collection of Chinese enamels and porcelains. Soon his home on Fifth Avenue became a museum of sorts, with more than one thousand Chinese porcelains, enamels, tapestries, sculptures, and paintings. During this time, Altman also amassed a significant library on the history of art. Gradually he turned over the management of B. Altman to a partner in order to devote his time to collecting art.

Benjamin Altman did not socialize; less than one hundred people knew him by sight. He died after a short illness in 1913, and his estate amounted to $35 million. He left a sizable portion of it to the National Academy of Design, to be used to encourage American painters. Altman's art collection, appraised at $20 million, was donated to New York's Metropolitan Museum.

"For a man may do his work with wisdom, knowledge and skill, and then he must leave all he owns to someone who has not worked for it."

Ecclesiastes 2:21

Father, in our labor and in our leisure, be with us. Teach us not only how to acquire but how to give back.

Jonathan Plummer, peddler and poet
July 13, 1761–September 13, 1819

When Jonathan Plummer was a boy, people told him he was "peculiar." To make money, he peddled halibut from a wheelbarrow. Because he was unhappy at home, he became a wanderer.

Despite his eccentricities, the young boy was gifted with a good memory and a desire to read. Plummer always made friends with people who owned books. After reading Shakespeare, Ovid, Dryden, Swift, and Cervantes, he became convinced that he, too, could write. He failed as a preacher but had some success as a peddler of sermons. At twenty-six, he decided he would find a rich woman to marry as a solution to his poverty. Two months and nine vigorous rejections later, Plummer concluded that celibacy was his lot in life.

About 1793, Timothy Dexter hired Plummer to be his poet laureate, which lasted until the benefactor died in 1806. Plummer spent most of his time writing one-page broadsides and pamphlets on such subjects as scandals, suicides, dying confessions, and smallpox inoculations. For many years, citizens could expect a daily oration by Jonathan Plummer in Market Square.

Plummer left about $1,500 in his estate, which he wanted used to publish his memoirs. His will was rejected.

"The quiet words of the wise are more to be heeded than the shouts of a ruler of fools."

Ecclesiastes 9:17

Father, remind us to be diligent in the use of our gifts.

Jerry Traylor, motivational speaker
July 14, 1954–

He made it! He had run 3,500 miles across the United States. But then, Jerry Traylor had run three dozen marathons, in hundreds of shorter races, and up rugged Pike's Peak. What was so special about this achievement?

Jerry ran on crutches.

Traylor was born two months premature, with cere-

"I can do all things through Christ which strengtheneth me."

Philippians 4:13 KJV

bral palsy. He had a dozen corrective operations by the time he reached his early teens. When he was fourteen, doctors replaced his steel braces with crutches.

"What a thrill it was to get those crutches," Jerry recalls. "There are two kinds of crutches—positive and negative. Mine are positive crutches. They help me, support me, and free me to get out and live life. But crutches can be negative, too, if people think that they are and let the crutches limit them or handicap them."

Jerry's crutches didn't keep him from a degree in business administration, from learning to dance or ski, from a position with the United States Department of the Treasury, or from quitting his job to begin a career as a motivational speaker.

"God really has blessed me," Jerry says. "I think what I do is just to live life and make the best of every single thing the Lord has given me to use. So long as I keep trying, I don't worry about falling down."

Father, the next time we fall, give us the courage to get back up.

July 15

Thomas Bulfinch, author
July 15, 1796–May 27, 1867

After graduation from Harvard, Thomas Bulfinch taught at Boston Latin School and then clerked in his brother's store. After his father was appointed Capitol architect, Bulfinch followed him to Washington and was in business for himself until 1824.

In 1825, he returned to Boston and repeatedly failed in each business he started. In 1837, he began clerking at the Merchants' Bank of Boston, a position he held until his death thirty years later.

During these years, Bulfinch was busy writing *Hebrew Lyrical History*; *The Age of Chivalry*; *Legends of Charlemagne*; *Poetry of the Age of Fable*; *Shakespeare Adapted For Reading Classics*; and *Oregon and Eldorado*.

He is best known for *The Age of the Fable*, published in 1863, a masterful book that makes mythology interesting for untrained readers. The work is still found in most libraries.

This bachelor lived with his parents, to whom he was devoted.

"There were giants on the earth in those days. . . . Those were the mighty men who were of old, men of renown."

Genesis 6:4 NKJV

Key Point: The ability to take a complex subject and make it more easily understood is a lasting feat.

Marion Reilly, educator and suffragist
July 16, 1879–January 27, 1928

Marion Reilly faced a formidable challenge in 1907: She had to follow the legendary Carey Thomas as dean of Bryn Mawr, her alma mater. Her graduate study in mathematics and physics had included stints at the University of Göttingen, Cambridge, and at the University of Rome.

In 1916, she resigned the deanship to pursue other interests, although she did join the college's board of directors and served there until her death.

During World War I, she organized the Bryn Mawr Service Corps, which sent a small army of social and educational experts to help in the war-ravaged nations of Europe. Reilly served on the administrative staffs of three other educational institutions and struggled with burnout because of her overwhelming workload.

She was a leading force in the American Association of University Women from 1907 to 1927, both at the board and committee levels, helping the group develop its contacts with university women in Europe.

Marion Reilly was committed to working for women's right to vote, serving on committees at the local, state, and national levels. She chaired the Philadelphia chapter of the League of Women Voters and invested a great deal of time and energy into the organizations she joined.

Miss Reilly was known for her anonymous generosity, particularly in helping deserving women complete their educations.

One biographer noted, "Her outstanding qualities were spiritual—sympathy, faith in the fundamentals of character, and a willingness to serve others."

"As we have opportunity, let us do good to all people, especially to those who belong to the family of believers."

Galatians 6:10

Key Thought: Marion Reilly illustrated the principle that variety is the spice of life. Just as there were organizations that needed her wit and wisdom, so there are organizations and causes that need ours today.

Isaac Watts, hymn writer
July 17, 1674–November 25, 1748

Isaac Watts was a scholar, poet, educational pioneer, and preacher, yet he is best remembered as "the father of English hymnology." Isaac began writing hymns at twenty. On the way home from church, he had complained about the dreary quality of the music that morning. "Then give us something better, young man!" his father admonished. The next Sunday Isaac Watts introduced his first hymn to the congregation. For the next two years, he wrote a new hymn each week.

It should be noted that Watts was innovative. At this time, only meterical psalms were sung in worship. Though these were somewhat stilted, some thought it sinful to sing anything else. But within a few years, this single adult's hymns had taken the religious world by storm. Watts gave the dissenters a new way to express their understanding of God's glory and grace.

To this day, no hymnal would be complete without a dozen or more Isaac Watts's hymns, such as "Joy to the World," "O God, Our Help in Ages Past," "When I Survey the Wondrous Cross," "I Sing the Mighty Power of God," "Alas, and Did My Savior Bleed?"

Isaac was only five feet tall and had a poor self-image. Though never married, he knew the heartbreak of love. He cared for Elizabeth Singer, a poet with whom he'd had a continued correspondence. Isaac hoped Elizabeth could eventually love him, since she had been enchanted by his writing and was complimentary. When they finally met, Watts proposed. Elizabeth reportedly answered that while she "loved the jewel she could not admire the casket which contained it!" No wonder Watts wrote:

> Forbid it, that I should boast
> Save in the death of Christ, my God.
> All the vain things that charm me most,
> I sacrifice them to His blood.

Isaac Watts's legacy to the church was 750 hymns.

"... I consider everything a loss compared to the surpassing greatness of knowing Christ Jesus my Lord, for whose sake I have lost all things."

Philippians 3:8

Father, what a legacy! One man's music is just as stirring today as two centuries ago. How barren our worship would be without Watts's contribution. Remind us of that the next time we think we cannot make a difference.

July 18

Paul Ambrose Oliver, soldier and inventor
July 18, 1830–May 17, 1912

Paul Oliver came to the United States from Germany at nineteen and became involved in the cotton business. When he was twenty-six, he headed the Fort Hamilton Relief Association, which was credited with preventing a yellow fever epidemic in New York City.

When the Civil War broke out, Oliver joined the Twelfth New York Volunteers and had a distinguished military career. He was recognized for his "coolness, bravery, and intelligence." Oliver was involved in twenty-five major battles, including one in which he may have saved a future president's life. In Resaca, Georgia, on May 6, 1865, Union troops became confused and began firing on one another. Oliver prevented disaster by stopping the shooting. The troops being fired on were commanded by Colonel Benjamin Harrison.

After the war, Oliver began to experiment with explosives. He developed new formulas and manufacturing processes that made the use of explosives safer and is generally credited with the discovery of dynamite.

"Moreover, when God gives any man wealth and possessions, and enables him to enjoy them, to accept his lot and be happy in his work–this is a gift of God."

Ecclesiastes 5:19

Father, give us the ability to enjoy all the gifts that You give us.

July 19

Mary Ann "Mother" Bickerdyke, nurse
July 19, 1817–November 8, 1901

"What can one person do?" asked Mary Bickerdyke, a young Illinois widow, as the casualties in the Civil War mounted. All around her, it seemed, soldiers were dying from lack of nursing care and food. Eventually Mary left her own children with family and set out to do her part to alleviate some of the suffering.

Mary began by distributing food supplies to the hungry troops. She collected supplies in the North, often by sending a simple note to the pastor just before his sermon. She was famous for her "cow and hen" missions, in which she delivered a hundred cows and a thousand hens to field hospitals to feed the wounded.

One officer described Mary as "strong as a man; mus-

"Do not withhold good from those who deserve it, when it is in your power to act."

Proverbs 3:27

cles of iron; nerves of steel; sensitive but self-reliant; kind and tender; seeking all for others, nothing for herself." Mary fought tenaciously for the rights and needs of enlisted men, whom she called "my boys." She loved to cut through bureaucratic red tape and often violated army policies.

The best-remembered incidence of Mary's tenacity occurred at Lookout Mountain, near Chattanooga, on New Year's Eve 1863. It was bitterly cold, and thousands of men were wounded. Many were freezing to death because fuel had run out, and the officer in charge thought little could be done until morning.

Mary was desperate to save the dying men. She surveyed the log breastworks that had been built for fortifications. Now that the campaign had been won, there was no use for such a defense, so Mary ordered that the breastworks be torn down and the wood burned to keep the wounded warm.

About daybreak, when the officer in command discovered what Mary had done, he yelled, "Madam, consider yourself under arrest!"

Mary calmly replied, "All right, Major! I'm arrested! Only don't meddle with me till the weather moderates; for my men will freeze to death if you do!"

Several hundred men survived that bitterly cold night because of Mary Bickerdyke's bold actions. No wonder thousands of Union soldiers called her "mother."

Lord, give us the insight to be bold when we see what has to be done.

July 20

Sarah Wister, diarist
July 20, 1761–April 21, 1804

The writing of history is often accomplished through the use of biographies and diaries of those who participated in the making of history. The study of daily life during the American Revolution has been enormously enhanced by the writing of Sarah Wister.

When the British threatened Philadelphia, Sarah's father moved his family to a small hamlet fifteen miles away. Sixteen-year-old Sarah promised to keep in touch with her good friend, Deborah Norris, so on September 25, 1777, she began keeping "a sort of journal of the time" describing the everyday experiences of a young woman during the war.

"They will beat their swords into plowshares and their spears into pruning hooks. Nation will not take up sword against nation, nor will they train for war anymore."

Micah 4:3

Ironically, Norris did not see her friend's writing until long after Sarah's death. She immediately recognized its value. Sarah's accounts were accurate, and she mixed both the dramatic and the humorous into her writing. Historians have labeled the diary "a human document."

After independence, Sarah occasionally published poetry in such periodicals as *Port Folio*. She invested her life in caring for her mother and became deeply religious.

Father, sometimes the value of our life is not noticed until after our death. Keep us faithful anyway.

July 21

Oliver Hazard Perry, capitalist
July 21, 1839–June 27, 1917

Oliver Perry left Yale after his sophomore year to fight in the Union army during the Civil War. By 1863, he had been promoted to colonel. Although seriously wounded at the battle of Chickamauga, he returned to service. After the horrors of the Atlanta campaign, Perry resigned his commission.

Perry went into the iron and oil industry and became a formidable competitor for Rockefeller. After Rockefeller formed Standard Oil, however, Perry joined the organization as treasurer. Eventually, Perry became the fourth largest stockholder in the Standard Oil Company.

Oliver Perry donated large sums of money to the Ohio Democratic party. His support of candidates like Henry B. Payne for the Senate produced heated controversy; more than once, Perry was accused of buying the seat or office.

Tired of wrangling with politics, Perry divested himself of his holdings in Standard Oil and moved to New York City, where he built the most luxurious yacht in the country. He spent his life sailing the *Aphrodite*, including one voyage around the world.

Perry was a quiet philanthropist. He launched Cornell Medical College with a half-million-dollar grant. During the ensuing years, he gave more than $7.5 million to establish the school as a leader in medical education.

Perry left $1 million each to the New York Public Library, Yale University, and Cleveland's Lakeside Hospital. Numerous others benefited from Oliver Perry's generosity.

"There was a man all alone; he had neither son nor brother. There was no end to his toil, yet his eyes were not content with his wealth."

Ecclesiastes 4:8

Father, help us to become generous people, realizing that "our" money is but a resource You have brought into our lives to help build Your kingdom.

181

July 22

Emma Lazarus, poet
July 22, 1849–November 19, 1887

A young woman who had published her first book of poetry at age seventeen, who was a friend of Emerson and received great encouragement from him to write, who grew up one of eleven children in a wealthy New York home, Emma Lazarus would be remembered not for her books, but for thirty-six words she wrote.

In 1883, to raise funds for the Statue of Liberty project, a literary auction was held. Writers contributed poems and articles, and the sum paid for them was donated to erecting the great monument to freedom in New York Harbor.

Emma Lazarus contributed "The New Colossus," a sonnet.

> Give me your tired, your poor,
> Your huddled masses yearning to breathe free,
> The wretched refuse of your teeming shore.
> Send these, the homeless, tempest-tost to me,
> I lift my lamp beside the golden door!

Emma was a shy woman, devoted to her father. His death in 1885 caused her to become deeply depressed, and she died of Hodgkins disease two years later. Emma Lazarus never knew what a legend her sonnet would become.

"Do not mistreat an alien or oppress him, for you were aliens in Egypt."

Exodus 22:21

Father, we come to You like immigrants, and we, too, yearn to breathe free. We are reminded that You turn no one away.

July 23

Samuel Henry Kress, merchant
July 23, 1863–September 22, 1955

Samuel Kress knew he didn't want to teach school as a career, so he saved enough money to buy a novelty store in Nanticoke, Pennsylvania. Three years later he bought a toy and novelty wholesale business. He and his brother, Claude, "lived to work" and poured all their time, energy, and profits into the business.

By the 1890s, Kress made a commitment to finance the company's expansion solely out of the profits; they

"If the ax is dull and its edge unsharpened, more strength is needed but skill will bring success."

Ecclesiastes 10:10

would not borrow. He decided to open nickel-and-dime stores and undercut his competition by buying stock directly from the manufacturers instead of through distributors. Although Kress could offer fewer items than his competitors, he could buy in larger volume and offer lower prices.

The plan worked. By 1901, Kress had fifty-one stores and grossed $3 million. He ran all of his stores uniformly; no deviation from his policies was permitted. Kress traveled constantly to spot-check his stores. He prided himself on permitting no waste and was one of the first to design a management training program.

With the same enthusiasm, Kress began collecting art in 1921. His incentive to collect was unusual: He wanted to draw customers. Kress displayed Geiorgione's painting, *The Adoration of the Shepherds*, in his Fifth Avenue store at Christmas. The display became a tradition of the season for many New Yorkers.

He used his profits to establish the Kress Foundation in 1939 to "promote the moral, physical, mental welfare and progress of the human race." The same year he donated his 375 paintings to the National Gallery of Art. At the time of his death, fourteen galleries contained art from his collection.

Father, give us wisdom as stewards of what You have provided us, so that our giving outlasts our living.

July 24

Mary "Suitcase" Bartelme, judge
July 24, 1866–July 25, 1954

Many people assume the decline of the family is a new crisis in our country. However, in 1929, Mary Bartelme declared, "The home is no longer what it used to be."

Mary was appointed public guardian in Chicago in 1897, based on her four years of service as the first woman probation officer. She was assigned to juvenile court to help wayward young girls.

"There are no bad children," Mary often said. "There are confused, neglected, love-starved and resentful children, and what they need most I try to give them—understanding and a fresh start in the right direction." Mary wanted homes where the young girls could be "helped, encouraged, connected" rather than "re-

"The Lord is compassionate and gracious, slow to anger, abounding in love."

Psalm 103:8

183

formed," so she converted her own three-story house on the city's West Side into a club where the girls could live. Two more homes were soon opened.

In 1923, only three years after women gained the right to vote in Illinois, Mary risked everything to run for judge. "I knew a woman could win," she said. Mary won. Judge Bartelme's court was humane; jurors often cried, and on more than one occasion took up a collection to help defendants.

Mary's judicial philosophy was simple: "I believe that the young girls of Chicago and all Cook County are entitled to at least one judge who can deal with them in terms of real sympathy and understanding rather than in terms of legal lore and technicalities."

She earned her nickname "Suitcase Mary" by filling suitcases with clothes, underwear, and necessities to give to the young girls when they left "Mary's club." A high percentage of those girls became productive citizens. Mary Bartelme's second-chance philosophy made a difference.

Father, we are so glad that You are the God of the second chance. Thank You for Your compassion.

July 25

Flora Adams Darling, patriot
July 25, 1840–January 6, 1910

Flora Adams married Colonel Edward Darling in March 1860. With war clouds all about, Flora moved to Louisiana. Immediately she struggled with divided loyalties between her Northern family and her Southern husband. When the Civil War broke out, she moved to her father's home in New Hampshire but eventually went to Richmond to be with her husband after he was wounded in battle.

After his death in 1863, Flora returned to their home in Louisiana and was arrested in New Orleans by Union officials who suspected her of being a Southern sympathizer and perhaps a spy. By the time she was released, much of her jewelry and money had been stolen. Flora returned North and after the war worked in a government office in Washington, D.C.

On October 11, 1890, Mrs. Darling and Mrs. Mary Lockwood organized the Daughters of the American

"The widow who is really in need and left all alone puts her hope in God and continues night and day to pray and to ask God for help."

1 Timothy 5:5

Revolution. Flora's tasks were to organize local chapters and to edit the society's official magazine, *Adams Magazine*. However, friction arose between Flora and the board when the board said that eligibility for membership could be determined by either the paternal or maternal side of an applicant's family.

Mrs. Darling resigned her membership and on August 20, 1891, founded a rival organization, the Daughters of the Revolution. Six months later she founded the Daughters of the United States of the War of 1812. Both organizations based their membership on paternal ancestry.

Father, as important as earthly genealogy may be, we are glad that we are Your children and that You say "whosoever will may come."

Donaldina Cameron, humanitarian
July 26, 1869–January 4, 1968

Donaldina Cameron was born in New Zealand. However, her father moved the seven children to San Jose, California, after their mother's death in 1874. He became manager of a sheep ranch near Los Angeles, which opened the door for Donaldina to take a teacher training program at Los Angeles Normal School. However, her father's death in 1887 ended her academic aspirations.

In 1895, Donaldina moved to San Francisco to teach sewing at a mission home for Chinese women. In 1900, she became the mission's superintendent. Donaldina became engaged to a student from Princeton Seminary, but both decided to put their work above marriage. (Later she would plan to marry a wealthy widower, but his sudden death would prompt her to recommit herself to mission work.)

From the mission home near Chinatown, Donaldina worked to destroy the Chinese slave trade, rescuing more than two thousand girls who had been smuggled into San Francisco by ship. On numerous occasions, Lo Mo, or Little Mother, as she was called, participated with police in raids on brothels. One police report noted, "Miss Cameron willingly has gone with us into the most dangerous and notorious of Chinese places, often helping us to chop through heavily paneled oaken doors in the work of rescuing 'slave girls.'"

Once Donaldina had the girls back at the mission,

"The Spirit of the Lord is on me. . . . He has sent me to proclaim freedom for the prisoners . . . to release the oppressed, to proclaim the year of the Lord's favor."

Luke 4:18, 19

she had to fight for legal custody and to expose the importers. She educated her foster daughters and played matchmaker in the Chinese tradition, helping many find husbands.

When the governance of the mission was shifted from foreign missions to the Board of National Missions, the center became more of a social service agency and Donaldina was forced to retire at the age of sixty-five.

She did, however, remain in San Francisco to assist her successor until the needs of her three unmarried sisters took her time and she moved to Oakland in 1939.

Donaldina's faith at times conflicted with Chinese cultural norms, but this single adult changed the future of many young women. One Presbyterian single adult made a difference.

Father, give us courage to be the kind of single adults who will tackle culture and greed to free the "slaves" of today.

July 27

Genevieve Rose Cline, federal judge
July 27, 1879–October 25, 1959

The first woman ever appointed a United States federal judge, Genevieve Cline gained valuable education and experience while working as a clerk in her attorney brother's office. During this time, she was active in women's club work in Ohio, organizing support for new child-labor laws, civil-service reform, and pure-food laws. Miss Cline lobbied in the Ohio statehouse and in Washington.

In 1917, Rose began law school at Baldwin-Wallace, graduated, and passed the bar in 1921. During these years, she became involved in the Republican party in Ohio and won President Harding's appointment in 1922 as appraiser of merchandise in Cleveland. Miss Cline—the first woman ever appointed to the position—inspected and appraised for tax purposes all foreign goods shipped through customs into Ohio and western Pennsylvania.

Through her service in the party and the National Association of Women Lawyers, she was nominated to the United States Customs Court by President Coolidge in 1928. Although there was opposition, she was confirmed by the Senate on May 25, 1928, as the first woman federal judge.

Judge Cline spent twenty-five years on the bench.

"He appointed judges in the land, in each of the fortified cities of Judah. He told them, 'Consider carefully what you do, because you are not judging for man but for the Lord, who is with you whenever you give a verdict.' "

2 Chronicles 19:5, 6

Father, for doors that open to admit those who have prepared themselves, we give You thanks.

July 28

John Gresham Machen, theologian
July 28, 1881–January 1, 1937

After graduation from Princeton Seminary and graduate study in Marburg and Göttingen, John Machen began teaching New Testament at Princeton in 1906. For the next twenty-three years, Princeton's halls were home to this bachelor scholar.

Around 1920, Machen became alarmed by the theological drift and growing liberal stance within the Presbyterian Church. He reminded the church of its need to reaffirm its traditional moorings: the virgin birth of Jesus, the plenary inspiration of Scripture, the vicarious atonement of Jesus, and the bodily resurrection of Jesus from the dead. He argued one could not truly call himself a Christian and reject such cardinal doctrines. Machen precipitated a great deal of debate among Presbyterians.

After a theological rift with leaders at Princeton in 1929, Machen resigned his professorship and became part of the founding faculty at Westminster Seminary in Philadelphia. Because of his concern over the theological convictions and commitments of Presbyterian missionaries, he founded the Independent Board of Foreign Missions. The General Assembly of the Presbyterian Church disassociated itself from the organization. When Machen continued to support it, he was stripped of his ordination in 1935.

In 1936, a new denomination, the Orthodox Presbyterian Church, was established under Machen's guidance. John Machen remained unshaken in his theological convictions and turned a great deal of his attention to sharing his convictions through *The Presbyterian Guardian.*

"You must teach what is in accord with sound doctrine."

Titus 2:1

Father: Thank You for the life of a man who found faith too precious to take casually.

July 29

Dag Hammarskjöld, U.N. general-secretary
July 29, 1905–September 18, 1961

Dag Hammarskjöld came from a distinguished family of Swedish diplomats and clergymen. After he earned a Ph.D. in economics, he became a top economist in the

"Do not pay attention to every word people say, or you

187

Swedish government. During World War II, he helped plan the economic reconstruction of Europe.

In 1953, the United Nations selected Hammarskjöld secretary-general because his experience as a dedicated civil servant had shown him to be a passive leader. He proved to be an aggressive yet effective diplomat. His flight to Peking to negotiate the release of twelve United States airmen and his marshalling of a peace force to develop a peacekeeping presence during the Suez Canal crisis stunned many of his supporters.

Hammarskjöld loved to slip quietly into Manhattan churches for worship. After his death, aides found beside his bed a diary called *Vagmarken*, or *Markings*. Many were stunned by its contents, which revealed the depth of the diplomat's faith.

"I don't know who-or-what put the question. I don't know when it was put. I don't even remember answering. But at some moment I did answer *Yes* to Someone or Something—and from that hour I was certain that existence is meaningful and that, therefore, my life, in self-surrender, had a goal. And from that moment I have known what it means 'not to look back,' and 'to take no thought for the morrow.' "

Hammarskjöld was slandered because he lived in a time when most single males were suspected of being homosexuals. Ugly rumors were spread by malicious colleagues anxious to see him ousted from his post.

Hammarskjöld never fought back. He responded that if the charge were true, he never would have accepted such responsibility as that of secretary-general. He explained that marriage and the post were totally incompatible pursuits. For Dag Hammarskjöld, peace came first.

> may hear your servant cursing you."
>
> **Ecclesiastes 7:21**

Father, remind us that faith is not evidenced only by words. Some people demonstrate faith by following the markings You set on the trail before them.

July 30

William Mackenzie, bibliophile
July 30, 1758–July 23, 1828

After graduation from Philadelphia Academy, William Mackenzie began working for the counting house of John Ross, a Philadelphia merchant and supplier for the Pennsylvania navy. As an apprentice, he learned a great deal about merchandising and shipping.

"Now go, write it before them in a table, and note it in a book, that it may be for the time to

However, his interest was elsewhere. When he was thirty, William inherited enough money to make him independently wealthy. He began to collect books. By the time of his death, he had one of the largest private libraries in the United States containing more than seven thousand volumes.

Mackenzie became well-known mostly because his will was innovative. He bequeathed his private library to several public libraries in the Philadelphia area. Those books that were not given were purchased. Many of them were extremely rare, published by the earliest European presses. Some of the books he gave to the Loganian Library were the only copies in the United States.

His lifelong friend James Abercrombie said William Mackenzie had no enemies. "From the purity of his principles and correctness of his conduct, I am sure he never deserved one."

come for ever and ever."

Isaiah 30:8 KJV

Key Thought: The gift of a book is a lasting gift.

July 31

Benjamin Foster, artist
July 31, 1852–January 28, 1926

After the death of his father, Benjamin Foster was forced into the world to make a living. He worked in New York for ten years as a salesman until, at age thirty, he decided to commit himself to painting. He studied with Abbott Thayer and at the Art Student's League. When the chance came to go to Paris, he took it. He studied with French masters Olivier Merson and Aime Merot.

Ben Foster returned to New York determined to ignore the contemporary theories on painting. He did not have to be recognized, he told himself. He spent six months each year on his Connecticut farm, memorizing sunrises and sunsets, walking, sketching, and observing life. Then in his studio, from memory, he recreated the landscapes. He attempted to paint nature in its abundance of beauty.

The Chicago's World Fair in 1893 gave Ben his first recognition; in 1900, he won a bronze medal at the Paris Exposition. The art world took serious notice of Foster when the French government purchased his *Lulled by the Murmuring Stream*, a landscape of a New England

"You care for the land and water it; you enrich it abundantly."

Psalm 65:9

village at night. Through the years Ben Foster won many other prizes for his paintings. Eventually he became an art critic for the *New York Evening Post* and a contributor to the *Nation*.

In the days before the development of the camera, Ben Foster gave his viewers a glimpse of what he had discovered.

Father, we thank You for those who have the ability to paint what we will never see. Thank You for the gift of imagination.

August 1

Maria Mitchell, astronomer
August 1, 1818–June 28, 1889

It was Maria Mitchell's good fortune to have a progressive astronomer for a father. Her curiosity about his work pleased him and he taught her everything he knew, valuing her assistance in his observatory.

In 1836, she took a position as librarian at the Nantucket Athenaeum. During the next twenty-four years, she intensely studied science and astronomy texts. She worked side by side with her father in the small observatory built on the roof of their home, making official observations for the United States Coastal Survey.

On October 1, 1847, Maria discovered a new comet, eventually named after her. Recognition from the American Association for the Advancement of Science, the Smithsonian, and the American Academy of Arts and Science gained her prominence in scientific circles in this country. Her reputation became even more widespread when she identified a second comet in 1858.

Although she had no degree, Maria was invited to join the faculty of Vassar College in 1865. The college provided her a twelve-inch telescope and a fully equipped laboratory, where daughter and father could continue their research.

Maria consistently challenged her pupils to excellence—"question everything," she reminded them. Twenty-five of her students were eventually listed in *Who's Who*.

Maria Mitchell pioneered in photographing sunspots and also studied the surfaces of planets. Finally, at Vassar she encouraged the use of scientific methods in investigating social problems.

As a single adult, she helped make women full participants in the advancement of science.

"The heavens declare the glory of God; the skies proclaim the work of his hands."

Psalm 19:1

Key Thought: Once the door of opportunity is opened, it invites all to come through it into the world of potential.

190

August 2

Pierre Charles L'Enfant, architect
August 2, 1754–June 14, 1825

Although Pierre L'Enfant had studied painting in Paris, he came to America and joined the army as a volunteer. He soon was promoted to major of engineers and came to the attention of George Washington when he designed an eagle emblem for Washington's Society of Cincinnati.

In 1788, the young American government commissioned L'Enfant to convert the New York city hall into a federal building. His work was so well received that, when the District of Columbia was created, L'Enfant was hired to design the city. He suggested that two buildings—the White House and the Capitol—dominate the city. He proposed thirteen major streets, named after the states, then sketched a host of statues, columns, and obelisks to commemorate the heroism of the leaders who led America to liberty.

In 1792, L'Enfant was dismissed from his assignment because he was dissatisfied with his salary. His last great project—a grand house for Philadelphia banker Robert Morris—was never completed. L'Enfant died in obscurity and poverty.

Almost one hundred years later, Secretary of State Elihu Root led a tribute at the dedication of the L'Enfant Tomb in Arlington National Cemetery. "Few men can afford to wait a hundred years to be remembered. It is not a change in L'Enfant that brings us here. It is we who have changed, who have just become able to appreciate his work" and his vision for a great city.

"Then they said, 'Come, let us build ourselves a city.' "

Genesis 11:4

Father, we are reminded that the last word is not always held by our critics. Help us to deal with criticism and competition in a healthy manner.

August 3

Rupert Brooke, poet
August 3, 1887–April 23, 1915

Everyone at King's College, Cambridge, agreed that young Rupert Brooke had a brilliant future. His undergraduate work had been outstanding. After travel across Europe and a vigorous study of John Webster and Elizabethan drama, Brooke received a fellowship at King's College ensuring him an academic career with ample time to write.

"Where, O death, is your victory? Where, O death, is your sting?"

1 Corinthians 15:55

His first book, *Poems*, published in 1911, drew favorable comments. At Christmas, twenty-four-year-old Rupert had a nervous breakdown, but time in Germany the next spring and summer restored his health. During that time he wrote "Grantchester," which many believe was his best work. He returned to England and helped compile *Georgian Poetry: 1911–1912*.

After extensive travel from 1913 to 1914, Rupert returned to England, accepted a commission in the Royal Navy, and was sent to the Dardanelles. On April 17, 1915, he had a sunstroke. His lip became infected and resulted in septicemia. On April 23 he died. His will directed that future royalties from his poetry be given to his poet friends. Brooke had written, "The worst friend and enemy is but Death." That enemy cut short his writing, but he remains a romantic legend.

Key Thought: The length of our life is not as important as the way we live.

If I should die, think only this of me:
That there's some corner of a foreign field
That is forever England.

August 4

Raoul Wallenberg, humanitarian
August 4, 1912–unknown

Budapest was a nightmare in November 1944. The Nazis had the remaining Jews barricaded; many realized that their time to live had run out. Into that tense arena stepped a young graduate of the University of Michigan, a member of one of Sweden's leading families who had been granted diplomatic title and privilege. Raoul Wallenberg would try to keep Hitler from carrying out his final solution. Wallenberg took drastic measures to stop German army regulars and the SS, who were fanatically trying to kill as many Jews as possible before the Allies reached Budapest. In a brazen move, he went to German headquarters and confronted the general. If he allowed the slaughter to take place, Wallenberg would hold him accountable. "Who are you to tell me what to do!" the military commander demanded.

But Wallenberg had already sent a message to Swe-

"Whoever wants to save his life will lose it, but whoever loses his life for me and for the gospel will save it."

Mark 8:35

den informing them of his daring action. Although the general was outraged, to save his own neck, he ordered German soldiers to stop the SS.

As a result, 100,000 Jewish lives were saved. One was a sixteen-year-old named Tom Lantos, who eventually came to the United States and was elected to Congress. His first act was to introduce legislation to make Wallenberg an honorary United States citizen.

Witnesses report that Wallenberg was arrested by the Soviet army in January 1945. The Russians first claimed he was killed by retreating Germans. In 1957, they said he had died in a Moscow jail in 1947. Since then there have been reported sightings of Raoul in Russian prisons.

What made Wallenberg risk his life? He "was imbued with a conviction that anything was within reach, any goal could be met if one just applied oneself, and all of one's God given gifts, to its fulfillment."

Father, when we die is not known to us, but how we die is a choice. Give us courage to do the right thing, even if it costs us our lives.

August 5

Ellen Culver Potter, physician
August 5, 1871–February 9, 1958

Ellen Potter studied art and worked in the Morning Star Mission in New York's Chinatown. She generally carried her art supplies in a small black bag, which caused many residents to assume she was a physician. That confusion influenced Ellen's decision to study medicine at Women's Medical College of Pennsylvania in 1899. By 1905, Dr. Potter was practicing obstetrics and gynecology in Philadelphia.

Ellen took an active role in the social justice movement in the city of brotherly love. She wanted the city's slogan to become a reality.

In 1920, Dr. Potter assumed responsibility for children's health in the Pennsylvania Department of Health. She organized some two hundred local child-health centers and developed the Bureau of Children in the Department of Public Welfare, which promoted organized but compassionate reform.

In 1923, she joined Governor Gifford Pinchot's cabinet as secretary of welfare. In her four-year term,

"He raises the poor from the dust and lifts the needy from the ash heap."

Psalm 113:7

193

Dr. Potter instituted significant social reforms. In 1927, she moved to New Jersey and served in senior administrative positions in a series of state correctional institutions. Three years later, she became medical director for the New Jersey Department of Institutions and Agencies and used the office to reform existing adoption procedures as well as to develop community health programs. She kept the post for nineteen years.

Ellen Potter spent the last years of her medical and humanitarian career calling attention to the needs of the chronically ill and the aged.

Key Thought: God today often "raises" the poor and "lifts" the needy through the loving compassion of single adults like Ellen Potter.

August 6

William Hyde Wollaston, scientist
August 6, 1766–December 22, 1828

From 1793 to 1800, William Wollaston practiced medicine, spending three years of that time in London. However, Wollaston was so sensitive to his patients that he found himself too emotionally involved to be competent, sometimes bursting into tears if asked about their condition. As a result, in 1801, he set up a laboratory in his home and began conducting experiments. Wollaston discovered a process for making platinum malleable, which made him very wealthy and financed his research into optics and chemistry. His work established his scientific reputation across Europe.

Wollaston's eyesight was so keen that it was said he could identify minute plants while riding on a horse. He was recognized as the most skilled chemist and mineralogist of his day. Other scientists regularly sought his advice.

Wollaston was not interested in scientific competition, but rather in cooperation. His lifelong goal was to satisfy his own questions. If others were helped by this, that was an extra blessing. He was specifically interested in finding practical applications for his research. He delighted in visiting factories. England would have had no Industrial Revolution without the creative genius of William Hyde Wollaston.

"The plans of the diligent lead to profit."

Proverbs 21:5

Father, thank You for the gift of curiosity and for creating this world so intricately. We praise You that You enable some to discover the secrets of Your creation.

194

Ellen Fitz Pendleton, college president
August 7, 1864–July 26, 1936

One of the by-products of the American Civil War was the recognition of the need of higher education for women. Ellen Fitz Pendleton was an advocate of this thinking.

Ellen graduated from Wellesley College in 1886 and assumed a position as tutor in mathematics. Other than a year spent working on her master's at Cambridge, she spent her career at Wellesley.

Ellen Pendleton became dean in 1901 and was appointed acting president in 1910; in 1911, she became president. Pendleton got the opportunity to demonstrate her administrative skills in March 1914, when fire destroyed a building that housed more than two hundred students, most of the classrooms and labs, all the administrative offices, and all the records of the institution.

After the fire, Pendleton ordered an immediate spring recess and within three weeks had secured a temporary classroom and administration building. She proceeded to build five dormitories, four apartment buildings, two academic buildings, and a student center. Then she built a new administration building.

During Pendleton's twenty-five-year tenure, Wellesley's endowment portfolio increased 800 percent. She resisted attempts to add vocational programs, standing firmly on the side of a liberal arts education for Wellesley graduates. She encouraged the growth of student and academic freedom, especially through sharing leadership responsibilities through committees.

As a Baptist who took her faith seriously, Ellen Pendleton worked hard to oppose intolerance and provincialism.

"Even on my servants, both men and women, I will pour out my Spirit in those days."

Joel 2:29

Father, in a world of short commitments and tenures, it is hard to imagine a person investing her entire life in one institution. If that is Your will for us, direct us to a place where we can invest ourselves.

August 8

Wesley Newcomb Hohfeld, legal scholar
August 8, 1879–October 21, 1918

Wesley Hohfeld graduated in 1901 from the University of California with a new academic record: He had earned the highest grade possible in every course he took. He enrolled at Harvard Law School, won high academic marks, and edited the *Harvard Law Review*. After passing the bar, Hohfeld returned to San Francisco, where he was offered a partnership in a major law firm. Instead, he joined the law faculty of Stanford University, where he taught from 1905 until 1914. Then Hohfeld joined the faculty at Yale Law School.

During this time, Hohfeld published *Fundamental Legal Conceptions as Applied in Judicial Reasoning*, in which he argued that confusion had resulted in the legal world because of semantics. Hohfeld proposed a system of precise legal concepts and definitions, particularly for concepts such as right, privilege, duty, and power. He was the first to provide a complete set of satisfactory legal terms and their fundamental relation to one another. The impact was enormous, both in legal practice and legal education.

Hohfeld's teaching method was to lead his students through hypothetical cases rather than lecturing, as was common in those days. He emphasized thoroughness and logic, and his technique was a breakthrough in legal education. He never seemed too busy to counsel students, discuss legal cases, or explain difficult concepts.

Wesley Hohfeld died of heart trouble at the age of thirty-nine.

"The Teacher searched to find just the right words."

Ecclesiastes 12:10

Father, words are all we have. Thank You for the gift of communication.

August 9

Kenneth Scott Latourette, historian
August 9, 1884–December 26, 1968

Kenneth Latourette might well have been a lawyer, if it had not been for his college involvement in the YMCA and Student Volunteer Movement for Foreign Missions.

"Not only was the Teacher wise, but also he imparted

He switched majors and colleges to enter Yale in 1905. He prepared for a career in the Orient and finished his doctorate in 1909. After a couple of years in China, he became seriously ill with amebic dysentery and returned home. Although he had planned to return to China, his health prevented that.

Instead, Latourette began teaching at Reed College and wrote *The Development of China* (1917), which became a standard text on Chinese history. At Dennison University, he taught a course on the history of missions that led to his epic *A History of the Expansion of Christianity*, tracing Christianity's expansion in seven volumes. After he was ordained, Latourette became chaplain at Dennison. In 1921, he joined the faculty of Yale Divinity School, where he taught Oriental history before becoming chairman of the department of religion.

Although he retired in 1953, he continued writing and speaking. At Yale, Dr. Latourette was affectionately called Uncle Ken. He spent a great deal of time organizing students into groups for prayer, Bible study, and conversation.

His thirty books and hundreds of articles made him the most respected American church historian of the mid-twentieth century.

Three key elements were characteristic of the Latourette research methodology: detailed verification of facts; careful interpretation of evidence; and illumination from his own deep faith.

knowledge to the people."

Ecclesiastes 12:9

Father, it is difficult to fully fathom the contribution Kenneth Scott Latourette made to understanding church history through its glory and its tragedy. Remind us that throughout history he found hope a vital ingredient to dynamic faith. So must we.

August 10

Samuel Dickinson Hubbard, postmaster general
August 10, 1799–October 8, 1855

Samuel Dickinson Hubbard was tired of his almost twenty years of studying and practicing law in Connecticut, so in 1837, he became a manufacturer. Then, from 1845 to 1849, he spent two terms in Congress. Alarmed by the growing division between North and South, he published *Letter from S. D. Hubbard of Connecticut, to his Constituents on the Alarming Crisis in the Affairs of the Country*.

In 1852 and 1853, Hubbard served President Tyler as postmaster general.

"The Lord gave the word: great was the company of those that published it."

Psalm 68:11 KJV

Key Thought: S. D. Hubbard believed that answers to the

197

After his retirement from government, S. D. Hubbard returned home to Middletown and became involved in the Middletown Bible Society and educational pursuits. He was one of the original trustees of Wesleyan University.

problems of life were found in Scripture. That still makes sense for single adults.

August 11

Logan Gran McPherson, statistician
August 11, 1863–March 23, 1925

Newspaper work didn't capture Logan McPherson's imagination the way railroads did, so the reporter switched careers and began working for the Pennsylvania Railroad in 1890. In 1904, McPherson became a statistician for the Rock Island Railroad. This was a time when railroads were under increased public scrutiny and the public was calling for government controls on rates and profits.

Railroads recognized the need for an improved public image. In 1905, McPherson played a key role in the organization of the Associated Railways of the United States. He spent two years gathering a mountain of statistics for Congress and for the public, in order to improve the reputation of railroads.

In 1905, McPherson began teaching transportation at Johns Hopkins University and devoted himself to analyzing the correlation between railroad shipping rates and American business cycles. McPherson's research was thorough and highly esteemed, contributing to the reform movement.

After a European study trip during which he examined the European rail systems, McPherson came back and organized the Bureau of Railway Economics. He served as the bureau's director until 1914, then spent the rest of his academic career writing, in an attempt to make the subject more understandable for laymen.

"They could find no corruption in him, because he was trustworthy and neither corrupt nor negligent."

Daniel 6:4

Father, thank You for the ability to make money and to be involved in a profession. Give us the diligence to be effective in our chosen arena of service, for there is no separation of secular and spiritual with You.

Katherine Lee Bates, poet and teacher
August 12, 1859–March 28, 1929

Katherine Lee Bates grew up in a single-parent home after her father's death but still received the best education available to women in the late nineteenth century. She received a B. A. from Wellesley and returned there five years later to teach English. In 1891, after a year's graduate study at Oxford, she was made full professor and head of the department.

With a group of teachers, she made a tour of the United States in 1893. They visited the Columbian Exposition in Chicago and viewed the beautiful White City, then traveled to Colorado. After a day of hiking in the mountains, Katherine and her friends talked into the night about the beauty they had witnessed on the trip.

When Katherine went to bed, she could not sleep. After hours of turning and tossing, she took a pencil and paper and began writing phrases: "O beautiful for spacious skies. . . . For purple mountains' majesties. . . ." Then her attention turned to "pilgrim feet . . . for heroes proved." Soon she had a poem.

For two years she carried the verses she had written that night in her purse. On July 4, 1895, the poem was published in the *Congregationalist*. Nine years later, a revised version appeared in the *Boston Evening Transcript* and touched a patriotic and sentimental place in the hearts of thousands of readers. In 1912, someone set her words to Samuel Augustus Ward's tune "Materna," and the song became a patriotic favorite, almost rivaling the national anthem.

Katherine Bates wrote other poetry but is remembered for "America the Beautiful." She spent her life teaching literature at Wellesley.

"Blessed is the nation whose God is the Lord, the people he chose for his inheritance."

Psalm 33:12

Father, for our country's beauty, we give You praise. Mend our flaws, refine our gold, and remind us that Your grace has made us a great nation.

Ashbel Smith, state surgeon general
August 13, 1805–January 21, 1886

After graduation from Yale Medical School, Ashbel Smith opened a practice in Salisbury, North Carolina, where he had previously taught school. Three years later he went to Paris for more medical studies and was decorated for meritorious service during an outbreak of Asiatic cholera. When he came home to North Carolina, he opened his practice and edited the *Western Carolinian*, a paper committed to states' rights.

In 1837, Smith moved to Texas and was appointed surgeon general of the young republic. He lobbied for the annexation of Texas by the United States, but the issue of slavery in Texas became a major barrier. In February 1845, he was named secretary of state and negotiated the Smith-Cuevas Treaty with Mexico, which recognized Texas's independence. Then President John Tyler signed a joint congressional resolution inviting Texas to join the Union. Public opinion turned against Smith and he was burned in effigy. Psalm 34 took on a whole new meaning for this single adult.

Smith served a stint in the Mexican War after statehood, then retired to his plantation. In 1848, he joined the board of visitors of West Point. In 1855, he was an active member of the Texas Legislature. During the Civil War, he was decorated for heroism at Shiloh and Vicksburg and promoted to brigadier general.

After the war, he was elected twice to the legislature and became known as a strong advocate of higher education. In 1881, as president of the board of regents of what was to become the University of Texas, he devoted himself to creating a university of first-class stature. Smith attracted some of America's finest scholars to the university.

The University of Texas today is one of the nation's finest state universities. It began with an idea in the mind of Ashbel Smith.

"Turn from evil and do good; seek peace and pursue it."

Psalm 34:14

Key Thought: Ashbel Smith reminds single adults that one can invest energies into great causes and great institutions that long outlive us.

Carrie Lou Goddard, Christian educator
August 14, 1911–

After graduation from Maryville College in Tennessee, Carrie Lou Goddard taught elementary school and worked in local Methodist churches. Her interest in Christian education led to her appointment as Director of Children's Work for the Methodist conference in East Tennessee. After four years, she became Director of Children's Work for the Methodist Board of Education for the Virginia Conference. In these assignments she worked to help Sunday school teachers and pastors in local churches improve their ministry to children.

In 1954, Miss Goddard moved to Nashville to teach Christian education at Scarritt College, an internationally known center for training Christian educators. Carrie Lou's students came from across the United States and around the world. Her message was the same to all: Love the Lord and serve your students.

In 1957, Carrie Lou resigned her position to become editor of children's materials for the Methodist Publishing House, but she returned to Scarritt in 1960. Four years later the Children's Center—a laboratory Christian school for students specializing in Christian education for children—was established under Miss Goddard's guidance. The center helped establish the reputation of the master's degree program in Christian education that was headed by Carrie Lou.

Miss Goddard authored several books: *We Go to Church*; *Learning to Live With Others*; *The Child and His Nurture*; and *Jesus Goes to School*, a reading book for children.

Carrie Lou Goddard helped bring progressive educational theory on child development into the world of Christian education, training a generation of Christian educators for both local church ministry and college teaching.

"He took a little child and had him stand among them. Taking him in his arms, he said to them, 'Whoever welcomes one of these little children in my name welcomes me.' "

Mark 9:36, 37

Father, for this woman's contribution to the lives of so many children, we give You thanks.

John Bankhead Magruder, soldier
August 15, 1810–February 18, 1871

John Magruder's military career began with his graduation from West Point as a second lieutenant in 1830. For sixteen years he served in scattered army posts, seeing action in Texas and in the Seminole War in Florida. He was known for his zest for battle. General Stonewall Jackson, who served under him, said, "If any fighting was to be done, Magruder would be on hand."

When the Civil War broke out, Magruder joined the Confederate army and took charge of the troops in the Virginia Peninsula. Not only was he a superbly trained, seasoned officer, he had an uncanny ability to inspire courage in his men. He won the first battle of the Civil War.

Later, in the Seven Days Battle near Richmond, Magruder was blamed for Lee's losses to General McClellan. Lee ordered Magruder to pursue the Union army, but the enemy escaped. When the troops finally did engage in battle, Magruder's troops suffered heavy losses. Lee was less than kind to the brilliant general.

When Lee censured him, Magruder fought back. Biographers have noted, "He was a disappointment to Lee, who desired not only good generals but men with whom he could work."

In October 1862, Magruder was transferred to Texas and ordered to defend the coastline. In January 1863, he captured Galveston and the Union ship *Harriet Lane* and broke up the Union blockade.

After the hostilities had ended, General Magruder refused to petition for a pardon; instead, he went to Mexico and became a major general under Emperor Maximillian.

John Magruder eventually returned to the United States and became a public lecturer. He died in Houston in 1871.

> "No one serving as a soldier gets involved in civilian affairs—he wants to please his commanding officer."
>
> **2 Timothy 2:4**

Father, to disappoint a leader is a fearful thing. Have we by our choices, our sin, by our cowardice, disappointed You? If so, forgive and restore us.

August 16

Sarah Porter, teacher
August 16, 1813–February 17, 1900

If Sarah Porter had been a male, she would have followed her brothers to Yale after her studies at Mr. Hart's Academy in Farmington, Massachusetts. Instead, she had to be content with a year of Latin studies in New Haven.

Over the next ten years, she taught in Springfield, Philadelphia, and Buffalo but continued her own vigorous studies, particularly in German.

In 1843, Sarah returned to her hometown of Farmington and opened a day school. Eventually she began accepting boarders, and the school and Miss Porter became key elements in the Farmington community.

Many girls from wealthy families attended the school, and Sarah thought it imperative to influence them to develop responsibility for their own learning and for the needs of others.

Despite a heavy teaching load, Miss Porter found time to keep in touch with the intellectual developments of the day, and many scholars and intellectuals made visits to the school.

One Yale professor described Sarah Porter as "the most magnificent example of symmetrical womanhood that I have ever known."

> "She speaks with wisdom, and faithful instruction is on her tongue."
>
> Proverbs 31:26

Father, help us to live our lives as single adults so that after our deaths we will be remembered for more than our single status.

August 17

Edgar Montillion Woolley, actor and director
August 17, 1888–May 6, 1963

Edgar "Monty" Woolley's family owned hotels, so he grew up with great economic advantages. At Yale, Edgar immersed himself in drama with his friend Cole Porter. After study at Harvard, Woolley returned to Yale in 1914 as a drama coach. An innovative director, he encouraged creativity in his students and staged two successful American drama premieres.

After World War I military service, Woolley returned to Yale to teach drama. However, due to academic pol-

> "There is a time for everything, and a season for every activity under heaven. . . . a time to weep and a time to laugh. . . ."
>
> Ecclesiastes 3:1, 4

itics, Woolley was passed over for both the directorship of the new Yale theater and a permanent academic post. Greatly hurt, he left Yale in 1927.

In 1929, in New York, he directed Cole Porter's *Fifty Million Frenchmen* and won critical acclaim for that and three other Porter works. When Porter fled New York for the lights of Hollywood, Edgar soon followed. He won the role of Sheridan Whiteside in *The Man Who Came to Dinner*, appearing in the role on Broadway (1939–1941) and in the film version. He won two Academy Award nominations: best actor for *The Pied Piper* (1942) and best supporting actor for *Since You Went Away* (1944).

His film and acting career peaked during World War II.

Edgar Woolley made a major contribution to academic theater and encouraged many writers and actors in their careers.

Key Point: Edgar Woolley demolished the notion that those who can't act, teach. He was successful on stage and in teaching the stage.

August 18

Winckworth Allan Gay, landscape painter
August 18, 1821–February 23, 1910

In an age before air travel was common and when quality photography was scarce, it was the task of the landscape artist to show the wonders of God's creation. Through their eyes, the world saw far-off places.

Most men go to West Point to become soldiers; Allan Gay went there to study drawing. In 1847, he moved on to study with Constant Troyon in Paris. Troyon was to have a lasting impact on Gay's style. Gay traveled in Europe, then returned to Boston to open a studio in 1850. He was one of the artists who introduced the French influence on landscape painting to American audiences.

Over the years he painted steadily, interrupting his devotion with a trip to Egypt in 1874. Three years later he had a large exhibition in Boston of one hundred landscapes he'd painted in Egypt, Holland, Italy, and America. Gay then spent five years living in the Orient, mostly in Japan.

His next major exhibit in Boston focused on the landscapes of Japan and was a sensation.

Gay lived to be eighty-nine but never received the public recognition many of his artist friends thought he deserved.

"Those living far away fear your wonders; where morning dawns and evening fades you call forth songs of joy."

Psalm 65:8

Key Thought: A good artist can invite people to travel in the theater of the mind.

Mary Belle Harris, prison reformer
August 19, 1874–February 22, 1957

Traditionally, jailers have been male, but Mary Belle Harris—armed with a Ph.D. in Sanskrit and Indo-European philosophy from the University of Chicago—changed that. On January 1, 1914, she began her work as the assistant warden of the New York City workhouse. Miss Harris installed changes in the daily lives of prisoners, creating a library and establishing daily exercise periods.

Later, Harris worked closely with architects to design the first federal prison for women, which opened in November 1928. She was then appointed its first warden. In Mary's prison, there were no massive walls and heavily armed guards. Instead, she instituted a classification system according to the seriousness of the offense, some self-governance by inmates, and major educational and social programs.

Harris believed that criminal actions by women were a result of economic need or psychological dependency upon men. She argued that reform would be more effective than punishment. Moreover, they could have a better future by building their self-respect and learning employable skills that would help them support themselves.

Mary Belle Harris also served as a trustee of the First Baptist Church of Lewisburg, Pennsylvania. She died at age eighty-two.

"At that hour of the night the jailer took them and washed their wounds; then immediately he and all his family were baptized."

Acts 16:33

Father, for those who can make differences in prisons, we give You thanks.

Francis Asbury, bishop
August 20, 1745–March 31, 1816

"I believe the devil and the women will get all my preachers!" Asbury moaned when he heard that one of his associates had fallen in love. "Marriage is honorable in all—but to me is a ceremony awful as death."

Francis Asbury came to America in 1771 planning to

"You, however, know all about my teaching, my way of life, my purpose, faith, pa-

205

spread Methodism throughout the New World. He was one of eight volunteers sent by John Wesley, but by the time of the American Revolution, only Asbury remained in America. For the next forty-five years, Asbury traveled from 4,000 to 6,000 miles a year, mostly on horseback. No trail was too rugged, no community too isolated, no village so sin ruined as not to expect a visit from Asbury.

Asbury recruited single males to be his circuit riders. He asked them to be ready at a moment's notice to saddle up a horse and ride to the newest section of the American frontier. The small salaries he offered kept most of his men from marrying.

When Wesley appointed Asbury superintendent of the church in America, Asbury accepted under the condition that he be approved by the American ministers. At a special conference in 1784, Francis Asbury was elected the first bishop of the American Methodist Church. When asked why he never married, Bishop Asbury explained:

> If I should die in celibacy, which I think quite probable, I give the following reasons for what can scarcely be called my choice. I was called in my fourteenth year; I began my public exercises between sixteen and seventeen; at twenty-one I traveled; at twenty-six I came to America: thus far I had reasons enough for a single life. It had been my intention to return to Europe at thirty years of age; but the war continued, and it was ten years before we had a settled, lasting peace: this was no time to marry or to be given in marriage. At thirty-nine I was ordained superintendent bishop in America. Amongst the duties imposed upon me by my office was that of traveling extensively, and I could hardly expect to find a woman with grace enough to enable her to live but one week out of fifty-two with her husband . . . if I have done wrong, I hope God and the sex will forgive me.

By the time of Francis Asbury's death, he was more than the bishop of the American Methodist Church—he was its father. Twenty thousand people attended his funeral.

tience, love, endurance, persecutions, sufferings."

2 Timothy 3:10

Father, Francis Asbury left a lasting legacy. Thank You for his life and his commitment.

August 21

Constance Green, historian
August 21, 1897–December 5, 1975

After attending the University of Chicago and graduating from Smith College in 1919, Constance Green married and started a family. She completed her Ph.D. at Yale in 1935 and began teaching at Smith College. In 1939, her first book, *Holyoke, Massachusetts: A Case History of the Industrial Revolution in America*, was published. From 1939 to 1946, she directed research for the Council of Industrial Studies, and part of that time was historian for the Department of the Army.

Constance was widowed in 1946, and as a single parent became historian for the American National Red Cross. In 1948, she became chief historian for the United States Army Ordinance Corps; then in 1951, Green moved to the Department of Defense as a historian. In 1954, she joined the Washington History Project, affiliated with American University.

Green wrote about the role of women as workers during the war, Eli Whitney, and the role of cities in the growth of the nation. In 1973, she won the Pulitzer Prize for her history of the nation's capital, *Washington, Village and Capital, 1800–1878*.

She published five more histories after she won the Pulitzer and served as a member of the landmarks committee of the National Capital Planning Commission.

Constance Green was a Congregationalist and will long be remembered for her love of the nation's capital city.

"A city on a hill cannot be hidden."

Matthew 5:14

Father, thank You for those who remind us of our past. Help us realize we are creating a past that will be remembered by a future generation of historians.

August 22

Nathaniel Harrison Harris, general
August 22, 1834–August 23, 1900

Nathaniel Harris began practicing law with his brother in Vicksburg, Mississippi, in the 1850s. When the Civil War broke out, he joined the Nineteenth Mississippi Regiment and was honored for his heroism at the battles of Williamsburg and Seven Pines. By 1863, he was promoted to colonel.

"Be strong and very courageous."

Joshua 1:7

207

Because of the gallantry of troops under his command in battles at Chancellorsville and Gettysburg, he was promoted to brigadier general in 1864. After his heroics in the Wilderness Campaign of 1864, he was assigned to command the inner line of defenses in Richmond in the final days of the war.

General Harris surrendered with Lee's army and returned to his law practice in Vicksburg. For a time he was president of the Mississippi Valley and Ship Inland Railroad but resigned to pursue his fortunes in the new territory of South Dakota. In 1885, Harris was appointed head of the United States Land Office in Aberdeen, South Dakota. He moved to San Francisco in 1890 and died while on a business trip to England in 1900.

Father, heroism is an admirable trait. Remind us that You want to be our source of courage.

August 23

John MacPherson Berrien, senator and attorney general
August 23, 1781–January 1, 1856

John Berrien began his law career in Louisville, Kentucky, but soon moved back to his home state of Georgia and began practicing law in Augusta. He was elected solicitor for the Eastern Circuit in 1809 and held the post until 1821.

Berrien served one term in the Georgia State Senate before he was elected as a Democrat to the United States Senate in 1824. Five years later he resigned and joined the Cabinet of President Andrew Jackson as attorney general. In 1841, Berrien returned to the Senate as a Whig and served four years; he resigned in May 1845, to accept appointment to the Georgia Supreme Court.

In *An Address to the People of the United States*, he argued that a compromise must be found on the slavery question. Berrien rejected secession but felt Northern states were demanding too much of the South. Twice more Berrien was re-elected to the United States Senate as a member of the Know-Nothing party.

His final political act was to preside over the Know-Nothing party convention in December 1855.

"Do not be in a hurry to leave the king's presence."

Ecclesiastes 8:3

Key Thought: Integrity sometimes demands tough choices on our part.

Carol Weiss King, lawyer
August 24, 1895–January 22, 1952

After graduation from Barnard College, Carol Weiss worked as a research assistant for the American Association for Labor Legislation, investigating the needs of workers. She became convinced she could make more of a difference as an attorney and entered New York University Law School.

She married Gordon King, a writer, in 1917. When she graduated from law school, no labor-law firm would hire a woman. Not to be deterred, Carol rented an office in a large firm that specialized in defending foreign-born workers. Mrs. King became involved in helping immigrants fight deportation. She was instrumental in changing the United States Immigration and Naturalization Service's policy on deportation, which deprived aliens of their rights of due process. In 1925, she became a full partner in the firm of Shorr, Brodsky, and King.

In 1930, Carol's husband died. She had a five-year-old son, and though her wealthy family urged her to stop her work, she refused. Instead she cared for her son and continued her career.

In 1932, Carol visited Russia and Germany. Alarmed by the growing Nazi influence, she came home and founded the *International Juridicial Association Bulletin*. The periodical published articles on immigration, labor, civil rights, poverty, and tenant-landlord law. Many attorneys considered it one of the best legal publications in America.

Throughout her career, Carol took on big cases and little cases. She defended the poor and the destitute. She tried to save the lives of nine blacks accused of rape in Scottsboro, Alabama. She petitioned the United States Supreme Court for relief on the exclusion of blacks from juries and the right of the poor to have competent court-appointed attorneys. King fought for such ideas long before they were popular in the legal or liberal communities.

One biographer wrote that Carol King "brought the Bill of Rights to Ellis Island and to many criminal and appellate courts where it had long been treated as alien."

"This is what the Lord Almighty says: 'Administer true justice; show mercy and compassion to one another. Do not oppress the widow or the fatherless, the alien or the poor.' "

Zechariah 7:9,10

Key Point: Single adults should be leaders in securing justice for all.

August 25

Cloe Annette Buckel, physician
August 25, 1833–August 17, 1912

Within a year of Cloe Buckel's birth, both of her parents died. She was taken in by her grandparents, who died soon after. Finally, Cloe was raised by two aunts who were strict with her; she turned to reading as an escape. By age fourteen, she was teaching school for $1.25 a week.

At some point in those teen years, Cloe decided she would become a doctor. She got a job in a burnishing factory, studied Latin at her workbench, and entered Woman's Medical College in 1856, living on money borrowed against her life insurance policy.

In 1858, after defending her thesis on insanity, she was awarded her degree and began postgraduate study with Dr. Marie Zakrzewska at New York Infirmary for Women and Children.

After opening a practice with another woman in Chicago, Dr. Buckel sensed the need for physicians in the Civil War and volunteered. The governor of Indiana sent her to Grant's army "to look after the condition and wants of Indiana's sick and wounded soldiers." Next she was assigned by the surgeon general to visit federal hospitals and advise staff on the selection and training of nurses.

In the fall of 1863, Cloe became chief of female nurses at Jefferson General Hospital, across the river from Louisville. However, the army would not allow her to be a physician to its male patients.

After opening a practice in Evansville after the war, Dr. Buckel joined the staff of the New England Hospital for Women and Children. She became ill in 1872 and took a two-year sabbatical in Europe, where she studied European surgery in Vienna and Paris. After her return, she became an attending surgeon. Two years later, another health relapse forced Dr. Buckel to resign and move to California.

In 1877, Cloe became the first woman member of the Alameda County (Oakland) Medical Society. She began devoting a great deal of her time to the needs of children and worked in a program to care for orphaned and delinquent girls.

Cloe Buckel had a host of friends and stayed busy

"Even while the boy was coming, the demon threw him to the ground in a convulsion. But Jesus rebuked the evil spirit, healed the boy and gave him back to his father."

Luke 9:42

Father, Dr. Cloe Buckel could have spent all her energies fighting the male medical establishment for full recognition of her

with her love of nature. Through her will, she established a trust fund to benefit feeble-minded children and a Buckel fellowship at Stanford for the study of child psychology.

degree, but she became a servant instead. Give us a faith like hers.

August 26

Annie Turner Wittenmyer, relief worker
August 26, 1827–February 2, 1900

What do you do when your dream collapses?

Annie Turner discovered early that life was hard. She married at age twenty; four of her children died in childhood; then, with war clouds coming, she found herself widowed.

When the Civil War touched Iowa, Annie was concerned about care of the wounded. She traveled to Keokuk, Iowa, to investigate the care of the soldiers and sent reports back to women, urging them to organize aid societies in their communities and send supplies. By the summer of 1861, she was an official agent of the state of Iowa, but by 1862, she had a string of male critics who thought a widow's place was by the hearth and not in a field hospital. In 1864, her appointment was repealed by the Iowa legislature, then reinstated. By this time, she was disgusted with bureaucracy and resigned.

She turned her attention to providing special kitchens as an alternative to army-issue rations. With the support of the United States Christian Commission, Annie devoted her energy to the growing problem of the orphans of dead soldiers.

After the war, she threw herself into organizing the Ladies' and Pastors' Christian Union to visit the sick and needy. In 1871, she established *Christian Woman* magazine. In November 1874, she was elected the first president of the Women's Christian Temperance Union and served for five years. Annie resisted attempts to involve the W.C.T.U in issues of women's rights and was defeated for president in 1879 by Frances Willard. Annie Wittenmyer invested the rest of her life in establishing homes for former nurses and widows of veterans.

"The Lord will keep you from all harm—he will watch over your life; the Lord will watch over your coming and going both now and forevermore."

Psalm 121:7, 8

Father, help us to realize that You are interested in our "comings and goings" and that You will keep us when we are committed to You. Even when defeat and death come, give us courage to rely on You for strength.

211

Richard Ward Greene Welling, reformer
August 27, 1858–December 17, 1946

After graduating from Harvard with classmate Theodore Roosevelt, Richard Welling wanted to go west to raise sheep, but his father forbade that idea. To please his family, Richard agreed to attend Harvard Law School. After graduation in 1880, he practiced law in New York City.

Welling became actively involved in the city's reform movement, joining Roosevelt's City Reform Club. For two decades he was involved in trying to overturn the crooked Tammany machine that ran the city. He and Edmond Holly organized Good Government Clubs in every legislative district in New York, which became a contributing factor in the 1894 election of reform mayor, William L. Strong.

Then Welling began investing his energies in educational reform. He organized the School Citizen Committee in 1904 to "develop a real love of democracy" in the nation's public schools. With the backing of prominent educator John Dewey, Welling lectured across the United States, calling for the introduction of civics curriculum and student government. He also was actively involved in implementing programs to combat juvenile delinquency in New York City.

In the 1930s, Welling again became active in municipal reform and actively supported the campaign of Fiorello H. LaGuardia. He also served as president of the Civil Service Reform Association.

Richard Welling, an Episcopalian, realized that reform was a continuing battle to be waged. His fifty years of work is credited with improving New York City's government.

"Be careful not to do your 'acts of righteousness' before men, to be seen by them. If you do, you will have no reward from your Father in heaven."

Matthew 6:1

Father, we need to take seriously our duties as citizens. Help us to be conscientious citizens.

Bryon Caldwell Smith, philologist
August 28, 1849–May 4, 1877

Bryon Smith studied at such prestigious universities as Heidelberg, Berlin, and Munich. When his sister died, he abandoned plans to complete his doctorate in Eu-

"Then I thought in my heart, 'The fate of the fool will

212

rope and joined his parents at home in Kansas. Within a few months he had been appointed to the faculty at the newly founded University of Kansas. Within a year, because of his brilliance, he was promoted to full professor.

Smith became engaged to one of his students, but in the summer of 1874 he was diagnosed with a kidney disease and sent to Philadelphia for treatment. By the time he had sufficiently recovered, he had been terminated by the university. Smith decided to remain in Philadelphia and took a position with the *Philadelphia Press*. He studied economics in his spare time.

In 1877, Smith contracted tuberculosis. He moved to Boulder, Colorado, having been advised that the mountain air would help him. He died there as a young scholar known for his gracious personality.

Bryon Smith is remembered today primarily through two collections of his letters: *A Young Scholar's Letters* and *The Love Life of Bryon Caldwell Smith*.

overtake me also. What then do I gain by being wise?' "

Ecclesiastes 2:15

Key Thought: The life of Bryon Caldwell Smith reminds us that we must live fully now.

August 29

Elisabeth Antoinette Irwin, educator
August 29, 1880–October 16, 1942

Elisabeth Irwin, although born into affluence, had such a bleak childhood that she eventually broke all her family ties. She graduated from Smith College in 1903, got a job in the Cottage Settlement House on New York City's lower East Side, but stayed for only a year. For the next four years, Miss Irwin traveled around the East.

In 1910, she became a visiting teacher and psychologist in New York City, paid by a citizen's community group interested in social reform. Based on her experience in testing children for intelligence, she continued her graduate education at Columbia.

In 1916, Elisabeth started a new program to identify and tutor gifted children, which led to the first schoolwide grouping by IQ. Six years later, Miss Irwin introduced "the Little Red School House," a redesigned curriculum for the first grade that introduced play and group activities into the school day. Her program developed an international reputation despite the con-

"Lo, children are an heritage of the Lord."

Psalm 127:3 KJV

cerns of school bureaucrats and immigrant parents who wanted a more traditional education for their children.

Eventually, the school board withdrew its support, so Miss Irwin opened a Little Red School House in Greenwich Village. During the Depression, Elisabeth argued that the social and emotional adjustment of children must be a top priority for educators.

Miss Irwin, a militant feminist, adopted one child and helped rear three others. She had wit, great common sense, and derived a great deal of pleasure from her work with children.

Key Point: Other people's children are vital in the mature development of any single adult.

August 30

Elva McAllaster, professor and poet
August 30, 1922–

"Sometimes, the easiest thing is to drift into matrimony." That's a startling statement unless one knows the compassionate concern of the speaker, Elva McAllaster. She understands student relationships, having spent forty years as a college professor.

Dr. Mac has been more than a grader of papers and lecturer on obscure points of Shakespeare. She has been a friend, a listening ear, and her concern did not end when a student completed an English 101 course or graduated with a degree. Dr. Mac has always reminded her students of her home phone number. Sometimes years have passed before a Greenville College alumni called to find a comforting voice.

McAllaster's poems have been published in more than three hundred publications. *Free to Be Single*, published in the late 1970s, was one of the pioneering books in the field of identity for single adults.

When she retired from the classroom, she was named poet in residence at Greenville. Letters of congratulations came from around the world. One paragraph from a letter written by a Greenville alumnus who now works at the United States embassy in Amman, Jordan, summarized the thoughts of many of her former students:

"I will never forget her listening ear, gentle counseling, and her faith in a bewildered sophomore ever so

"Have I not commanded you? Be strong and courageous. Do not be terrified; do not be discouraged, for the Lord your God will be with you wherever you go."

Joshua 1:9

Father, Elva McAllaster is a reminder of the influence of one life fully com-

many years ago. She may have had the title of professor of English, but she was really an inadequately disguised professor of the human heart."

If Elva had married, I wonder if as many students would have been touched by her life?

mitted to You. Remind us today of the need for the human touch, whatever our occupation.

August 31

Anna Barlett Warner, hymnist
August 31, 1824–January 22, 1915

Her hymn is the first one learned by many children, and its words are a lasting theology to Jesus' love: "Jesus Loves Me, This I Know."

Anna Warner and her sister, Susan, made their home on Constitution Island, near the United States Military Academy at West Point, New York. For twenty years the two sisters conducted Bible classes for the cadets; their tenure matched that of any professor. When Anna died, she was buried with full military honors.

Anna wrote several novels under her pen name of Amy Lathrop and two collections of poetry: *Hymns of the Church Militant* (1858) and *Wayfaring Hymns, Original and Translated* (1869).

"People were bringing little children to Jesus to have him touch them. . . ." 'Let the little children come to me, and do not hinder them, for the kingdom of God belongs to such as these.'

Mark 10:13, 14

Father, the simple song of our childhood reminds us of one great truth: You love us, even when no one else does, even when we don't love ourselves. Give us grateful hearts.

Elizabeth Harrison, educator
September 1, 1849–October 13, 1927

After the marriage of her sisters and the death of her mother, thirty-year-old Elizabeth Harrison needed a way to support herself. Friends suggested she go to Chicago and study the new education program called kindergarten. Elizabeth enrolled in a teachers' program and graduated in 1880; she remained at the school the next year as an assistant.

Next she studied with two pioneers in the kindergarten movement: Susan Blow in St. Louis and Marie Klaus-Boelte in New York. In 1883, Elizabeth returned to Chicago and organized the Chicago Kindergarten Club for teachers. The following year she offered free kindergarten training in a mission kindergarten.

In 1886, Elizabeth and Mrs. John Crouse opened a school to train kindergarten teachers and young mothers. This evolved in 1891 into the Chicago Kindergarten College and eventually the National Kindergarten and Elementary College. Harrison was president of the two institutions for thirty-three years.

In 1890, she studied the kindergarten movement in Germany and published her book, *A Study of Child Nature*, which went through fifty editions and was translated into eight languages. Miss Harrison became the first woman to address the National Education Association.

In 1894, Elizabeth was involved in creating what became the National Congress of Parents and Teachers. In 1912, she went to Rome to study the work of Madame Montessori and published *Montessori and the Kindergarten* in 1913.

Elizabeth Harrison's biographers have noted that she had an "elasticity of the mind" that allowed her to stay abreast of rapid changes in the field of child development. She always integrated the most up-to-date material into her teaching.

"Let the little children come to me, and do not hinder them, for the kingdom of heaven belongs to such as these."

Matthew 19:14

Father, remind us of Your single Son's love for children. Thank You for all those who work with children.

September 2

Lucretia Peabody Hale, author
September 2, 1820–June 12, 1900

Coming from a newspaper family, where even children could be expected to write book reviews or essays, it was no surprise that Lucretia Hale became a writer. Her first piece that gained notice was "The Queen of the Red Chessmen," which appeared in _Atlantic Monthly_. She wrote on the Lord's Supper, lacework, needlework, and games. However, her literary reputation is based on her Peterkin novels, which were stories she initially told to amuse the daughter of a friend.

She invented "the Lady from Philadelphia," who seemed to be able to settle any problem a child could face. _The Peterkin Papers_ (1880) and _The Last of the Peterkins_ (1886) were enormously successful.

After a visit to Egypt where her brother was a diplomat, she returned to Boston and took up causes related to the advancement of women. Lucretia was one of the first female members of the Boston School Committee.

Through writing, she enriched the imaginations of thousands of children.

"Then little children were brought to Jesus for him to place his hands on them and pray for them."

Matthew 19:13

Father, remind us of the needs of the children of our world—and that we don't have to have children of our own.

September 3

Edward Albert Filene, merchant and reformer
September 3, 1860–September 26, 1937

Edward Filene walked with a limp from a childhood incident. Because of his declining health, he was forced to give up plans to attend Harvard. Instead he and a brother took over their father's Boston store. Edward was the generator of ideas, while his brother handled the daily details of the business. Because of their aptness, by 1891 Filene's was a prominent and immensely profitable department store in Boston.

Because of their success, Edward's father turned the entire company over to the sons, which gave Edward the freedom to innovate. One idea that changed the business world was his "automatic bargain basement,"

"All hard work brings a profit, but mere talk leads only to poverty."

Proverbs 14:23

where the prices fell as the merchandise failed to sell. Other stores had to create their own bargain basements to compete for customers.

Most of Edward's sales experiments were successful, based on his conviction that "the efficient performance of a needed social service would bring the best long-run business profit." His brother did not agree, and by 1928, Edward was stripped of his responsibilities, although he retained the title of president. He was forced to abandon his plan to turn the ownership of the store over to the employees through a cooperative program.

As a result, Edward turned his attention to civic opportunities. He took the lead in organizing the first chamber of commerce in Boston, the Massachusetts Chamber of Commerce, and eventually the United States Chamber of Commerce.

Always a friend to workers, Filene argued for high wages, unemployment and medical insurance, and minimum wage laws. He believed such incentives would be good for the worker and for the employer as well. Filene had a vision of the future: He predicted installment buying, chain stores, and more efficient distribution systems. His lasting contribution may be the credit union movement, which he saw as more democratic than banks. He also organized what became the Twentieth Century Fund, endowed it with trust funds, and eventually left most of his sizable estate to it. The fund was instrumental in developing federal stock market legislation in the 1930s.

Despite his achievements, Edward Filene died believing he was a failure. He despaired because he had not known how to pass on more of his business ideas to his employees and the business world.

Key Point: Our definition of success and our perception of our own success is not always shared by our friends; most of the time we think too poorly of ourselves.

September 4

Phoebe Cary, poet and hymn writer
September 4, 1824–July 31, 1871

Twenty-five years of farm life did much to shape the thinking found in the poems that Phoebe Cary contributed to *Poems of Alice and Phoebe Cary*, published in 1849. As a young woman, Phoebe left the farm for New

"But Martha was distracted by all the preparations that had to be

218

York, where she cared for her sister Alice, who was ill. Their home was a popular gathering place on Sunday nights; many of New York's influential citizens considered Phoebe one of the wittiest women in the country.

The sisters' writing temperaments were quite different: Alice wrote regularly, while Phoebe wrote only when the mood struck. Alice's poetry was read by contemporaries, but Phoebe's writing has endured the test of time.

Phoebe is best remembered for a poem she composed on a Sunday in 1852. Inspired by a morning worship service, she wrote:

> One sweetly solemn thought
> Comes to me o'er and o'er;
> I am nearer home today
> Than I ever have been before.

"One Sweetly Solemn Thought" was set to music and became a popular song of her day.

Alice's death in February 1871 was an incredible blow to Phoebe, who had invested so much energy in caring for her. Phoebe died only five months later.

Phoebe also published *Poems and Parodies* (1854) and *Poems of Faith, Hope and Love* (1868). She collaborated with Charles Deems in compiling *Hymns for All Christians*, published in 1869.

made. She came to him and asked, 'Lord, don't you care that my sister has left me to do the work by myself? Tell her to help me!' "

Luke 10:40

Key Thought: Taking care of ill loved ones is tough. Phoebe said: "Although hard be the task, 'Keep a stiff upper lip.' "

September 5

Anna Euretta Richardson, home economist
September 5, 1883–February 3, 1931

Since Anna Richardson was named for an unmarried schoolteacher aunt, no one was surprised when she declared, "I will be an old maid and teach school because all Anna Richardsons do that." By nineteen she had a degree from George Peabody College for Teachers and had begun a career that included high school and college teaching.

After she received her master's degree at Columbia in 1911, she planned to specialize in nutrition, but because of her administrative skill, she was appointed to

"Remember your leaders. . . . Consider the outcome of their way of life and imitate their faith."

Hebrews 13:7

the newly created Federal Board for Vocational Education. Her assignment was to expand home economics services and educational programs in this country. Eventually, Anna headed the board, and many thought her innovations were generations ahead of her peers. She recognized the need to combine "homemaking" and wage earning. The woman of the future, Anna contended, would need skills in both areas.

In 1922, she became dean of the home economics division of Iowa State University. During her four years of leadership, the program gained national prominence. In 1926, she resigned to begin a new program promoting child development. The next four and a half years, as a field worker for the American Home Economics Association, she consulted for colleges, conducted conferences on family life, and lobbied for the recognition of child development as an academic discipline. Anna Richardson died unexpectedly while working on a White House conference on education for home and family life.

Key Thought: One woman—neither wife nor mother— laid a crucial foundation for family life education in this country.

September 6

Jane Addams, reformer
September 6, 1860–May 21, 1935

Jane Addams began studying medicine at Philadelphia's Woman's Medical College but dropped out after a few months. After major surgery to correct spinal curvature, she battled long periods of depression. For twenty-seven months she toured Europe, seeking a purpose for her life. Jane found what she was searching for when she visited Toynbee Hall, a social service agency in London. The encounter convinced her that educated people, by living in poor neighborhoods, could improve the futures of the residents.

Addams and a college friend, Ellen Gates Starr, opened Hull House on Chicago's Halstead Street on September 18, 1889. Jane attempted to design programs she thought the neighborhood needed and would appreciate—mainly literary parties. Soon, at the neighbors' request, programming at Hull House included classes, clubs, a day nursery, and social events.

In the 1890s, Jane began to study the causes of pov-

"Defend the cause of the weak and fatherless; maintain the rights of the poor and oppressed."

Psalm 82:3

erty and poor adjustment to city life. She criticized many labor practices, especially after her involvement in the bitter Pullman strike in 1894. She believed that corporations were destroying the neighborhoods and harming the health of residents.

By the end of the century, Miss Addams had developed a keen interest in children and had urged the city of Chicago to create more playgrounds and parks. Her work on the Chicago Board of Education prompted her to champion the cause of vocational and industrial education. She also lobbied hard for the regulation of child labor.

Jane seconded Theodore Roosevelt's nomination in 1912 at the Progressive party convention. The growing threat of war in Europe led her to become involved in peace issues. In 1915, she teamed with Carrie Catt to launch a National Woman's party because she felt the other political parties were ignoring the needs of women. That same year she initiated an international women's political caucus that evolved into the Woman's International League for Peace and Freedom, which she served as president until 1929.

Her peace efforts during World War I led many to question her patriotism. The Daughters of the American Revolution went so far as to revoke her lifetime membership. In 1931, her efforts were recognized when she was awarded the Nobel Peace Prize.

Father, remind us that You do care about the poor, their housing, and their working conditions.

Jane Addams led the progressive reform movement in this country, skillfully balancing her social theories with a pragmatic sense of reality. She motivated hundreds of young women to begin careers in social work.

September 7

Edith Sitwell, poet and critic
September 7, 1896–December 9, 1964

Edith Sitwell first attracted public attention when she and other poets issued *Wheels* in 1916. In 1923, she gave a public poetry recital behind a screen to illustrate her contention that poetry should be disassociated from the personality of the poet.

Miss Sitwell had a long love affair with words, ignoring dictionaries and traditional usage. Some friends and critics teased her habit of making words say what she wanted them to say.

"My mouth will speak words of wisdom; the utterance from my heart will give understanding."

Psalm 49:3

Sitwell's poetry, she said, were "hymns of praise to the glory of life."

September 8

Gordon Norton Ray, author
September 8, 1915–December 18, 1986

After earning a Ph.D. in literature at Harvard, Gordon Ray served in the navy in the Pacific during World War II. After the war, he published his four-volume work, *The Letters and Private Papers of William Makepeace Thackery*, which became a standard of excellence in research for other scholars. In 1946, he joined the faculty of the University of Illinois and rose to department chairman in just four years.

Ray became the world's authority on Thackery. In 1952, he published *The Buried Life*, a study of the link between Thackery's fiction and his private life. In 1955, he published *The Use of Adversity*, the first volume of his comprehensive biography of Thackery, and in 1958, the second volume, *The Age of Wisdom*. The work was heralded as an "indisputable masterpiece of literary biography."

Ray helped the University of Illinois acquire many of the papers of H. G. Wells and studied the relationship Wells had with Henry James, which led to another book, *H. G. Wells and Henry James*. Ray also edited Wells's *Desert Diary* and *The History of Mr. Polly*, which were published after his death.

Ray was convinced of the importance of literature being passed from generation to generation. With so much debate in his day on the emergence of the electronic media, he responded with *The Future of the Book*.

On more than one occasion, Gordon Ray reminded libraries they are more than just "repositories of books" but "mind-saving" stations.

"My heart took delight in all my work, and this was the reward for all my labor."

Ecclesiastes 2:10

Key Point: "The real case for books is that they give the reader something more precious than information . . . they encompass the 'literature of power.' "

Gordon Ray

September 9

Ferdinand Morton, politician
September 9, 1881–November 8, 1949

Life was tough for Ferdinand Morton. This son of a former slave was forced to drop out of Harvard University and Boston University Law School for lack of funds.

In 1908, Ferdinand lived in New York City, working as a butler. He spent his spare time preparing for the bar exam, which he passed in 1910. During this time he became active in the Democratic party, speaking at rallies for William Jennings Bryan. He joined the United Colored Democracy and helped recruit Republican blacks to switch parties. In 1915, Morton became head of the UCD.

In 1920, Morton became assistant district attorney for New York County. In 1921, he resigned to become the first black member of the Municipal Civil Service Commission, where he carefully worked to increase the number of blacks employed by New York City. His strategy for change was to seek the attainable and ignore the impossible. He once explained his political philosophy: "politics . . . is but a theoretical bargain counter to buy wares and get the best we can in bargains."

Eventually, Ferdinand Morton became the most powerful black politician in New York City. Clearly, he opened the door for many blacks to become fully involved in the political process.

"Then Peter began to speak: 'I now realize how true it is that God does not show favoritism but accepts men from every nation who fear him and do what is right.' "

Acts 10:34, 35

Father, remind us that discrimination because of the color of a person's skin is wrong. Help us to make opportunity for participation, not only in the political world, but in the church world as well.

September 10

Nicholas Biddle, naval officer
September 10, 1750–March 7, 1778

Nicholas Biddle went to sea for the first time at thirteen. After several years in the merchant marine, he joined the British navy in 1772. Biddle volunteered to serve on one of the ships being commissioned by the Royal Geological Survey to chart the poles; when he was rejected, he became a stowaway. On that expedition, he met Horatio Nelson, who was destined to become England's greatest naval hero.

"But now I urge you to keep up your courage . . . only the ship will be destroyed."

Acts 27:22

223

The expedition to the poles was a tremendous success, but the growing war clouds between England and the colonies caused turmoil in Biddle's life. On which side would he fight? At the first opportunity, Biddle quit the British navy, sailed to Philadelphia, and joined the ragtag colonial forces.

Although only twenty-five, he initially served on the *Franklin* but soon assumed command of the *Andrea Doria* (with 14 guns and 130 men). Captain Biddle sailed the North Atlantic, seizing a number of His Majesty's ships, which were loaded with military supplies. He captured two ships carrying Highlanders, crack British troops, and was promoted to command of the *Randolph*.

In 1778, Biddle took charge of four small vessels with which he planned to break up the British blockade of Charleston. Though the captain found himself up against a sixty-four-gun ship, he opened fire. For an incredible twenty minutes the battle raged, but Biddle's flagship was hit and he was wounded.

Despite his wounds, twenty-eight-year-old Captain Biddle ordered a chair placed on the deck and continued to direct the battle. While a doctor was examining him, the *Randolph* exploded. Biddle and most of his men went down with the ship.

"Ardent, ambitious, fearless, intelligent, and persevering" were terms Biddle's men used to describe him. "He had ever been successful until the fatal moment when he so gloriously fell."

Eventually, the Charleston blockade was broken and the Americans won their independence—but only through the blood of heroic single adults like Nicholas Biddle.

Father, our freedoms came at a great price. We thank You for Nicholas Biddle and the thousands of single adults who died in the Revolution, their heroism unknown to us.

September 11

Sydney George Fisher, lawyer and historian
September 11, 1856–February 22, 1927

After two years at Harvard Law School, Sydney Fisher passed the Pennsylvania bar in 1883 and began his law practice in Philadelphia.

"So I saw that there is nothing better for a man

His avocation, and the real joy in his life, was writing history. *The Making of Pennsylvania* came first in 1896, followed by *Pennsylvania: Colony and Commonwealth* and *The Evolution of the Constitution* the following year. Two of his books that proved popular were *The True Benjamin Franklin* and *The True William Penn*; in both of these, Fisher tried to debunk some of the historical myths being taught as fact. His *The True Story of the American Revolution* was an immediate success with readers, going through five editions before being re-released as the two-volume *The Struggle for Independence*.

Fisher was also interested in church-supported colleges and wrote *Christian Colleges: Their History, Position and Influence* in 1895. He served as a trustee and president of the board of Trinity College for many years. The Institution for the Education of the Blind received Fisher's enthusiastic support.

Fisher raised significant intellectual questions about the writing of the history of the American Revolution. He reminded readers that factual errors in history were more the result of political ideas and material interest than of religious issues. While there was a place in folklore for myth, Fisher believed historians should be more cautious in their writing.

than to enjoy his work."

Ecclesiastes 3:22

Father, what is true and what is false and what is somewhere in between? Examine my heart today and take from me all that is false.

September 12

Florence Kelley, social worker and reformer
September 12, 1859–February 17, 1932

Florence Kelley, a single parent with three children in the 1890s, experienced life differently from most of her contemporaries. Florence invested her life in improving working conditions for women and children, beginning in Chicago at Jane Addams's Hull House. In 1891, she wrote her study of sweatshops and slums, which resulted in a new child-labor law.

It was one thing to pass legislation but another to see it enforced. Florence was appointed chief factory inspector in the state of Illinois. She was so unpopular with factory owners that one almost shot her. To complicate the problem, city attorneys would not file

"The Lord showed [Moses] the whole land. . . . 'I have let you see it with your eyes, but you will not cross over into it.' "

Deuteronomy 34:1, 4

225

charges against wealthy factory owners, so Florence enrolled at Northwestern Law School, where she graduated with a law degree in 1894.

In 1899, Florence Kelley moved to New York and became secretary for the National Consumers' League. She used that position to push for a minimum wage, women's suffrage, and financial aid for mothers and children. Historians recognize Kelley as one of the prime movers in the adoption of the minimum wage.

In 1904, Florence helped organize the National Child Labor Committee with the goal of eliminating child labor in the United States. The result was the Keating-Owen Child Labor Act, passed by Congress in 1916. When Keating-Owen was overturned, Florence demanded: "Why are seals, bears, reindeer, fish, wild game in the national parks, buffalo, migratory birds, all found suitable for federal protection; but not the children of our race and their mothers?"

Florence Kelley—who called herself Mrs. Kelley to protect her children—was no gentle saint. One associate described her as a guerrilla warrior fighting for women and children in the wilderness of industrial wrongs.

Father, thank You for toughness. Are there issues in our lives about which we should become warriors?

September 13

Sarah Louise Cady, educator
September 13, 1829–November 8, 1912

Sarah Cady's father was a prominent Massachusetts coachmaker who built a luxurious coach for President Pierce. Sarah spent several years as a schoolteacher in small communities before marrying Henry Cady, a merchant, in 1850.

Mr. Cady died in 1863, leaving Sarah with three small children and little money. She opened a small school, then taught at Maplewood Hall, a prominent boarding school for women. In 1870, she opened her own school, West End Institute, in New Haven, Connecticut. Mrs. Cady wanted her school to be more than just a finishing school for girls from wealthy families. She was a natural

"So I counsel younger widows to marry, to have children, to manage their homes and to give the enemy no opportunity for slander."

1 Timothy 5:14

administrator and disciplinarian and built a fine faculty. She also started one of the first kindergartens in Connecticut.

In 1899, after disputes with Yale University, the owner of the building in which her school was housed, Sarah closed the school and moved to New York. There she became involved in several women's clubs, was an active member of the Broadway Tabernacle, and served on the executive boards of the Y.W.C.A. and the Women's Christian Temperance Union.

Key Thought: In the tragedies of life, single parents must find the strength not just to survive but to thrive.

Sarah Cady did much to improve the standards of college preparation for women and gave the enemy no opportunity for slander.

September 14

Julia Magruder, novelist
September 14, 1854–June 9, 1907

Julia Magruder never escaped her Southern heritage; her childhood reflected the ideas and prized virtues of the Old South. Julia published her first articles in the *Baltimore Sun* at eighteen. She won a contest with a $300 prize, a sizable amount in those days.

"Look to the Lord and his strength; seek his face always."

Psalm 105:4

Julia Magruder's writing was influenced by her avid reading and study of other writers, particularly Tennyson, Eliot, and Emerson. Her twenty novels include *Princess Sonia*, regarded as her best. Julia relied on two plots: the hero and the heroine who successfully triumph over the barriers to their marriage and the woman who marries the wrong man but after his death or disappearance finds her true love.

Julia's short stories appeared in many leading magazines of the day and focused on the interests and needs of women in society. Julia Magruder wrote her last novel, *Her Husband*, on her deathbed. It was published after her death and capped a successful writing career.

Father, good writing comes out of good thinking. Thank You for the life of Julia Magruder, who, despite her writing, still made time for her friends.

Eva Burrows, Salvation Army general
September 15, 1929–

The gathering of leaders composing the world council of the Salvation Army was hushed. For several days they had been voting for a new general to head the army of 1.5 million Salvationists around the world and 3 million supporters in ninety countries. On May 2, 1986, one candidate had the majority.

"We have a General . . . Eva Burrows." Overnight her name became a household word. While the Anglicans were debating whether a woman could be in charge of a handful of people in a local church, a single woman headed a worldwide church.

DON'T CALL THIS GENERAL SIR and THE GENERAL IS A LADY ran the headlines in the tabloids. Some, including Eva, wondered what all the fuss was about. After all, Eva was not the first woman general; from 1935 to 1939, Evangeline Booth had held the office, and the founder of the Salvation Army, William Booth, had once quipped, "Some of my best men are women."

Eva Burrows's work for the Salvation Army in Australia, Zimbabwe, London, Scotland, and Sri Lanka had prepared her well for this awesome responsibility. She was an excellent administrator, teacher, musician, and encourager.

Soon it was evident to all that the Salvation Army was in for a shake-up. She reminded members of their roots: "You can only show a caring God by action. People are far more impressed by what you do than by what you say. It's an indictment of us all when we don't live up to our faith."

Known for her aggressive yet fair style, Eva does not hide her sense of humor. Once, after a flattering introduction, she responded, "After a welcome like that I can hardly wait to hear myself speak."

Some have pitied her single status, but Eva Burrows will have none of that. "God gives more than enough back to you when you give up something for Him. He is nobody's debtor. You find your comfort and solace in Him."

How does she meet all the demands of her office?

> **"And He is the head of the body, the church, who is the beginning, the firstborn from the dead, that in all things He may have the preeminence."**
>
> **Colossians 1:18** NKJV

I am always thrown back on the resources of God. When you are at the end of your own strength you lean so much more on God. The Holy Spirit seems to get hold of you in those times in such a way that afterwards you say, "Wasn't that amazing? My resources are limited, but God's resources are unlimited."

Give us courage to recognize our limits and Your limitlessness, Lord.

September 16

James Walker Lowrie, missionary
September 16, 1856–January 26, 1930

James Walker Lowrie was a third-generation missionary born in Shanghai, China. After his father's death when James was four, his mother returned to the United States to supervise James's education. Although everyone assumed James would be a missionary, he waited until he had a clear sense of "call." He received his B.A. and M.A. from Princeton, graduated from seminary in 1883, was ordained by the presbytery of New York City, and appointed to China.

"Fight the good fight of the faith."

1 Timothy 6:12

James spent eight years in Peking and became fluent in the Chinese language. Joined by his mother and a married sister, he developed a permanent home among the Chinese at a mission station in Paotingu. However, while he escorted his mother to the coast for a trip to the United States, the Boxer Rebellion swept across China. Paotingu was particularly impacted, and most of Lowrie's missionary colleagues were killed by the Boxers.

Marooned in Peking, James worked as a translator for the allied army sent to end the disturbance. When he discovered that an allied general planned to level Paotingu in retribution, Lowrie convinced him to spare the city and its residents. His action won the hearts of many Chinese.

In 1903, James Walker Lowrie was made a mandarin by the Chinese government. In 1910, he headed the China Council, the executive body of the seven Chinese missions sponsored by the Presbyterian Church.

Father, Lowrie's name is not on the tip of our tongues; he is one of the forgotten missionaries of yesterday. Remind us that no life of service is forgotten by You.

229

Friedrich Wilhelm von Steuben, Revolutionary hero
September 17, 1730–November 28, 1794

The confrontation could no longer be postponed; the best of the king's redcoats would fight the American patriots. War would be costly, with untrained American farmers facing disciplined shooters. Indeed, the American Revolution might have failed had it not been for the genius of a German single adult who had been discharged from the Prussian army.

Friedrich Wilhelm von Steuben was looking for an opportunity when a friend introduced him to Benjamin Franklin in 1777. Frenchmen secretly financing the Americans had urged him to volunteer for service with the underdogs.

Baron von Steuben met with the Continental Congress on February 5, 1778, and waived all claims to high rank or monetary compensation. If the Americans won the war and felt von Steuben had helped them, he trusted Congress to compensate him. He was ordered to report to General George Washington immediately.

Washington promptly appointed von Steuben inspector general and placed him in charge of training the troops. This was no small task, since von Steuben did not speak English, but he used interpreters to direct his intense drills and created a crack unit of one hundred men whom he personally trained as models of military precision and discipline. Eventually, von Steuben created a fighting force that humbled the best of the British.

In 1778, von Steuben wrote *Regulations for the Order and Discipline of the Troops of the United States*, popularly known as "the blue book" or military bible of the army. By the end of the war, von Steuben was Washington's trusted confidant, helping him plan the future defense of the young nation.

Washington's last act as general was to write a letter of thanks to the Prussian. Because of his contribution, the Pennsylvania legislature made von Steuben a United States citizen.

"Look! It is Solomon's carriage, escorted by sixty warriors . . . all of them wearing the sword, all experienced in battle, each with his sword at his side."

Song of Songs 3:7, 8

Father, von Steuben asked so little and gave so much. Remind us of his example.

John Hessin Clark, Supreme Court justice
September 18, 1857–March 22, 1945

John Hessin Clark was born in 1857 to Irish immigrant parents who had settled in Ohio. John's father, an attorney, was active in the Democratic party.

John passed the bar in 1878, when he was twenty-one years old. For two years, he practiced with his father. In 1880, he moved to Youngstown to specialize in corporate law, purchasing the *Vindicator* and committing the newspaper to political reform.

In 1897, Clark joined the prestigious firm of William and Cushing and became general counsel for the Nickel Plate Railroad. He was a strong advocate of antitrust and antirebate legislation, supporting women's suffrage, mandatory civil service, and public disclosure of campaign finances.

In 1894, Clark ran for the Senate but was defeated. In 1914, he withdrew from a second Senate campaign when another Irishman announced his candidacy. Later that year President Woodrow Wilson appointed Clark to the federal district bench. Two years later, based on Clark's progressive record, Wilson nominated him to the Supreme Court.

Clark resigned his post six years later to lobby for America's participation in Wilson's dream, The League of Nations. When asked why, Clark explained, "I will die happier working for world peace rather than devoting my time to 'determining whether a drunken Indian had been deprived of his land before he died or whether the dragging of a ditch was constitutional.' "

John Clark did not live to see his dream of a world peace organization. He died six weeks before the start of the San Francisco Conference that launched the United Nations.

"Let the wise listen and add to their learning, and let the discerning get guidance."

Proverbs 1:5

Father, peace seems impossible in our world, but it must have seemed just as impossible in Justice Clark's day. Give us the same zeal to work for peace and justice.

Rosetta Sherwood Hall, physician
September 19, 1865–April 5, 1951

Rosetta Sherwood wanted more of life than what she found through teaching school in Chestnut Ridge, New York. After hearing Isabella Thoburn's sister-in-law tell of the needs of women in India, Rosetta entered the Women's Medical College of Pennsylvania in 1886, graduating in 1900.

Soon she met Dr. William Hall, a candidate for a medical appointment to China. They became engaged and Rosetta applied to the Women's Foreign Mission Society of the Methodist Church, expecting to be appointed to China, too, but the society needed her in Korea.

She arrived in Korea on October 10, 1890, and Dr. Hall—who had switched mission boards—arrived soon after. They were married on June 27, 1892, and had a son two years later. When the child was only one, William Hall came down with typhoid fever and died. Rosetta, with a one-year-old and seven months pregnant, returned to the United States. Four days after her arrival, she gave birth to a daughter. She spent the next years lecturing, raising money for Korea, and preparing a biography of her late husband.

Dr. Hall and her children returned to Korea in 1897. Within a year, her daughter, Edith Margaret, died of amoebic dysentery. In her grief, Rosetta wrote: "The thought that God loves these Koreans as He loves His own son stimulates me to want to tell everyone I meet of the 'Good news.' "

Dr. Hall poured herself into rearing her son (who later became a missionary doctor to Korea) and building the Women's Hospital of Extended Grace. Perhaps in memory of her daughter, she financed the American medical education of a young Korean woman, Esther Kim Pak. With Rosetta's help, Esther became the first Korean physician trained abroad to practice Western medicine in Korea.

Dr. Hall also helped establish the Women's Medical Institute in Seoul in 1928 and headed the Institute for the Blind and the Deaf, developing a Braille-like system for the Korean language.

Rosetta Hall's ministry and singleness were domi-

"And the Father himself, which hath sent me, hath borne witness of me."

John 5:37 KJV

Key Point: "It seems too high, too altogether great, but God does not ask anything He does not give the strength to perform; Jesus said, 'I am not alone'—

nated by this thought: "I don't understand how or why the Father could love us so, but He must have done so or He would never have sent Jesus to suffer for us."

September 20

Charles Zeuner, organist
September 20, 1795–November 7, 1857

Charles Zeuner studied with prominent German organists before his immigration to the United States in 1830.

Perhaps because of its great musical tradition, Zeuner settled in Boston, where he was soon elected organist for the Handel and Haydn Society. A number of his compositions were first performed by the society; some were written specifically for the group.

Unfortunately, Zeuner often found himself at odds with the board of trustees of the Handel and Haydn Society. Eventually he resigned and moved to Philadelphia to play at St. Andrew's and Arch Street Presbyterian Church.

Zeuner's contribution to musical literature was significant. He wrote *Church Music, Consisting of New and Original Anthems, Motets and Chants* (1831) and *The American Harp* (1832), both collections of church music. *Ancient Lyre* (1833) was a compilation of hymns. He wrote many popular songs and pieces for the piano and contributed to Lowell Mason's *Lyra Sacra.*

Zeuner is best known for his *The Feast of the Tabernacles*, a two-part oratorio, the first written in America.

Mental illness forced Charles Zeuner to retire from the stage; he committed suicide in 1857.

"While David was playing the harp, Saul tried to pin him to the wall."

1 Samuel 19:9, 10

Father, we do not understand why sometimes those with such enormous musical talents struggle with emotional pain. Thank You for the gift of composition, which is a legacy to the next generation of musicians.

September 21

Ethel Percy Andrus, teacher and founder of AARP
September 21, 1884–July 13, 1967

Ethel Andrus was the first woman in California to become a principal. She served in this role at Los Angeles's Abraham Lincoln High School for twenty-eight years.

"I was young and now I am old, yet I have never seen the righteous for-

Lincoln High was an ethnic and cultural melting pot where Miss Andrus devoted herself to helping her students blend their pasts with their futures. She did not demand they forget their heritage but accelerated their adjustment to America. Miss Andrus also won recognition for her work in reducing juvenile delinquency.

Miss Andrus completed her Ph.D. at USC. During the summers, when others took vacations, she taught educational philosophy and administration at USC, UCLA, and Stanford. Then, in 1944, she abruptly resigned to give full-time care to her mother.

In retirement, Miss Andrus had quite a shock: After forty-one years of teaching, she was entitled to a pension of only sixty dollars a month. Although she had some investments, she wondered how other teachers lived on such a small pension. She launched an ad hoc investigation of teachers' pensions that resulted in a national organization to improve teachers' benefits—the National Retired Teacher's Association. As president, she stunned school boards, policy makers, government officials, and especially legislators with her expectations and tenacity.

NRTA started a journal, a retirement home, and an insurance program in 1956. The programs were so successful that retirees from other professions wanted to join.

So, in 1958, Andrus, at the age of seventy-one, launched the American Association of Retired Persons and opened it to anyone over fifty-five. Soon the organization's power was being felt at every level of American government.

Anticipating "the graying of America" long before others, Andrus also founded the Retirement Research and Welfare Association to emphasize research and philanthropy. She also founded and edited a national magazine for retirees, *Modern Maturity*, which currently has the largest subscription of any magazine in the country.

A strong opponent of mandatory retirement, Andrus crisscrossed America at every opportunity, challenging stereotypes of the aged.

Most of the achievements of Ethel Andrus came after she was sixty.

saken or their children begging bread."

Psalm 37:25

Key Point: It's never too late to make a difference.

September 22

Frederick Knab, entomologist
September 22, 1865–November 2, 1918

In 1889, Frederick Knab sailed to Europe to study painting in Munich. He returned to the United States in 1891 and made a living as a landscape painter for more than a decade. Later, Knab began to devote his time to the study of insects, a boyhood fascination. He had once spent sixteen months collecting specimens along the Amazon River.

In 1903, Knab became an inspector and collector of mosquitoes for the Carnegie Institution. His research expanded existing information about mosquitoes. In 1904, he moved to Washington, D.C., and thereafter worked as an entomologist. His field assignments included Central America and Saskatchewan.

Frederick Knab wrote and illustrated most of the four-volume series *The Mosquitoes of North and Central America*, a major scientific reference work. He also wrote for many of the leading science journals of his day, publishing almost 177 papers during his career.

A keen observer, Knab used his art to enhance his writing.

"We constantly pray for you, that our God may count you worthy of his calling, and that by his power he may fulfill every good purpose of yours."

2 Thessalonians 1:11

Father, You created all things, even insects. This is Your world. Increase our curiosity.

September 23

Joseph Thomas, lexicographer
September 23, 1811–December 24, 1891

Although he dropped out of Yale without a degree, Joseph Thomas graduated from the University of Pennsylvania Medical School in 1837. However, for some unknown reason, he did not practice medicine. Instead, Thomas taught elocution at Haverford College, then spent sixteen years editing reference books at J. P. Lippincott, becoming a recognized specialist in pronunciation.

Thomas was instrumental in the founding of Swarthmore College and became known for his address advocating higher education for women. He eventually headed the English department and taught until his retirement in 1887.

"All right, say, 'Shibboleth.' If he said, 'Sibboleth,' because he could not pronounce the word correctly, they seized him and killed him at the fords of the Jordan."

Judges 12:6

235

Thomas was one of the world's authorities on pronunciation and etymology, working to insure a high standard of usage in reference works. He contributed the pronunciation vocabularies of the biographical and geographical names in the 1867 edition of *Webster's Unabridged Dictionary*.

His strong advocacy of the liberal arts, although considered radical in his day, led to many curriculum innovations in higher education.

Father, You who created languages has blessed us with people who can teach us to speak correctly.

September 24

Charles Simeon, pastor
September 24, 1759–November 13, 1836

Fifty years is a long time to pastor one church, but that was the tenure of English pastor Charles Simeon. On his fiftieth anniversary, he said, "I can appeal to all who have ever known me, that to proclaim a suffering and triumphant Messiah, as revealed to us by Moses and the prophets, has been *the one object of my life, without any variation . . . without ever turning aside* after novelties, or fond conceits or matters of doubtful disputation."

Charles Simeon was "soundly converted" in 1779 during his first term at King's College, Cambridge. After his death, a letter was found that described his conversion:

"Yea, I think it meet, as long as I am in this tabernacle, to stir you up by putting you in remembrance."

2 Peter 1:13 KJV

> The light of God's countenance then first visited me, and in his great mercy he has never wholly withdrawn it from me during 56 years. I was then enabled by his grace to set my face towards Zion, and though I have had much to lament and mourn over, and for which to be confounded before God, yet, blessed be his name, I have never turned my face away from Zion.

Simeon was appointed vicar of Holy Trinity Church in Cambridge in 1782 but retained academic connections at King's College. He was clearly an evangelical, without apology, in the Church of England. He had an independent mind and a deep personal devotion. Over the

"Almighty and everlasting God, who by thy holy servant, Charles Simeon, didst mould the lives of many that they might go forth and teach others also; mercifully

236

course of Simeon's ministry, he edited twenty-one volumes of his sermon outlines, which are still used by pastors around the world. He was a specialist in expository preaching and in teaching others how to use Scripture effectively in sermons.

Simeon was a friend to hundreds of students at Cambridge and influenced their careers. He was a moving influence in the formation of the Church Missionary Society, a strong supporter of the English Bible Society, and encouraged ministry to the Jews.

Thousands turned out for the funeral of one pastor who had more influence over the Church of England than any of its archbishops.

The prayer at right is prayed in the chapel of King's College every November 13 to commemorate his death.

grant that as through evil report and good report he ceased not to preach thy saving Word, so we may never be ashamed of the Gospel of Jesus Christ our Lord, who with Thee and the Holy Spirit liveth and reigneth one God, world without end."

September 25

James Harvey Rogers, economist
September 25, 1886–1939

Armed with a Yale Ph.D., James H. Rogers taught at the University of Missouri, Cornell, and Yale. A brilliant teacher, Rogers could translate intricate economic theories into proposals for action on social problems. As an adviser to Franklin D. Roosevelt, along with George F. Warren, he studied government fiscal policies in view of the major political reorganization of the New Deal.

Rogers recommended that the United States go off the gold standard. He encouraged large-scale public works programs, coupled with foreign lending and expanded trade overseas.

He authored *Stock Speculation and the Money Market* (1927); *The Process of Inflation in France, 1914–1927* (1929); *America Weighs Her Gold* (1931); and *Capitalism in Crisis* (1938).

Few men have had such a profound influence on economic policy.

"He designated the weight of gold for all the gold articles to be used in various kinds of service."

1 Chronicles 28:14

Father, thank You for those who give sound advice. Give us ears to discern.

Edith Abbott, social worker
September 26, 1876–July 28, 1957

Edith Abbott called herself "a child of the old frontier." She grew up in Grand Island, Nebraska; her mother was a Quaker who was very committed to women's rights. Edith completed a Ph.D. in political economics at the University of Chicago in 1905. She specialized in studying the wages of unskilled laborers from 1830 to 1900. After additional study at the prestigious London School of Economics, where she was influenced by British reformer Beatrice Webb, Dr. Abbott returned to the United States to teach at Wellesley.

In 1908, her former professor at Chicago, Sophonsiba Breckenridge, invited her to join the faculty. For the next ten years, Edith resided at Hull House with her sister, Grace, a well-known social worker. Edith was concerned with the economic protection of juveniles and immigrants as well as housing improvement. She wrote *Women In Industry* in 1910 and collaborated with Miss Breckenridge on *The Delinquent Child and the Home*, which examined the impact of compulsory education on homelife and child labor.

In 1920, Abbott and Breckenridge negotiated the merger of the School of Civics and Philanthropy into the University of Chicago as the graduate School of Social Service Administration. The two single adults envisioned a graduate program that would train professionals and encourage research. In 1924, Miss Abbott was named dean of the school, where she served until 1942. During her tenure, she trained several hundred public welfare administrators and policy makers.

Edith Abbott was never timid about expressing her opinions on issues relating to women, children, or immigrants. Helen Cody Baker observed, "the main drives in Edith's life have been toward broadening and stengthening our public welfare services and the adequate preparation of students to do the job."

"The needy will not always be forgotten, nor the hope of the afflicted ever perish."

Psalm 9:18

Father, the needy are still with us. We are never more like You than when we remember them.

Lillian Thrasher, missionary
September 27, 1887–December 17, 1961

Just ten days before her marriage, Lillian Thrasher went to hear a missionary speak. She had no idea that within hours she would break her engagement and make a decision to become a missionary to Egypt. Previously she had worked in an orphanage in North Carolina where she said she "learned how to trust God for the needs of everyday life."

In those days, there were no formal missionary appointments in some denominations. Lillian gathered her money and possessions and headed for a missionary convention in Pittsburgh, confident that God would provide the finances and direction for her passage to Egypt.

Lillian annoyed her missionary supervisors in Cairo when she insisted on keeping a baby whose mother had died. "Take her back!" she was ordered.

After prayerful consideration, Lillian said, "I will take her back, but I will go back with her."

The missionary leader laughed. "An American woman, unmarried, alone in the Arab world? Why, you'll be killed or starve to death."

"No, I won't be alone," Lillian responded. "I'll have God with me."

Lillian rode a donkey from village to village, begging money for her orphanage that kept growing, earning her nickname of Lady on the Donkey. If no hospitality was offered in a town, she stayed in the nearest jail.

Despite two wars, the Suez crisis, numerous epidemics, always having more children than financial resources, Lillian would turn away no child.

During her five decades in Egypt, Lillian cared for more than eight thousand orphans and widows. The orphanage she founded–renamed the Lillian Thrasher Memorial Orphanage–thrives today in Assiout. Did she have any regrets? "If the Lord allowed me to live my life over, I would do the same thing for another 50, another 100 years."

"I have seen, I have seen the affliction of my people which is in Egypt, and I have heard their groaning, and am come down to deliver them. And now come, I will send thee into Egypt."

Acts 7:34 KJV

"O God, since You have enabled me to do the simple things I can do, I have full trust in You to do the great things which I cannot."

Lillian Thrasher

Frances Willard, temperance leader
September 28, 1839–February 17, 1898

Frances Willard grew up in a strict, nondrinking Protestant home. She graduated from Northwestern Female College, later studied at the Sorbonne in Paris, and then pursued a career in education and was named dean of women at Northwestern University.

Miss Willard became interested in the women's movement in 1873 and decided to make temperance her life's work. She helped found the Women's Christian Temperance Union, became its president in 1879, and served there until her death.

As a writer, lobbyist, and orator, she helped build the antiliquor movement, not only in the United States but also in Canada and Western Europe.

Under Willard, the W.C.T.U. had two rallying cries: to rescue the problem drinker and pass preventive social measures. Willard believed it was easier to prevent someone from becoming an alcoholic than it was to heal one. Through prohibition, she argued, the American family would be preserved from the evil influences of alcohol.

She argued persuasively that drinking was linked to prostitution, social diseases, poverty, and other evils. "Drinking father/drinking son" was a cycle that prohibition would stop.

Miss Willard declared that women were "the guardians of the sanctity of the home" and, therefore, had to become involved politically in promoting social reform. This led to a tie-in with other reform movements, particularly women's suffrage.

Toward the end of her life, Miss Willard began to modify some of her more radical statements. She had come to believe that alcoholism was as much an effect as a cause of poverty.

After Frances Willard's death, the W.C.T.U. restricted itself to prohibition and abandoned the auxiliary causes. Prohibition became the law of the land through passage of a constitutional amendment in 1919.

"You armed me with strength for battle; you made my adversaries bow at my feet."

Psalm 18:39

Key Thought: Whether or not we live to see a cause succeed during our lifetime is immaterial. Our task is to commit ourselves to giving life to the cause now.

September 29

Naomi Norsworthy, psychologist
September 29, 1877–December 25, 1916

After teaching third graders for three years, Naomi Norsworthy enrolled at Teacher's College, Columbia, and completed her Ph.D. in 1904. The publication of her doctoral dissertation, *The Psychology of Mentally Deficient Children*, in 1906 greatly enhanced her academic career at Columbia. Norsworthy demonstrated that feeblemindedness was a matter of intelligence not a type of mental illness. She was a pioneer in the study of mental age.

Two of her books, *How to Teach* (1917) and *The Psychology of Childhood* (1918), were significant contributions to the educational psychology field. However, Naomi was more remembered for her classroom skills. As a teacher at Columbia, she helped popularize the theories of Thorndike, Dewey, and McMurray.

Naomi Norsworthy found time to be an adviser, counselor, and friend to an emerging generation of educational psychologists.

"We who are strong ought to bear with the failings of the weak."

Romans 15:1

Father, for those who help us understand the intricacies of the human mind, we thank You. Remind us that some of the labels we use—based on perceived mental capacity—may be discriminatory and hurtful.

September 30

Anne Henrietta Martin, suffragist
September 30, 1875–April 14, 1951

When women gained the right to vote through the prolonged efforts of suffragists like Carrie Catt, Mabel Vernon, and Gail Loughlin, some people appreciated the logical next step of women running for office. Although Jeanette Rankin had already been elected to the House of Representatives, Anne Martin was the first woman to run for the United States Senate.

Her name was not a new one in Nevada politics. Anne had participated in the militant suffragist movement and had headed the Nevada Equal Franchise Society, which had worked for the successful ratification of the state suffrage amendment. In 1916, she became chairman of the National Women's Party. In that position,

"On my servants, both men and women, I will pour out my Spirit in those days."

Joel 2:29

Key Thought: In a world that had concluded a woman's

241

Miss Martin organized intense congressional lobbying and adopted the British strategy of holding those in office responsible for delays in passage.

Anne was arrested in 1917 for picketing the White House but used the situation to arouse public indignation against Woodrow Wilson.

Though she only pulled 20 percent of the vote in 1918, she ran again and lost in 1920. However, her campaigns were laboratories for women to test their political skills in a male-dominated world.

Martin's dream was that women would not just vote but would get involved in every stage of the political process.

place was in the home, Anne Martin countered, "the Senate, too." Though she was never elected to political office, Anne Martin was not discouraged from trying. Help us, Father, to have that type of tenacity.

October 1

Esther Boise Van Deman, archaeologist
October 1, 1862–May 3, 1937

Esther Van Deman, although engaged three times to be married, could never get comfortable with the loss of freedom she thought occurred in marriage. She graduated from the University of Michigan in 1892 and earned a master's degree the following year. During the next fourteen years, she taught at Wellesley, then worked on her doctorate at the University of Chicago. After completing her Ph.D. and three more years teaching at Mount Holyoke, she studied in Rome as a fellow at the American School of Classical Studies. When Miss Van Deman returned to the country, she was annoyed by the restrictions on faculty and fought several battles with administrators at Goucher College. Then, in 1906, Dr. Van Deman joined the faculty at the American School in Rome and spent the rest of her life teaching in Italy.

Van Deman's career took an important turn in 1907 when she realized that the bricks in the doorway of the Atrium Vestaem differed from those in the walls. She concluded that periods of construction were demonstrated by varieties of bricks. Later in life, fearing that she would not live to publish her work on the construction of antiquities, she organized her notes so that the compilation could be completed by other scholars after her death.

"To all in Rome who are loved by God and called to be saints."

Romans 1:7

Loyalty was a strong theme of Esther's life. She felt her friends could do no wrong. With a colorful personality, she was an inveterate talker, perhaps a result of her loneliness.

Miss Van Deman gave freely of herself and her time to scholars and students from around the world. Her system of dating ancient construction was a significant contribution to the field of archaeology.

Key Thought: The past has lessons to enrich the present. However, it shares its secrets only with the diligent and persistent thinker.

October 2

James Wilson Bright, philologist
October 2, 1852–November 29, 1926

Growing up in a single-parent family, James Wilson Bright desperately wanted a college education. He graduated from Lafayette College and earned a Ph.D. at Johns Hopkins in 1882. After teaching and additional study in Germany, he eventually returned to Johns Hopkins and helped develop the English department's reputation in philology, the study of the use of language in literature.

In his long tenure as professor, Bright trained fifty-five Ph.D. candidates and helped them launch careers as teachers and scholars. They in turn developed outstanding academic English departments in their respective universities.

Bright served on the board of editors of *Modern Language Notes* for twenty-nine years and as editor in chief for nine years. He wrote *The Anglo-Saxon Reader, The Gospel of St. Luke in Anglo-Saxon, The Gospel of St. John in Anglo-Saxon*, and *The Gospel of St. Mark in Anglo-Saxon*.

James Bright is primarily remembered as the founder of the scientific study of English. One biographer observed, "James Bright lived all his life as a graduate student"—writing, reading, and modeling excellence.

"And the words of the Lord are flawless, like silver refined in a furnace of clay, purified seven times."

Psalm 12:6

Key Point: Learning cannot be bequeathed. However, a commitment to excellence can be given away like a prophet's mantle.

Clara Dutton Noyes, nurse
October 3, 1869–June 3, 1936

At the onset of the American Civil War, nurses were scarce. Nursing was a profession for men only; women were forced to watch from a distance. That changed through the efforts of Dorothea Dix and others. After the war, nursing became a profession open to women, particularly single women.

Clara Noyes was one of the outstanding nurses at the turn of the century. After graduating from the Johns Hopkins School of Nursing in 1896, Clara was asked to stay another year as head nurse. In 1897, she left Baltimore to head St. Luke's Hospital in New Bedford, Massachusetts. Under Miss Noyes's leadership, the hospital went through a large expansion and revised its nurses' training programs.

For three years she headed the National League of Nursing Education, which monitored and established standards for nursing programs in the United States. As war in Europe seemed more likely, Jane Delano asked her to supervise the military relief operations for the American Red Cross. Miss Noyes acted decisively to recruit, mobilize, and deploy thousands of nurses for fifty-four base hospitals.

After the war, Clara became director of field nursing, and in 1919 she followed Miss Delano as head of the nursing division of the American Red Cross, a position she held until 1936.

She also gave leadership to the American Nursing Association as its president from 1918 to 1922 and chaired the National Committee of the Red Cross Nursing Service. In 1923, Clara Noyes received the prestigious Florence Nightingale Medal from the International Red Cross.

"Many women were there, watching from a distance. They had followed Jesus from Galilee to care for his needs."

Matthew 27:55

Father, we take nursing care for granted today. Thank You for those early pioneers who established schools and curriculums and standards, who gave themselves to making nursing an honorable profession of servanthood. Thank You for those who do the same today.

Harriet Auber, hymn writer
October 4, 1773–January 20, 1862

In Hoddesdon, England, Harriet Auber lived a secluded life, rooming with another single adult, Mary Jane Mackenzie, who was also a poet.

Harriet had a deep concern that many of the psalms sung in churches of the day were too stilted. One Sunday, as she sat alone in her bedroom reflecting on the pastor's sermon, the phrase "our blest Savior" kept coming to mind. Unable to find paper or pen, Harriet took her diamond ring and scratched some words on a windowpane. That poem became the British hymn "Our Blest Redeemer, Ere He Breathed."

Years after her death, an antique dealer tried to buy the windowpane, but the owner of the home refused. Eventually it was stolen.

Harriet Auber wrote many hymns but seldom shared them with others. However, Charles Spurgeon included twenty of her hymns in his *Collection of Hymns*, which was popular in the last part of the nineteenth century in Britain.

The hymn Harriet Auber scratched on a windowpane is a reminder to single adults to be prepared "in season and out of season," because we never know when one of those life-changing thoughts will strike.

"Be prepared in season and out of season; correct, rebuke and encourage—with great patience and careful instruction."

2 Timothy 4:2

Father, teach us to be ready for that moment of inspiration so we will not waste it.

Frank Harris Hitchcock, postmaster general
October 5, 1869–August 25, 1935

After graduation from Harvard University in 1891, Frank Hitchcock began working for the Treasury Department, then later worked as a biologist for the Department of Agriculture. He earned his law degree from Columbian University and was admitted to the District of Columbia bar in 1894.

For the next seven years he worked in the Department of Commerce and Labor. In July 1904, he was

"All a man's ways seem right to him, but the Lord weighs the heart."

Proverbs 21:2

245

chosen assistant secretary of the Republican National Committee and in 1908 became an assistant postmaster general.

Hitchcock managed William Howard Taft's presidential campaign in 1908 and in June of that year became chairman of the Republican National Committee.

With Taft's victory, he was appointed postmaster general. Between 1909 and 1913, he initiated airmail delivery, instituted the postal savings system, and managed the budget so that the post office was left with a small surplus (it was in deficit when he took office).

Hitchcock moved to New York City to practice law in 1914 and managed the preconvention political campaigns of Charles Hughes in 1916, Leonard Wood in 1920, and Senator Hiram Johnson in 1924—all of which were unsuccessful.

In 1928, he moved to Tucson, Arizona, and became owner and publisher of the Tucson *Daily Citizen*.

Key Thought: In the world of politics, it is assumed you have to be married. Hitchcock proved otherwise. Am I missing opportunities to make a difference because I am waiting for a spouse?

October 6

William Batchelder Bradbury, musician
October 6, 1816–January 6, 1868

William Bradbury inherited his musical ability from his parents, who were known as excellent singers. As a boy, Bradbury quickly mastered any musical instrument he touched, but he never saw a piano or organ until he moved to Boston when he was seventeen.

In 1841, Bradbury became the organist at the First Baptist Church of New York City. He organized free singing classes patterned after those of Lowell, with whom he studied in Boston. He also organized music festivals with as many as one thousand musicians performing.

William wrote singing books for his schools, his first being *The Young Choir* (1841), followed by *Mendelssohn Collection* (1849) and *Psalmista* (1851). Many of the books were incredible sellers: *The Jubilee* (1858) sold 200,000 copies; *Fresh Laurels* (1867) sold 1.2 million; and *The Golden Chain* sold approximately 2 million. More than fifty books were prepared under

"Show me Your ways, O Lord; Teach me Your paths. Lead me in Your truth and teach me. . . ."

Psalm 25:4, 5 NKJV

his editorship. Although many music critics of the day blasted Bradbury's "sugared American psalmody," the people who were singing were singing Bradbury's tunes.

In 1854, William and his brother founded the Bradbury Piano Company, which became highly successful.

Two of his compositions have remained all-time favorites for believers: "Just as I Am" and "He Leadeth Me, O Blessed Thought."

Key Thought: Bradbury became an organist although he had never seen a piano before the age of seventeen. It's never too late to accept new challenges.

October 7

Martha McChesney Berry, college founder
October 7, 1866–February 27, 1942

If anyone seemed to have a bright future, it was Martha Berry. Someday she would marry well, have many children, and be the mistress of a large plantation home. All her friends in northern Georgia expected as much from Miss Martha.

One Sunday, Martha was surprised to find three mountain children admiring the playhouse in her yard. She invited them into the playhouse and taught them stories from the Bible. The next Sunday they returned with more children. When more than forty children began attending these informal sessions, Martha moved her class to an abandoned church.

By age thirty, Martha, who was a devout Episcopalian, determined to spend her life giving mountain children "ways to help themselves." She broke her engagement and set out to open her school, paying one teacher personally and supplementing the salaries of two others. Because the weather and distance kept many children from attending, Martha decided to open a boarding school for boys. The students would earn their educations by working at manual labor.

The Boys' Industrial School opened on January 13, 1902; applications flowed in from Georgia and other states. Martha could not begin to meet the need. As the school grew, so did Miss Berry's visits to Northern philanthropists. In no time, Andrew Carnegie and Theodore Roosevelt were writing checks for her school. Eventually, Henry Ford gave more than $4 million and

"Many women do noble things, but you surpass them all."

Proverbs 31:29

spent time teaching folk dancing on campus. Although some were against dancing, Miss Berry contended, "We take Mr. Ford's money. We're going to have to dance to his music."

In 1909, Martha opened a school for girls, realizing that her graduates were having trouble finding good wives. By 1926, her Sunday school class had become a junior college; by 1930, a senior college. By that time, the Berry schools had an annual enrollment of 1,000 and a waiting list of 3,000.

Miss Berry was often a bridesmaid in weddings of her students. Five times she was a bridesmaid "and thought that one day I would have the most beautiful wedding of all. Instead I stepped across the road and married my schools."

More than 14,000 people have graduated from Berry College in Rome, Georgia.

Father, from small beginnings come great dreams. We thank You for the legacy of Martha Berry. Remind us that the dream begins with obedience.

October 8

Mary Ruth Pennington, refrigeration specialist
October 8, 1872–December 27, 1952

Mary Pennington surprised her teachers in Nashville, Tennessee, when she announced she wanted to study chemistry. That was a strange request for a twelve-year-old girl in the 1800s.

In 1892, Mary completed the requirements for a degree in chemistry and biology at the University of Pennsylvania but was denied the degree because she was female. Instead, she was awarded a certificate of proficiency. By 1895, she finished her Ph.D. in chemistry under a catalog clause that allowed for "extraordinary cases." Mary soon discovered the great prejudice in hiring women scientists. Not to be defeated, she opened the Philadelphia Chemical Laboratory and began conducting bacteria sampling for area physicians. Soon Mary received an appointment to teach at the Woman's Medical College and became head of Philadelphia's bacteriology labs, where she was assigned to research the problem of impure milk that was being sold throughout the city.

After exhaustive research, Mary proposed standards for milk inspection that were adopted across the coun-

"She is like the merchant ships, bringing her food from afar."

Proverbs 31:14

try. She accomplished this by demonstrating that cleanliness and improved preservation ensured increased profits.

The head of the Bureau of Chemistry of the Department of Agriculture asked Mary to do independent research on refrigeration of foods. Her work impressed Dr. Harvey Wiley, who wanted to hire her. Mary took her civil service exams as M. E. Pennington and was appointed before the department discovered she was a female. In 1908, she was appointed chief of the food research laboratory.

Mary's laboratory had power over the warehousing, packaging, transporting, and distributing of food. Although her administrative load grew as her department increased, Miss Pennington remained a fixture in the labs. She gained notoriety during World War II by riding refrigerator cars across the country in order to monitor their temperatures; her standards on railroad refrigeration prevailed for a quarter of a century.

In 1922, Mary opened her own consulting firm. She still dabbled in the labs, turning her attention to frozen foods. She believed the freezing process would allow fruit, vegetables, and meat to be available all year, rather than just in season. Her research on refrigerators and frozen food processing resulted in the frozen foods industry of today.

Key Thought: One person can make a difference!

October 9

Bradford Torrey, ornithologist
October 9, 1832–October 6, 1912

After high school, Brad Torrey made shoes and taught school for several years. He worked in several Boston stores, but finally found a position as a clerk with the American Board of Commissioners of Foreign Missions. Although he had been curious about nature as a child, in Boston he became interested in birds. His first article, "With the Birds on Boston Common," was published in *Atlantic Monthly* in 1883, and that led to his first book, *Birds in the Bush*, in 1885.

In 1886, after sixteen years with the mission board, Brad joined the editorial staff of *Youth Companion*, which gave him the chance to write and travel. A string of nature books followed.

"Look at the birds of the air; they do not sow or reap or store away in barns, and yet your heavenly Father feeds them. Are you not much more valuable than they?"

Matthew 6:26

Torrey also edited the fourteen-volume journal of Henry David Thoreau, published in 1906.

Although he had no formal training in ornithology, Torrey was recognized as "a faithful and accurate field observer." He was the foremost authority on hummingbirds in the United States.

Brad Torrey's conversational essays delighted thousands of readers. He lived a solitary life, not unlike Thoreau, dying in his cabin near Santa Barbara in 1912.

Father, this is Your world. Thank You for those who remind us of the brilliance of Your creation. We are awed by Your love for us.

October 10

Arthur Lovejoy, philosopher and historian
October 10, 1873–December 30, 1962

After his first course in philosophy at the University of California, Arthur Lovejoy knew he'd discovered his life's work: philosophy. Despite his father's skepticism, Arthur entered Harvard graduate school to study with Josiah Royce and William James, the latter of whom had a profound impact on his philosophical writings and teachings. In 1897, with his master's, Lovejoy went to Paris and studied at the Sorbonne but never completed his doctorate.

After returning to teach at Stanford University, he resigned in 1901 in a controversy over academic freedom. Lovejoy was a lifelong advocate of the teacher's freedom. Over the next ten years, he taught at Washington University, Columbia, and the University of Missouri before finding an academic home at Johns Hopkins in 1910.

During those years, because of his father's influence, Lovejoy was involved in settlement-house work, which he described as "a mission of the trained to the untrained."

Lovejoy published frequently on issues related to the history of ideas, particularly the history of religious thought. He concentrated on the history of time, noting the Judeo-Christian concepts. However, in 1909, Lovejoy concluded that eternity was an obsolete concept.

Although born in Germany, Lovejoy was a strong patriot. As early as 1914, he warned of the German menace and threat of war. During this time, he was elected

"He has also set eternity in the hearts of men; yet they cannot fathom what God has done from beginning to end."

Ecclesiastes 3:11

president of the American Philosophical Association and advocated more scientific philosophical study and a more rational settlement of disputes between philosophers.

His major works were *The Revolt Against Dualism* (1930) and *The Great Chain of Being* (1936). Lovejoy argued that we lack the capacity for direct knowledge of the world; therefore, everything we know is indirect. He theorized that the absolute was obsolete.

After his retirement in 1938, Lovejoy again warned the nation of approaching war. He worked to get American financial assistance to the Allies as early as 1939. During the war, he was involved in sponsoring discussions of political and foreign policy issues.

He continued to write, capping his career with *Reflections on Human Nature*, in which he stated that the desire to be praised and the desire for self-esteem motivated all behavior. He believed these desires could be channeled into ethical behavior that benefited the individual and society.

Father, keep our ideas in line with Your Word and Your revelation to us through Your son, Jesus Christ.

October 11

Stark Young, critic and writer
October 11, 1881–January 6, 1963

Stark Young wanted to be an artist, but his Mississippi aristocrat father said no, such a life was inappropriate for a man of his social stature. Stark attended the University of Mississippi and went on to receive a master's degree from Columbia. For some sixteen years he taught at the University of Mississippi, Texas, and Amherst.

In 1921, Stark ended his academic career and moved to New York to become a free-lance writer. In 1922, he affiliated with *The New Republic*, a relationship that lasted twenty-five years. He critiqued theater and edited culturally related articles, quickly carving out a niche in the New York literary scene. In 1926, Young published his first novel, *Heaven Trees*, about life on a plantation in northern Mississippi.

Two other novels on the South, *The Torches Flare* (1928) and *River House* (1920), revealed Young's deep-

"The Lord blessed the latter part of Job's life more than the first."

Job 42:12

seated conflict over his Southern roots. In 1934, he published his best novel, *So Red the Rose.* The *New York Tribune* called the novel "a memorial wreath laid before a cherished tradition and way of life."

Although Young had been denied art lessons, in his sixties he took up painting. His work was well received in exhibits. Stark Young died at eighty-one.

Father, with You we always have a future. Make this day a good day.

October 12

Mabel Thorp Boardman, Red Cross leader
October 12, 1860–March 17, 1946

Mabel Boardman attended private schools and spent most of her twenties in travel and volunteer work. A four-year stint in Europe while her uncle was ambassador to Germany sparked Mabel's interest in politics and international affairs.

When she returned to the country, Mabel became involved in efforts to recruit and supply army nurses for the Spanish-American War. She became concerned by efforts to reorganize the American Red Cross, which, under the direction of founder Clara Barton, had performed poorly in the war. Mabel joined the board of the Red Cross and began lobbying for change. In 1902, she suggested expanding the board to diffuse the power of Miss Barton and her followers. Barton and her supporters countered with a resolution making Miss Barton president for life.

Mabel enlisted the support of President Taft, who promptly severed all government ties with the Red Cross. Then Congress investigated charges of mismanagement, which resulted in Barton's resignation. A new board was elected in 1904.

Mabel returned to serve on the board. Under a new congressional charter, she traveled the country, recruiting prominent citizens to local and state committees. Mabel launched the Red Cross lifesaving and first-aid programs, involved the Red Cross in military preparedness planning, and hired a professional staff to develop disaster and relief programs. She built the national headquarters in Washington, D.C., and raised a permanent endowment for the organization.

"Give her the reward she has earned, and let her works bring her praise at the city gate."

Proverbs 31:31

Boardman served as a volunteer, declining the chairmanship of the executive committee. During the days before the United States entered World War I, the Red Cross sent supplies to all countries in Europe. Boardman had difficulty ensuring the neutrality of the Red Cross, and others stepped in to guide the organization through a newly created Red Cross War Council. After the war, Mabel devoted herself to organizing Red Cross Volunteer Special Services and occasionally participating in the debate about the future of the Red Cross.

Boardman retired from the National Red Cross in 1940, convinced that younger hands would be needed to lead the organization through the next war.

Mabel Boardman "salvaged a floundering organization, drastically reformed its structure, and transformed it into a major and highly respected national institution."

Father, in the midst of a large organization, it's hard to believe we can make a difference. Remind us of the contribution of Mabel Boardman.

October 13

Arethusa Hall, educator and author
October 13, 1802–May 24, 1891

Arethusa Hall was raised by her half-sister, Apphia, after the death of her parents. Apphia's husband, a newspaper editor, tutored Arethusa and encouraged her to read and to think for herself. She began teaching in area academies until a carriage accident in 1831 made her an invalid for a number of years.

Arethusa was influenced by her cousin, Samuel Hall, a well-known educational innovator. She joined the faculty of Brooklyn Female Academy in 1849 and two years later helped found the Brooklyn Heights Seminary, an innovative school for girls. There Arethusa instituted one of the nation's first courses in the history of English literature—the forerunner of today's required classes in English literature—and also in the history of art.

Arethusa Hall also found time to contribute to the religious literature of the day, writing *Thoughts of Blaise Pascal* (1846) and *A Manual of Morals* (1849), the latter a book of ethics designed for children.

"I tell you the truth, unless you change and become like little children, you will never enter the kingdom of heaven."

Matthew 18:3

Key Point: If you can read this, thank a teacher.

253

Laura Askew Haygood, missionary
October 14, 1845–April 20, 1900

Laura Haygood was born into a prominent Methodist family and was heavily influenced by Atticus, her brother, who became an influential bishop. Laura graduated from Wesleyan College in 1864. Soon she opened a private school for girls in postwar Atlanta; in 1872, she began teaching at the Girls' High School and then spent seven years as its principal. In 1882, Laura became the first president of the Trinity House Mission Society, which established a training school that taught sewing skills to poor unemployed women and offered child care and residence for the homeless.

When her mother died in 1883, Laura felt free to move on to another phase of service. She accepted a call from the Women's Board of Foreign Missions of the Methodist Church, South, to serve in China. In November 1884, Laura arrived in Shanghai and immersed herself in language study. With her educational background, she was assigned to supervise day schools and to develop a normal school to train Chinese women teachers. She established a home for missionaries and a boarding school for children of upperclass Chinese families. Laura financed the program by selling ten-dollar "stocks" through missionary societies across the South.

Eventually, Laura became director of missions for the Women's Board in China. Because of the climate, she was soon forced to return to the United States for two years to regain her health. She spent the time raising funds to support the mission. In 1896, when Miss Haygood returned to China, she became the Women's Mission Board agent over all of China. The work was spread across five cities, and the travel demands of the job affected Laura's health. By 1899, she was confined to her room but continued to work.

Laura Haygood's death in April 1900 was mourned by the Chinese, who had lost a much-loved friend and advocate.

"O Lord save us; O Lord, grant us success. Blessed is he who comes in the name of the Lord."

Psalm 118:25, 26

Key Point: Just before death, Laura Haygood said: "Had I a thousand lives, I would willingly give them all to save China."

John Vanderlyn, artist
October 15, 1775–September 23, 1852

A blacksmith and wagon painter's shop is hardly a place to launch a career as a portrait painter, but that was the starting point for John Vanderlyn. He worked for two years as a print seller and took lessons from Archibald Robertson. One method of training in that day was copying the masters. John's copy of Gilbert Stuart's portrait of Aaron Burr was so good that Burr sent him to study with the original artist in Philadelphia. Burr then paid Vanderlyn to study five years in Paris.

John returned to the United States and painted two pictures of Niagara Falls that became quite popular. He returned to Paris, creating no small stir with his *Marius Amid the Ruins of Carthage*. After Napoleon honored him with a gold medal, Vanderlyn settled in Paris, painting copies of several masterpieces in the Louvre. In 1812, *Ariaone*, a nude, was a sensation in Europe.

Vanderlyn's popularity declined somewhat when he returned to America in 1815. He concentrated on painting portraits of Presidents Madison, Monroe, Jackson, and Taylor and such prominent Americans as John C. Calhoun, George Clinton, and Robert R. Livingston.

In 1832, Congress commissioned the artist to do a full-length copy of Stuart's *George Washington* for the Capitol rotunda. Five years later, he was commissioned to paint *The Landing of Columbus*. A stream of criticism and controversy erupted when it was disclosed that Vanderlyn hired a French painter to assist him.

The artist never recovered from the flap. Although his panoramas of Paris, Athens, and Versailles were exhibited in New York City, they did not win the acclaim of their audiences. He died, alone, in a rented room in 1852.

". . . whatever you do, do it all for the glory of God."

1 Corinthians 10:31

Help us to live so that our work will be consistent throughout our lives.

October 16

Frederick Lucian Hosmer, hymn writer
October 16, 1840–June 6, 1929

After graduation from Harvard in 1862, Frederick Hosmer spent seven years teaching before attending the Harvard Divinity School. Ordained in 1869, he pastored churches in Massachusetts, Illinois, Ohio, and Missouri before finally settling in Berkeley, California.

Hosmer was a radical liberal thinker, somewhat drawn to mysticism. He wrote a large number of hymns. With his friend William Channing Gannett he wrote *The Thought of God in Hymns and Poems* and *The Way of Life*.

He also lectured on hymnology at Harvard.

"Let the word of Christ dwell in you richly as you teach and admonish one another with all wisdom, and as you sing psalms, hymns and spiritual songs with gratitude in your hearts to God."

Colossians 3:16

Father, we thank You for all those past and present who have been gifted with the art of writing hymns.

October 17

Richard Mentor Johnson, vice president
October 17, 1780–November 19, 1850

Not all politicians set examples worthy of following. Richard Johnson, like many Southern slave owners, fathered children by two of his slaves. He passed the bar in 1802, and two years later entered the Kentucky House. In 1807, he was elected to Congress, where he served until 1819. During the War of 1812, he remained in office but obtained a commission as a colonel in the army and served under General W. H. Harrison. At the battle of Thames, he reportedly killed the great Indian chief Tecumseh.

Johnson served in the Senate from 1819 until 1829, when he was defeated for re-election. That same year

"Like a city whose walls are broken down is a man who lacks self-control."

Proverbs 25:28

he was elected to the House of Representatives, where he served until 1837.

Richard Johnson was the first vice president to be elected by the Senate, which chose him in 1836 when no candidate won a majority of the electoral votes. He served with President Martin Van Buren. In 1840, he ran on his own for vice president but lost.

Johnson returned to Kentucky and organized Columbian College, which is now Georgetown College of Kentucky. Just before his death, Richard Johnson was again elected to the Kentucky legislature.

Key Thought: You win some and you lose some. The important thing is to keep involved in the political process. Johnson could have retired from politics several times, but he didn't.

October 18

Ellen Browning Scripps, newspaper editor
October 18, 1836–August 3, 1932

After the death of her newspaperman father, schoolteacher Ellen Scripps began working in the family newspaper business. She invested heavily in the *Detroit Advertiser and Tribune*, which was managed by her brother James. After a disastrous fire, Ellen helped start a new paper, the *Detroit Evening News*; her involvement helped make the project a success. She also became a stockholder and writer for brother Edward's *Cleveland Penny Press*, in what became the Scripps-Howard chain of newspapers. On more than one occasion, Ellen's money saved the chain from financial disaster.

In 1891, Ellen moved to San Diego and lived on a ranch named Miramar. With careful investments in real estate, she made a sizable fortune, which she used to finance her philanthropy. She founded Scripps College and contributed substantially to Knox College and Bishop School for Girls.

Ellen gave several hundred acres of her ranch to the state of California for the creation of Torrey Pines State Park. She helped found the Marine Biological Association of San Diego, which in 1925 became the Scripps Institute of Oceanography at the University of California.

Ellen Browning Scripps helped shape the twentieth-

"She sees that her trading is profitable, and her lamp does not go out at night."

Proverbs 31:18

Key Thought: What a difference Ellen Scripps made—not only through her work in the newspaper world, but also through her generous

century newspaper world. She also pioneered the development of San Diego County. The writer of Proverbs would have marveled at her trading skills.

stewardship. Single adults can do the same today.

October 19

Amanda Theodosia Jones, inventor and poet
October 19, 1835–March 31, 1914

As early as 1854, when she was only nineteen, Amanda Jones's poems were recognized. She published *Utah and Other Poems* in 1861 and *Poems* in 1867. During the Civil War, a number of war songs written by Miss Jones appeared in Frank Leslie's *Illustrated Weekly* and were sung by the troops.

In 1873, Miss Jones began to research ways to preserve uncooked food in a vacuum, which had tremendous implications for the canning industry. Soon Miss Jones had patents for preserving fruits. In 1873, she perfected the process for removing air from fruit cans, thus reducing spoilage. Collectively, these patents made up the Jones Preserving Process.

Eventually Jones and some other women founded the United States Women's Pure Food Vacuum Preserving Company. Almost all the employees and managers were female. Eventually, Miss Jones sold her patents.

Amanda Jones returned to Kansas in 1882 and again began writing poetry. She also found time to subsidize reform programs for unhappy women and the protection of young girls.

Amanda Jones introduced something new: the idea that food did not have to be fresh to be eaten.

"Is there anything of which one can say, 'Look! This is something new'?"

Ecclesiastes 1:10

Father, we thank You that we can eat vegetables and fruits, not just during their natural growing season, but any day of the year. Make us thankful for that blessing in a world where so many go to bed hungry.

October 20

Ben Milam, Texas pioneer
October 20, 1788–December 7, 1835

The Texas we know today is a far cry from the Mexican colony where Ben Milam lived in 1835. The Mexicans had put military hero Steven Austin in a prison in Mex-

"He stood at the entrance to the camp and said,

ico. They were brutalizing the Anglo colonists. Now a group of Texas volunteers sat by their campfires, afraid.

That cold December night, a single adult walked into the camp. Ben Milam had helped Mexico gain its independence from Spain and had endured the hardships of battle in the name of freedom, but now he had a longing for Texas to be free.

Twice the soldiers around the campfire had voted against launching an attack against the Mexican soldiers in San Antonio. "It would be suicide!" some had said, lest their courage be questioned.

Ben had returned from a scouting expedition. If he didn't persuade them to fight, many would be headed home by daybreak. Milam drew a line on the ground and turned to face the men. "Who," he demanded, "will go with old Ben Milam to San Antonio?"

Three hundred and one men jumped to their feet. Ben Milam had an army and an enemy. Within hours they had marched on San Antonio, and they didn't stop until they had driven every Mexican soldier out. Within days, the Alamo had become the prize of the Texans.

Without courageous single adults like Ben Milam, Texas might still be part of Mexico. But it began with a challenge.

'Whoever is for the Lord, come to me.' And all the Levites rallied to him."

Exodus 32:26

Father, so often I want to know if You are on my side. But the question is: Am I on Your side?

October 21

William Henry Allen, naval officer
October 21, 1784–August 18, 1813

Even in short lives, some men leave an awesome example of courage under fire. William Henry Allen became a midshipman in the navy in April 1800. After several years of duty, he was assigned to the *Chesapeake*, which had several British navy deserters on board. When the British demanded they be turned over, Commodore James Barron refused. After a brief battle, Barron surrendered the prisoners and the ship.

Allen drew up a petition to the secretary of the navy protesting the commodore's behavior, which led to Barron's suspension from the navy. It was a gutsy action by a twenty-three-year-old lieutenant who planned on a navy career.

"How the mighty have fallen in battle!"

2 Samuel 1:25

A few years later, Allen's father approached him to protect some friends whom the navy had charged with violating the Embargo Act. Lieutenant Allen responded, "Nothing, my dear Sir, could give me more pleasure, but, Sir, had this been *your* vessel, the situation would have been precisely the same. It is impossible that I can be of the least service."

Promoted to full lieutenant, Allen joined the frigate *United States* and in the War of 1812 was instrumental in disabling the British frigate *Macedonian*. After its surrender, many assumed the *Macedonian* would sink, but Allen kept it afloat and got it back to port.

In 1813, he was assigned the command of the sloop *Argus* and sailed to France with the newly appointed American ambassador aboard. The British maritime fleet suffered enormous losses because of Allen.

Later in the same year, the *Argus* took on the British brig *Pelican*. During the battle, a cannonball blew off Allen's leg. He refused to leave the deck during battle but eventually lost consciousness. Although the *Argus* continued to fight after severe damage, the officer who was second in command surrendered.

William Allen died in a British prison at twenty-eight and was buried with full military honors.

Father, the temptation to compromise comes to all of us, sometimes in the voice of friends or family. Give us courage to stand firm for what is right.

October 22

Annie Louise Cady, contralto
October 22, 1831–April 4, 1921

When the great American politician James G. Blaine heard this young schoolteacher sing at a graduation, he urged her to immediately switch careers. Annie Cady heeded his advice, studied briefly in Portland, Maine, then went to Boston in 1859, where she was a student and church soloist for the next six years.

Loans from friends and a benefit concert provided funds for her European study, which was necessary for an operatic career. After one year of tutoring with Giovanni Corsi, motivated by her financial instability, she debuted in Copenhagen, performing as the gypsy Azucena in Verdi's *Il Trovatore*.

On April 12, 1870, Miss Cady appeared as Mafio Orsini

"Shout with joy to God, all the earth! Sing the glory of his name; make his praise glorious!"

Psalm 66:1, 2

in *Lucrezia Borgia*. She joined the Strakosch Concert Company and returned to the United States, where she made her American debut on September 19, 1870. Critics agreed that her long years of preparation had paid off. Anton Rubenstein, noted Russian pianist and composer, exclaimed after hearing her, "Miss Cady's voice is the most beautiful I have ever heard in the whole world."

She sang the role of Amneris in the first American performance of *Aida* and in 1877 sang Ortrud in *Lohengrin*, becoming the first American woman to sing a Wagnerian role in the United States.

In 1889, after lengthy trouble with her throat, she retired from the stage but continued to sing church music. In 1891, she retired completely from performing and married.

Father, for those voices that make musical notes on staffs become incredible beauty, we thank You.

October 23

Henrietta Mears, Christian educator
October 23, 1890–March 22, 1961

Henrietta Mears served as Christian education director of the First Presbyterian Church of Hollywood, California, from 1929 to 1961. Her first joy was the college class that attracted hundreds of college students and young adults on Sunday mornings and evenings and Wednesday nights. More than four hundred of her students went into full-time Christian ministry, and hundreds of others became active lay workers in local churches.

Henrietta was also concerned with children. In those days, all children, regardless of their age, were in the same classroom. Henrietta ended that by developing a graded curriculum and then founding Gospel Light Publishing Company to publish the materials. Because she believed in the value of camping, she founded the Forest Home Conference Center in the San Bernardino mountains of Southern California. There one Sunday afternoon she counseled a young discouraged minister named Billy Graham. He has often said Miss Mears was one of the three most influential people in his life.

When asked why she hadn't married, Henrietta said

"Let the redeemed of the Lord say this."

Psalm 107:2

261

she hadn't lived in the same time as the Apostle Paul and had not found anyone to match him. Henrietta added that she was in love once. She had cared for a young banker, but he had not shared her strong religious convictions and commitment, so she ended the relationship. She once wrote about her years as a single:

The marvelous thing has been ... that the Lord has always given me a beautiful home; He has given me thousands of children; the Lord has supplied everything in my life and I've never felt lonely ... I've never missed companionship. Through one experience after another the Lord has shown me that He had something peculiar and special for me to do. After I went through that final door, where it was just the Lord and myself, I've gone out into wide open spaces of people and things and excitement, and life has been an adventure. It has been a tremendous thing to see how the Lord has filled my life so abundantly with all these things and I just want to witness to the fact that *wherever* the Lord puts you, if He puts you on an island of the sea some place with Himself, He absolutely satisfies you.

Father, give us the courage to find out that You can absolutely satisfy us, too.

October 24

Sarah Josepha Hale, editor
October 24, 1788–April 30, 1879

The year 1822 looked dark and dismal for Sarah Hale, a young widow with five children. Her first effort to support her family was a millinery business, which failed in 1824. Then she decided to try writing, publishing her first novel, *Northwood*, in 1827.

Later that year, Mrs. Hale moved to Boston to edit *Ladies' Magazine*. Her literary skills attracted the attention of Louis A. Godey, who had established *Godey's Lady's Book*, and he offered her its editorship in 1837. Sarah Hale devoted herself and the magazine to "the progress of female improvement." Tremendously popular, it became a guidebook for women of the day. She

"Then little children were brought to Jesus for him to place his hands on them and pray for them."

Matthew 19:13

continued to write and is best known for her nursery rhyme, "Mary Had a Little Lamb."

Sarah was committed to the idea of a national day of thanksgiving, which she believed should be as traditional a celebration as the Fourth of July. November issues of her magazine carried strong editorials calling for such a day.

Each year, Sarah Hale personally wrote the governor of each state, requesting that he declare a thanksgiving holiday. Many rejected her idea on the basis of separation of church and state. The governor of Virginia called her ideas "theatrical claptrap."

Still, Sarah Hale lobbied on. By 1859, thirty states had Thanksgiving holidays on the last Thursday of November. Sarah turned her attention to a national declaration. On September 28, 1863, she wrote President Lincoln, asking him to proclaim an annual day of thanksgiving. On October 3, 1863, the persistence of one single adult paid off: Lincoln, on the heels of decisive Union victories at Gettysburg, proclaimed the last Thursday of November 1863 a day of thanksgiving.

Sarah wrote her last editorial at ninety.

And now, having reached my ninetieth year, I must bid farewell to my countrywomen, with the hope that this work of half a century may be blessed to the furtherance of their happiness and usefulness in their Divinely appointed sphere. New avenues for higher culture and for good works are opening before them, which fifty years ago were unknown. That they may improve these opportunities, and be faithful to their high vocation, is my heartfelt prayer.

Father, it took Sarah Hale thirty-six years to sell the idea of Thanksgiving Day. The next time we are tempted to give up on an idea, remind us of her persistence.

October 25

John Mankey Riggs, dentist
October 25, 1810–November 11, 1885

John Riggs had a habit of thinking for himself. He started a career as a blacksmith, then decided to prepare for the Episcopalian priesthood. He graduated from Hartford College in 1837, but because he had doubts about his call, he abandoned the pursuit of the ministry and became a school principal. Riggs next studied medicine

"He went to him and bandaged his wounds, pouring on oil and wine."

Luke 10:34

263

at Jefferson Medical College. Although he did not graduate, he took up the study of dentistry with Dr. Horace Wells, a noted dentist. He began practicing dentistry in 1840, and during the next twenty-five years, he was associated with several Hartford dentists. He opened his own practice at the age of sixty-seven.

Riggs was a strong promoter of preventive dental care. He specialized in treating *pyorrhea alveolaris,* eventually called Riggs' disease, and developed a special treatment approved by the American Dental Association. Riggs was recognized as an expert and spoke often to medical and dental societies.

On December 11, 1844, Riggs made dental history by participating in an experiment. He removed a tooth from his colleague Horace Wells's mouth while Dr. Wells was anesthetized with nitrous oxide gas. The experiment was judged a success when Wells testified that he had felt absolutely no pain. A new day in dental care had dawned.

Father, for those singles like John Riggs, who make medical and dental care more comfortable, we thank You.

October 26

Louisa Lee Schuyler, welfare worker
October 26, 1837–October 10, 1926

Born into a family of great wealth, Louisa Schuyler became a volunteer teacher for the Children's Aid Society at twenty-three. A year later, with the outbreak of the Civil War, there were tremendous opportunities for young women. Louisa went to work for the organization that became the United States Sanitary Commission, a forerunner of the American Red Cross. She gave of herself tirelessly during the war and was sent to Europe to rest at its conclusion.

However, when she returned from Europe in 1871, she became interested in the care and treatment of people in New York City's poorhouses. Louisa formed the State Charities Aid Association in 1872 to promote public visitation and inspection of state facilities. The group became responsible for the regulation of facilities and the advocacy of their patients.

In 1874, Miss Schuyler was involved with the lobby-

"The King will reply, 'I tell you the truth, whatever you did for one of the least of these brothers of mine, you did for me.' "

Matthew 25:40

ing that led to the creation of the nurses' training program at Bellevue Hospital, the first such program in America.

Then Louisa turned her attention to the needs of the insane. Although progress had been made since the days of Miss Dorothea Dix's scathing reports, much needed to be done, particularly in smaller cities. Through her insistence, conditions were improved.

Louisa was a trustee of the Russell Sage Foundation and active in its commitment to the prevention of blindness. She chaired the committee that eventually became the National Committee for the Prevention of Blindness. Ironically, Miss Schuyler went blind.

Associates described Louisa Schuyler as having "the mind of a lawyer and the willpower of a captain of industry." She gave sixty-six years of her life to remembering the needy.

Father, how could one woman have accomplished so much? Dare we ask why we have accomplished so little?

October 27

Sharlott Hall, historian
October 27, 1870–April 9, 1943

A child of the trail west, Sharlott Hall pinned her Christmas stockings on the side of her parents' covered wagon, hoping that Santa Claus would find her. Her father bought a ranch in Arizona, and Sharlott loved the outdoor life. Where others saw only desert, the young girl saw beauty. "I do enjoy everything—just the sunshine on the sand is beautiful enough to keep me giving thanks for eyes to see with. And all day long, I'm so glad . . . that God let me be an outdoor woman."

Sharlott found success with the publication of some of her poetry in Phoenix and Prescott papers as well as Eastern periodicals. In 1903, she moved to Los Angeles to become an editor of *Land of Sunshine* magazine. That assignment brought her into contact with many prominent Western writers.

When she returned to Arizona, she joined in the battle to prevent Arizona and New Mexico from being made into one state. Her poem on the subject became part of the congressional debate and was instrumental in defeating the proposal.

"The desert and the parched land will be glad; the wilderness will rejoice and blossom."

Isaiah 35:1

Sharlott wanted to be appointed clerk of the territorial legislature in 1909 but was defeated. She continued to lobby for better care of Arizona's historic and prehistoric artifacts. What the state needed was an official historian; however, some were reluctant to have a woman in that position. A state historian's office was created, but a man was chosen. Two days later, President Taft appointed a new governor, and in October, Sharlott Hall was appointed state historian.

The appointment became something of a political *cause célèbre* and led to bold headlines in the *Los Angeles Times,* WOMAN GETS PUBLIC OFFICE. Disgruntled legislators then tried to create a plank in the first draft of the constitution for statehood that would bar a woman from holding political office.

The next year Sharlott's *Cactus and the Pine: Songs of the Southwest* was published to great reviews. But soon she returned to her family's small ranch to care for her mother. She went through great depression there.

Over the years Miss Hall collected artifacts, which she moved into the old governor's mansion in Prescott in 1928 to create a museum.

Key Thought: "No generation lives for itself alone, but tomorrow rests upon the shoulders of today—as today rests on the shoulders of yesterday."

Sharlott Hall

October 28

Anna Elizabeth Dickinson, orator
October 28, 1842–October 22, 1932

After her conversion in a Methodist church, Anna Dickinson became concerned about the issue of slavery. As early as 1856—at fourteen years of age—she wrote an article for William Lloyd Garrison's *The Liberator.* In 1860, the eighteen-year-old made her first public speech before the Pennsylvania Anti-Slavery Society and won immediate encouragement from abolitionists. Her lecture on "The Rights and Wrongs of Women" created quite a stir across New England in 1861–1862. She lost her job at the United States Mint when she publicly denounced General McClellan.

After working with soldiers in field hospitals, Anna spoke on hospital life to large audiences. She was also

"My heart is stirred by a noble theme as I recite my verses for the king; my tongue is the pen of a skillful writer."

Psalm 45:1

effective on the stump for Republican candidates, drawing some five thousand to hear her speak at New York's Cooper Institute.

On January 16, 1864, she spoke in the House of Representatives, to an audience that included Abraham Lincoln and legislators who had won their office through her support.

She made about $20,000 annually from her lectures in which she attacked Mormonism, the double standard, assorted social evils, and large corporations.

Miss Dickinson's popularity faded, due to her age and her involvement with many controversial causes.

However, in 1888, the Republican National Committee brought her out of retirement to campaign against President Grover Cleveland, whom she denounced as "the hangman of Buffalo."

She spent the last forty years of her life in obscurity.

Father, remind us of the gifts You have given all of us, and make us wise stewards.

October 29

Othniel Charles Marsh, paleontologist
October 29, 1831–March 18, 1899

Othniel Marsh was raised by a single aunt after his mother's death when he was three. The aunt had a strong positive influence on the child. He graduated from Yale, then went on to study in Berlin, Breslau, and Heidelberg, Germany.

In 1866, he was appointed a professor of paleontology at Yale, the first endowed professorship in this field in America. In 1870, Marsh and thirteen associates, under military escort, traveled through the West, exploring the Pliocene deposits in Nebraska and the Micene in Colorado. They traveled across Wyoming and into California. The trips gained him recognition as the major American vertebrate paleontologist. Marsh was so enthusiastic, one biographer noted, that he gathered artifacts more rapidly than he could analyze them. One associate observed, "He not only had the means and the inclination, but entered every field of acquisition with the dominating ambition to obtain everything there was in it, and leave not a scrap behind."

"The eye never has enough of seeing."

Ecclesiastes 1:8

Although he published many articles, Marsh was known for his *Introduction and Succession of Vertebrate Life in America.*

Marsh was instrumental in making the collecting of fossils a scientific pursuit. Due to his influence (and that of the students he trained), museum displays were not simply a collection of bones but of entire skeletons.

Othniel Marsh was president of the National Academy of Sciences from 1883 to 1895 and was affiliated with the United States Geological Survey for seventeen years.

Father, guard our eyes today and our hearts.

October 30

Adelaide Ann Procter, poet
October 30, 1825–February 2, 1864

Having a father who was a poet opened the door for Adelaide Procter to explore her gift of writing. Miss Procter became a friend of Charles Lamb and Charles Dickens. Her first poetry was published under the pen name Mary Berwick in *Household Words*, edited by Dickens. She wrote a number of popular songs and hymns, such as "My God, I Thank Thee, Who Hast Made."

She is most remembered for the words to "The Lost Chord."

"How good is a timely word!"

Proverbs 15:23

> Seated one day at the organ,
> I was weary and ill at ease,
> And my fingers wandered idly
> Over the noisy keys.
>
> But I struck one chord of music
> Like the sound of a great Amen.

Adelaide Procter helped found the Society for Promoting the Employment of Women. Her collection of poems, *A Chaplet of Verse*, was sold to raise funds for a women's shelter, a cause close to her heart. In her day, her poetry was as popular as Tennyson's.

Father, for the gift of words, we give You thanks. For those who can take words and turn them into music, we praise You.

October 31

Josephine Louise Newcomb, philanthropist
October 31, 1816–April 7, 1901

Josephine Newcomb's mother and father died when she was a child; as an orphan, she went to New Orleans to live with a sister. Life was hard for Louise. She married young, lost a son in infancy, and was widowed at age fifty. Her husband's family contested the will and made relationships strained for the single parent. The final blow came in 1870, with the death of her beloved daughter, Sophie, at fifteen.

To deal with her grief, Josephine traveled. Eventually she decided to participate in another's dream. Paul Tulane, a Presbyterian bachelor, had given money in 1884 to convert the University of Louisiana into a private institution. Newcomb decided to finance a women's college as part of that university. Her initial gift of $100,000 in October 1886 made the women's program a reality.

For the last fifteen years of her life, the H. Sophie Newcomb College of Tulane University had first priority in her life. She gave money throughout those years and left $2.7 million in her will for the school's future.

Louise Newcomb was a careful steward of the money her husband had left her. She loved to give. Her biographer noted, "Wherever she saw that money was needed, she gave freely." The college she founded has educated thousands of women. She and her daughter have not been forgotten.

Josephine Louise Newcomb died on Easter 1901.

"For the living know that they will die, but the dead know nothing; they have no further reward, and even the memory of them is forgotten."

Ecclesiastes 9:5

Father, help us to invest our lives and our resources in things that will outlive us.

November 1

Mary Adelaide Nutting, nurse and educator
November 1, 1858–October 3, 1948

Mary Nutting graduated in the first class of nurses trained at Johns Hopkins Hospital and eventually became principal of the school of nursing, where she introduced many reforms. In 1895, she instituted the

"And in the church God has appointed . . . those having gifts of healing,

269

eight-hour day for nurses and developed a three-year training program for nursing education.

In 1907, Mary became the first professor of nursing in the world, accepting a position at Columbia University. During the next eighteen years, her contributions were enormous. She elevated the standards of basic nursing education and established professional organizations. She co-authored a four-volume *History of Nursing*, developed administrative models, and coordinated nursing services during World War I. Nutting also helped found the *American Journal of Nursing* in 1900.

One biographer noted that nursing developed as a respected profession because of Nutting's "devotion, courage, skill and magnificent perseverance."

Nutting "held many nurses to irksome and difficult tasks long after their own desire for release was most compelling—yet not quite so compelling as the urge of her example and advice."

those able to help others, those with gifts of administration."

1 Corinthians 12:28

Father, thank You for all those single adults—past and present—equipped with the gift of healing and the gift of helping others.

November 2

Mollie Bailey, circus owner
November 2, 1844–October 2, 1918

"The show must go on." When Mollie Bailey's husband, Gus, died in June 1896, she knew that somehow their circus had to continue. To quit would disappoint thousands of fans in small towns across Texas.

Some circuses in those days had a poor reputation, but not Mollie Bailey's. She made no claims of ferocious animals, unusual freaks, or death-defying acts. She offered a clean show in each small town where she stopped.

Mollie always had free seats available for orphans and Confederate veterans. She insisted on buying all her supplies locally and returned a percentage of the profits to the town, mainly to Confederate veterans' needs, charities, and churches. She financed fifty church buildings in Texas.

Molly required her performers to maintain high standards. She did not smoke, drink, or use slang. If she smelled whiskey on a worker's breath, he was fired; on his second use of profanity, he was unemployed.

"Do not grieve, for the joy of the Lord is your strength."

Nehemiah 8:10

Molly's work was tough. In one town a constable named Fred Cook met her train and told her she couldn't stay in town for more than an hour. She reminded him that Texas was in America. When he wouldn't budge, she snapped, "You are narrow, ignorant and mean. I'll move the show to the next town and lose this night. I'd rather not show anything after this insult."

Then she ordered him off her train, warned him never to speak to her again, and told him that if she were his size she would have thrown him out personally. Mollie's circus never played the town again.

As a widow, Mollie Bailey dedicated her life to bringing some excitement to the folks of Texas.

Father, when we are tempted to quit, give us the courage to continue. Let us meet our challenges with joy, and let us leave the results to You.

November 3

Stephen F. Austin, founder of Texas
November 3, 1793–December 27, 1836

In January 1822, a twenty-nine-year-old single adult, Stephen F. Austin, planted the first legal settlement of Anglo-Americans in Texas. From 1822 to 1828, before the establishment of constitutional government, Austin was the government. "My ambition," he wrote, "has been to redeem Texas from its wilderness state . . . in spreading over its North American population, enterprise, and intelligence; in doing this, I hope to make the fortunes of thousands and my own. . . ." If only he could see Texas today!

Biographers credit Austin's success to his patience and intelligence. He pushed back the Indians, mapped the Texas Territory, and kept a steady influx of settlers coming for a fresh start. That meant settling boundary disputes, establishing schools, and maintaining law and order.

In 1834–1835, Austin spent eighteen months as a prisoner in a Mexican jail for his involvement in the growing movement for Texas's political independence from Mexico. Later, the first provisional government sent him to Washington to negotiate recognition and financing, and Austin enlisted sympathy from the Jackson administration for eventual annexation.

"Then Caleb silenced the people before Moses and said, 'We should go up and take possession of the land, for we can certainly do it.' "

Numbers 13:30

271

He returned to Texas in June 1836 but was defeated for the presidency of the independent state of Texas by General Sam Houston. Austin served with distinction as secretary of state until his death.

Stephen Austin "opened the doors to colonization" for thousands of ambitious American families who wanted land at cheap prices. When asked why he didn't marry, Austin explained, "I was married to my colonists."

Father, it's easy to forget that some things are accomplished only when someone is willing to pay the price. Remind us of that principle.

November 4

James Montgomery, hymn writer
November 4, 1771–April 30, 1854

James Montgomery was dismissed from school because he wouldn't concentrate on his studies; he was always writing poetry. As a young man, he had a succession of jobs. He became an assistant editor of the *Sheffield [England] Register* in 1794, when he was twenty-three. Eventually he became owner and changed the name to *The Iris*.

Montgomery was a man of strong convictions; he was imprisoned for printing a poem celebrating the fall of the Bastille in France. He was a blistering opponent of slavery and a great supporter of various missionary enterprises and the Bible Society.

James's one desire was to write poetry, and his work was praised by leading poets such as Wordsworth, Byron, and Emerson. Some thought he might eventually be England's Poet Laureate. Toward the end of his life, when asked which of his poems he thought would be best remembered, Montgomery responded, "None, sir. Nothing except perhaps a few of my hymns."

Montgomery was a strong advocate of using hymns in worship in a time when many conservatives insisted on singing only the psalms. He and Thomas Cotterill composed the first hymnal endorsed by the Archbishop of New York around 1814. Montgomery is best known for his Christmas hymn:

"The Lord is my strength and my shield; my heart trusts in him, and I am helped. My heart leaps for joy and I will give thanks to him in song."

Psalm 28:7

> Angels, from the realms of glory,
> Wing your flight o'er all the earth;
> Ye who sang creation's story,

Now proclaim Messiah's birth:
Come and worship, come and worship,
Worship Christ, the newborn King.

Montgomery composed four hundred hymns. Just before he died, he said, "I would rather be the anonymous author of a few hymns which should become an imperishable inheritance to the people of God, than bequeath another epic poem to the world, which would rank my name with Homer, Virgil or Milton."

Father, "imperishable inheritance" sounds so sober in our disposable, toss-away society. Remind us that our days count and that we will be remembered for something.

November 5

Ida Tarbell, muckraker
November 5, 1857–November 8, 1944

Although she was keenly interested in biology, Ida Tarbell discovered there were no positions in that field for women. She taught school for two years instead and then began writing for a local paper in Pennsylvania.

In 1891, Ida traveled to Paris and researched the role of women in the French Revolution at the Bibliotheque Nationale. During this time she sent stories to a group of Midwestern newspapers. In 1892, she went to work at *McClure's* magazine, one of the leading periodicals of the day. Ida stayed with *McClure's* for twelve years and developed a wide readership.

In 1901, with *McClure's* encouragement, she began researching the business activities of John D. Rockefeller. Her work lasted five years and resulted in nineteen magazine articles and a two-volume history in 1904. Miss Tarbell indicted Rockefeller and the corporate arrogance, dishonesty, and political power of his Standard Oil Company. *The History of Standard Oil* was a literary bombshell that fueled political reformers such as Theodore Roosevelt.

The business world soon feared Miss Ida Tarbell. However, feminists criticized her because she would not support their movement. Tarbell thought women's rights could not be gained by laws, movements, and systems. She felt the movement was tainted by urban political bosses and trade unionists.

In 1912, Henry Ford hired Miss Tarbell to examine

"Like a partridge that hatches eggs it did not lay is the man who gains riches by unjust means."

Jeremiah 17:11

factory conditions. The muckraker was overwhelmed by Ford's mass production system, wage policies, and fair treatment of workers. She encouraged adoption of similar policies by other industrialists.

Ida Tarbell helped create a healthy distrust of big business.

November 6

Jeannie Maas Flexner, librarian
November 6, 1882–November 17, 1944

In 1905, Jeannie Flexner joined the staff of the Free Public Library in Louisville, Kentucky. From 1908 to 1909, she studied librarianship at Western Reserve University. After completing her studies, Miss Flexner returned to Louisville and was named supervisor of the circulation department.

Jeannie wanted to be more than a custodian of books. Her goal was to facilitate getting readers and good books together. She believed all citizens should have free access to books. As a result, she helped establish the first library for blacks in the South.

In 1928, Jeannie joined the staff of the New York City Public Library to formulate a reader's advisory service. She empathized with the plight of the immigrants, the poor, and the needy and worked tirelessly to get library cards for minorities and foreign-born readers.

In the 1930s, Miss Flexner and her staff spent a great deal of time helping the growing number of European immigrants fleeing the Nazis. She organized large shipments of books to the troops and to prisoners in German concentration camps. As the number of immigrants increased, Jeannie worked with the National Relief Service to develop a list of books designed to enhance adjustment to American life. She also made time to assess the reading needs of the poor in Harlem.

Jeannie Flexner contributed a great deal to the science of librarianship through articles and her *Making Books Work: A Guide to the Use of Libraries* (1943). She found a way to enrich the lives of the poor through reading.

"There will always be poor people in the land. Therefore I command you to be openhanded toward your brothers and toward the poor and needy in your land."

Deuteronomy 15:11

274

November 7

Lotta Crabtree, actress
November 7, 1847–September 25, 1924

Lotta Crabtree made her first appearance on stage in a California miners' camp at the age of eight. She was showered with gold nuggets. The next year Lotta and her mother joined a troupe of actors that traveled through the gold fields entertaining miners. In 1859, when she was twelve, Lotta moved to the variety halls of San Francisco, then went East.

Eventually she attracted the attention of John Brougham, who helped develop her dramatic skills. After her opening at Wallack's Theatre in New York City in 1867, her name became synonymous with theatrical success. Her triumphs included *Little Nell, The Little Detective, Nan the Good for Nothing, The Ticket of Leave Man, Heartsease*, and *Zip, Musette*.

Lotta's capacity to laugh and keep an audience laughing made the redhead a popular attraction to thousands of audiences during her career.

Offstage, she lived a lonely life, making few friends, perhaps because of her hectic travel schedule. Her companion for many years was her mother, who acted as her manager. Lotta left a large fortune to charity.

"Even in laughter the heart may ache, and joy may end in grief."

Proverbs 14:13

Key Thought: Laughing singles can still be hurting singles.

November 8

Eartha Mary Magdalene White, social worker
November 8, 1876–January 18, 1975

The sentence, "Put Your Duds In Our Suds!" was painted on the trucks of the Service Laundry Company, owned by a single adult named Eartha Mary Magdalene White. "We wash everything but a dirty conscience!" The laundry was only one of several enterprises in Jacksonville, Florida, owned and operated by Miss White.

The granddaughter of a slave, Miss White graduated from a women's finishing school in New York. She returned to Jacksonville and fell in love; however, one month before she was to marry, her fiancé died. In her grief, she poured herself into serving Jacksonville's

"If ye abide in me, and my words abide in you, ye shall ask what ye will, and it shall be done unto you."

John 15:7 KJV

black community, living her life by this motto: "Do all the good you can for all the people you can."

Throughout her life, Eartha raced from social project to project. In an era of no government funding, she became an accomplished fund-raiser. Once when a project needed money and she sought out a bank loan, the bank officer asked her marital status. He wanted a co-signer but was not prepared for her answer: "Being married only to Jesus and the cause of the kingdom . . . I have no husband but I am doing a good work and will surely repay the loan." Often when a project became accepted by the public, she turned it over to a board and moved on. "The Master has need of us in other fields," she would explain.

During World War I, when Florida's governor wanted to exclude blacks from the draft, Eartha fought for their right to serve in the army. She helped sell $300,000 in war bonds and coordinated recreation for black soldiers.

Eartha opened a tuberculosis hospital after she found a poor man dying in a car. She also founded the Clara White Mission, named for her mother, long before United Way was organized.

This angel of mercy became the "dumping ground and last resort" for the city's poor. Because she worried about boys becoming juvenile delinquents, she started a teen program and hired a director with her own funds. During the Depression she paid for soup kitchens.

Eartha was honored twice at the White House as the outstanding volunteer in America. She told reporters: "Get out of yourselves and let God use you. He has the solution to all of our problems."

At ninety-five, Eartha White testified, "God has worked wonderfully with me. He has miraculously taken care of me and He is going to continue to do so."

Key Point: "Today we must live as God's mouthpiece and prove to Him that He can depend on us."

Eartha White

November 9

Sally Louise Tompkins, nurse
November 9, 1833–July 25, 1916

When the Confederate army in Virginia had desperately wounded soldiers, it always sent them to Captain Sally's hospital.

"A good name is more desirable than great riches;

A prominent fixture in antebellum society in Virginia, Sally Tompkins had responded promptly to the plea for Richmond families to open their homes after the battle of Manassas in July 1861. Sally leased Judge John Robertson's large home and converted it, at her own expense, into a hospital. Demure, diminutive, and frail, Sally was at her hospital day in and day out. With a medicine chest strapped to her side and a Bible in her hand, she worked endlessly, directing volunteers, ordering supplies, and caring for the critically wounded. Late in the war, her only medicines were whiskey, turpentine, and loving care.

Still, Miss Tompkins's record speaks for itself: In 42 months she had 1,333 patients and lost only 79. When Confederate hospitals were placed under government control, President Jefferson Davis intervened to commission Sally a captain in the Confederate army, the only woman to hold a commission. Captain Tompkins returned her meager salary to the government and generously paid the costs of the hospital herself. She used her rank only when it was necessary to get supplies for her wounded men.

Although she was not physically attractive, Sally had many offers of marriage, which she graciously declined. After the war, she gave of herself and her money generously to the Episcopal Church.

At her death, Captain Sally Tompkins was buried with full military honors.

to be esteemed is better than silver or gold."

Proverbs 22:1

Father, this woman faithfully put others first. Help us to keep our priorities clear, even in times of crisis and confusion.

November 10

Alfred Howe Terry, general
November 10, 1827–December 16, 1890

Everybody loves a volunteer. Alfred Terry volunteered for the army after the Civil War broke out and fought at the first battle of Bull Run. Although he was a New Haven attorney, after his three-month enlistment was up, he returned to Connecticut and recruited enough volunteers to form the Seventh Connecticut Volunteers. By October 1862, Terry commanded all Union forces on Hilton Head Island, South Carolina. He won a decisive

"Do not pay attention to every word people say, or you may hear your servant cursing you."

Ecclesiastes 7:21

Union victory at Fort Fisher, North Carolina, which earned him Grant's praise, a transfer to the regular army, and a promotion to brigadier general.

After the war, Terry headed army operations in the Dakota Territory. His reputation was tarnished by his involvement in the massacre of General George A. Custer's troops on June 25, 1876. Had Custer exceeded Terry's orders? Terry chose silence rather than attempt to defend himself, accepting responsibility for the massacre. Following the incident, Terry transferred to the Northwest and provided army protection for the railroad-building crews. He also supervised the development and settling of what is now North and South Dakota and Montana.

Terry finished his military service with the rank of major general. He was a skilled strategist, known for his ability to obey superiors, cooperate with equals, and lead subordinates. Alfred H. Terry was the first general officer in the army who had not graduated from West Point.

Father, in the midst of criticism, remind us of the luxury of silence. Remind us of the need to accept responsibility and leave the rest to You.

November 11

David Ignatius Walsh, senator
November 11, 1872–June 11, 1947

David Walsh's life became hard when his father died. The eleven-year-old was able to continue in school only through the persistence of his Irish mother and his sisters, who worked in the mills. After graduation from Boston University law school in 1897, he and his brother launched a law firm, but politics captured David's heart.

Walsh delivered the keynote address at the Massachusetts State Democratic Convention in 1910. In 1914, he was elected governor. As a reformer, he created a coalition of Democrats, Progressives, and working-class Republicans. His two greatest accomplishments were a revitalization of the state labor code and developing a state system of higher education to make a college education possible to the youth of wage-earning families.

Walsh, as an Irish Democrat, capitalized on a growing disenchantment with Yankee-Protestant-business-dominated politics in the Bay State. He was the first

"Do not deprive the alien or the fatherless of justice."

Deuteronomy 24:17

non-Yankee governor. In 1915, he lost his re-election campaign, but in 1918, he was elected to the United States Senate, becoming the first Democrat senator from Massachusetts since 1851. Walsh was initially a strong supporter of Woodrow Wilson, until the president's peace plans alienated his constituents.

Walsh was defeated in the Republican landslide of 1924 (by only 19,000 votes) but made a comeback in 1926 by forming a new political alliance with Polish, Jewish, Irish, and black voters. He constantly spoke up for the rights of minorities and immigrants. Walsh committed himself to political issues that were important to a growing urban industrialized population.

Key Thought: Any dream can be accomplished if you enlist enough people to share the work.

In 1946, he was defeated by Henry Cabot Lodge.

Senator Walsh opened the door to participation in politics for minority Americans.

November 12

Harry T. Burn, legislator
November 12, 1895–February 19, 1977

In the summer of 1920, lobbyists were looking for a man among the Tennessee House of Representatives—a man who could make a difference when the Susan B. Anthony Amendment, giving women the right to vote in all federal elections, came up for ratification. Only one more state needed to ratify the amendment; the long battle of thousands of women to get the right to vote was hanging by a thread. The Tennessee senate had already passed the amendment; now it was up to the house. Would Tennessee be the thirty-sixth state to ratify?

The speaker announced his opposition; after stormy debate, one representative moved to table. That was defeated 48 to 48. Now the amendment itself had to be voted on.

Harry T. Burn, a twenty-eight-year-old bachelor from McMinn County, had voted to table the motion, but when the amendment itself came before the house, he voted yes. The amendment giving women the right to vote passed because this one man changed his vote. Pandemonium broke out. The next day, Harry T. Burn

"I looked for a man among them who would build up the wall and stand before me in the gap."

Ezekiel 22:30

rose in the house chamber, aware of accusations that he had been persuaded to change his vote by a young woman.

He said:

> I changed my vote in favor of ratification because:
>   1. I believe in full suffrage as a right;
>   2. I believe we had a moral and legal right to ratify;
>   3. I know that a mother's advice is always safest for her boy to follow, and my mother wanted me to vote for ratification;
>   4. I appreciated the fact that an opportunity such as seldom comes to mortal man— to free 17,000,000 women from political slavery—was mine;
>   5. I desired that my party, in both State and Nation, might say that it was a Republican from the mountains of East Tennessee ... who made National Woman's Suffrage possible at this date; not for any personal glory, but for the glory of his party."

With that, Harry T. Burn sat down.

The voters of his district did not return him to the legislature in the next election. Fifty years later, Burn said, "I am glad that I was able to do something for the millions of fine American women. If I had it to do over, I would do it again."

Father, give us Harry Burn's kind of courage.

November 13

Helen Archibald Clarke, author and musician
November 13, 1860–February 8, 1926

Helen Clarke's exposure to music began in early childhood. As a young woman, she was encouraged by her parents to pursue her talent. When she was twenty-three, she received a certificate of proficiency in music from the University of Pennsylvania. Although she played and composed throughout her life, music was an avocation for her.

"There is no remembrance of men of old."

Ecclesiastes 1:11

280

In 1888, with the assistance of Charlotte Endymion Porter, Helen Clarke launched *Poet Lore*, a journal "devoted to Shakespeare, Browning, and the Comparative Study of Literature." She worked diligently to publish unknown or little-known Europeans such as Ibsen, Strindberg, Gorky, D'Annunzio, and Maeterlinck. In the 1890s, the Misses Clarke and Porter moved to Boston and spent their lives writing, speaking, and editing.

Despite her own publishing career, most of Clarke's devotion was focused on the poetry of Robert Browning. In 1896, the women edited a new *Browning* edition. In 1898, they completed the ambitious project of publishing Browning's complete poetical works in twelve volumes; two years later they added Mrs. Browning's complete works.

Helen assisted her friend in editing the first three volumes of the First Folio Shakespeare (eventually forty volumes). Although they sold *Poet Lore* in 1903, they continued to edit the journal. Among Helen's works were: *A Child's Guide to Mythology; The Poet's New England; Browning and His Century; Browning's Italy; Browning's England*; and *Longfellow's Country*.

Although the writer of Ecclesiastes says that there is no remembrance after one's death, Helen Clarke gave her life to keeping the name of Robert Browning alive.

Key Thought: Helen Clarke's life may be summed up by this passage from her beloved Robert Browning: "Speak to me—not of me."

November 14

Isabel Bevier, home economist
November 14, 1860–March 17, 1942

Isabel Bevier's heart was broken in 1888 by the death of her fiancé. She moved to Pittsburgh to be near her college roommate and began teaching science at Pennsylvania College for Women. Over the next nine years, she taught geology, physics, and botany and conducted research under the direction of Wilbur Atwater, a noted agricultural chemist.

In 1900, Isabel was appointed by the president of the University of Illinois to revitalize the university's home economics program, with carte blanche freedom to redesign the curriculum. Bevier wanted a nationally recognized academic program and instituted rigorous

"So I counsel younger widows to marry, to have children, to manage their homes."

1 Timothy 5:14

chemistry requirements, wanting the program to be more than college-level cooking and sewing classes.

Her insistence on chemistry as a requirement for admission to the university, and her emphasis on scientific curriculum rather than practical, alienated many influential supporters of the program. Bevier also rejected the advice of the Illinois Farmers' Institute, which lobbied for more practical-based training. In 1914, Isabel established extension courses in agriculture and home economics across Illinois under the Smith-Lever Act.

Bevier was the first vice president of the American Home Economic Association and went on to serve as president between 1910 and 1912. During World War I she chaired the Illinois Committee on the Preservation of Food.

Father, none of us could survive without a homelife. Thank You for those who make housekeeping easier for us.

Bevier's publications included *Food and Nutrition, Selection and Preparation of Food; The House: Its Plan, Decoration and Care*; and *Home Economics in Education.*

Isabel Bevier made a lasting contribution to the recognition of home economics as an academic discipline.

November 15

William Cowper, attorney and hymn writer
November 15, 1731–April 25, 1800

William was born in a Christian home; his father was chaplain to King George II of England. Yet after his mother died, William had a hard time with life. He was bullied as a child and was quite timid. After he earned a law degree, the preparation for his bar exam gave him so much anxiety that he attempted suicide. From 1763 to 1765, he was in an asylum.

"But it was your own eyes that saw all these great things the Lord has done."

Deuteronomy 11:7

After his brother's death, William became involved with John Newton (author of "Amazing Grace") in writing for the new *Olney Hymns*. Cowper wrote sixty-eight hymns.

Still he wrestled with depression, despaired of living, and decided to take his life. He ordered his coachman to drive him to the river. The coachman, however, lost his way; sometime later they arrived back at Cowper's house. By this time the temptation to commit suicide had passed. The experience led him to write what many consider to be the greatest hymn on divine providence, "God Moves in a Mysterious Way."

> God moves in a mysterious way
> His wonders to perform;
> He plants His footsteps in the sea,
> And rides upon the storm.
> Ye fearful saints, fresh courage take;
> The clouds ye so much dread
> Are big with mercy, and shall break
> In blessings on your head.
> Judge not the Lord by feeble sense,
> But trust Him for His grace;
> Behind a frowning providence
> He hides a smiling face.

Today you, like William Cowper, may be fearful. You may be facing the dreaded clouds of depression or anxiety. Remember to "trust Him for His grace." The blessing won't be far behind.

Father, give us the vision, even in the thick clouds of depression, to see You.

November 16

Emma Lee Benedict, author and educator
November 16, 1857–Unknown

Emma Lee Benedict had an incredible thirst for knowledge; by age twelve she had read almost all the books in her father's library. By seventeen, she was teaching school and had decided to enter the New York Normal School at Albany to prepare for a career in teaching. Because of her writing skills, she joined the editorial staff of the *New York School Journal.*

Emma's first book, *Stories of Persons and Places in Europe,* was published in 1887. She joined the first class in advanced educational studies at the University of the City of New York. Miss Benedict was instrumental in kindling a new interest in educational reform in New York City.

On one occasion, Miss Benedict was asked to study the effects of alcohol on the body and prepare appropriate textbook materials. She became a recognized authority on the physiology of alcohol.

"Whatever your hand finds to do, do it with all your might."

Ecclesiastes 9:10

Father, make us well-rounded. Shape in us the de-

283

Emma Lee Benedict was a forceful speaker and an excellent writer. She was also a well-rounded person, willing to contribute in a variety of disciplines.

sire to use any area of our life to glorify You.

November 17

Oliver Newberry, merchant and ship builder
November 17, 1789–July 30, 1860

Many single adults, not encumbered with a family, are free to seize an opportunity when they see it. One visit to Detroit in 1826 caused Oliver Newberry to sell his store in Buffalo, New York, and move there. He set up a new store in Detroit and sold everything from oxbows to hairpins.

Oliver's ambition didn't stop in Detroit. He soon became an agent for the American Fur Company and began selling supplies to the government. Next he began building ships for trading along the Great Lakes.

Newberry's shipbuilding experience led him to Chicago. Sensing the city's bright future, he opened another business, buying and salting meat that he shipped to Detroit. His steamship *Michigan* was the largest on the Great Lakes. In 1835, Newberry established regular steamship service between Chicago and Detroit. Eventually, he opened the Chicago River to large ships through dredging.

Oliver Newberry loved to sell; nothing was too small or large. He invested heavily in real estate and built large warehouses to complement his shipping. He always had money to invest in a new idea.

Today, single adults need some of Oliver Newberry's enthusiasm for seizing opportunities.

"Again, the kingdom of heaven is like a merchant looking for fine pearls. When he found one of great value, he went away and sold everything he had and bought it."

Matthew 13:45, 46

Father, help us to see the opportunities You bring into our lives. Give us the courage and strength to do something with them.

November 18

Rose Knox, manufacturer
November 18, 1857–September 27, 1950

"Sell the business. It's too much for you!" This was the advice everyone was giving Rose Knox. How could a widow run this business? Rose had married a glove

"She also rises while it is yet night, and provides

284

salesman, Charles Knox, back in 1883, when between them they had eleven dollars. However, they had worked hard and invested in a process to manufacture gelatin. Charles concentrated on the advertising and marketing; Rose focused on new product development.

For a while after her husband's death, Rose turned the Knox Gelatin Company over to new management; then an audit uncovered dishonest practices. Rose decided to resume management of the company but was worried about the public's reaction. She announced she would only run the company until her son, who was in school, could take over. When Charles, Jr., died, Rose kept the job until her ninetieth birthday, running the company "in what I call a woman's way, because . . . after all, it was women who purchased gelatin."

Mrs. Knox invested heavily in establishing experimental kitchens and industrial research. She endowed fellowships to fund research on new uses for gelatin.

In 1913, Mrs. Knox began a five-day workweek for employees who agreed to do as much work as they did in five and one-half days. She pioneered with innovations such as two-week paid vacations, sick leave, and pensions. Rather than lay off workers during the Depression, she expanded.

Mrs. Knox loved her city of Johnstown, Pennsylvania, and donated a public swimming pool for the YMCA, an athletic field, and funds for the library. She made significant contributions to the Presbyterian, Slovak, Catholic, and African Methodist churches. In addition, she established the Willing Hands Home for Women.

Rose Knox balanced single parenting with business. "From my own experience," she wrote, "I know it is possible to happily blend home life and business life."

food for her household, and a portion for her maidservants."

Proverbs 31:15 NKJV

Key Thought: The Rose Knox motto: "Think about the things you can help; do not think about those you cannot!"

November 19

George Rogers Clark, general
November 19, 1752–February 13, 1818

Those familiar with American history know that, once England had been defeated, Americans had an incredible hunger to claim their western frontier (what is now

"If one falls down, his friend can help him up. But pity

285

Ohio, Indiana, Illinois, and Michigan). But the pioneers were concerned about their safety against the Indians, the Spanish, the British, and the French.

The brilliant George Rogers Clark realized that, as long as the British held the Northwest, expansion could never be accomplished. He persuaded the Virginia legislature to support the frontiersmen of Kentucky with militia, supplies, and money.

By the sheer force of his personality and will, Clark developed a style of leadership that led his small bands of men to incredible feats of endurance and courage. On more than one occasion in the Illinois Territory, he stopped a mutiny by some courageous act.

Clark received no pay for his services. Moreover, the Virginia legislature refused to reimburse the general for his expenses for gunpowder, food, and supplies.

Clark fell in love with a young Spanish woman named Terese deLeyba. However, when Virginia refused to reimburse his expenses, forcing him to sell his property to pay his debts, Clark thought it less than honorable to marry a woman without having any means to support her. Eventually, Terese returned to Spain and entered a convent.

Late in his life, Clark fell into a fire and severely burned his leg. When it became infected, it was necessary to amputate it. Captain G. R. C. Floyd marched his field band up outside the house of the local surgeon. The band played as the doctor amputated General Clark's leg; Clark tapped his fingers in time with the music. He was a man of great personal courage.

George Clark saved the Northwest Territory for the United States but lost almost everything he valued in the process.

the man who falls and has no one to help him up!"

Ecclesiastes 4:10

Father, **sacrifice** *is* **not an easy word for us to understand, let alone implement. If that be Your will for us, give us the courage to say yes.**

November 20

Henry Newman, philanthropist
November 20, 1670–June 26, 1743

Henry Newman was orphaned as a child and reared by his maternal grandmother. After graduation from Harvard, he considered entering the Congregational min-

"Command them to do good, to be rich in good deeds, and

istry but became an Episcopalian instead. Newman worked at a variety of jobs, from librarian at Harvard to a merchant in Newfoundland.

He moved to London in 1703 and became a commissioner for the Relief of Poor Proselytes, helping converts from Catholicism. Newman was also a leader in the Society for Promoting Christian Knowledge (SPCK), which worked to fund charity schools, mission programs in India, and the emmigration of Protestant Salzburgers to Georgia.

Newman periodically worked as a colonial agent in the New Hampshire colony. His avocations of mathematics and astronomy led him to publish two books: *Harvard's Ephemeris* and *News From the Stars*.

However, Newman is best known for his contributions to world evangelization through SPCK. He gave generously and joyfully to people in need, and his organization financed the work of David Brainerd among the American Indians.

to be generous and willing to share."

1 Timothy 6:18

Key Point: Money invested in building the Kingdom of God keeps on giving.

November 21

Allen Barlitt Pond, architect
November 21, 1859–March 17, 1929

Allen Pond was twenty-eight before he began to study architecture in the office of his brother. Eventually he was involved in the design of buildings of all kinds, from Chicago's Hull House to the Memorial Student Union at Purdue University.

Pond made several trips to Europe to study architecture and zoning. From 1923 to 1927, he was chairman of the board of appeals for zoning in the city of Chicago. He worked to ensure fairness in zoning in a city noted for its kickbacks. At times Pond struggled to be impartial.

Pond worked to better the city of Chicago through lobbying in the legislature for acts relating to architecture, playgrounds, public planning, zoning, and parks. He also invested a great deal of interest and energy in social and civic responsibilities. He was a close associate of Jane Addams at Hull House, serving for thirty-four years as a trustee.

Allen Pond made Chicago a more livable city for *all* of its residents.

"To show partiality in judging is not good."

Proverbs 24:23

Father, we thank You for our great cities that provide places for us to live, play, work, worship, and be. Remind us of our civic responsibilities.

Abraham Baldwin, political leader
November 22, 1754–March 4, 1807

Abraham Baldwin tutored at Yale and served as a chaplain in the Continental army between 1779 and 1793. After the Revolution, he studied law and was admitted to both the Connecticut and Georgia bars. In 1785, he was elected to the Continental Congress, and in 1787 to the Constitutional Convention.

Georgians elected him to the first five congresses, from 1799 to 1807. In 1802 he served as United States commissioner in resolving the boundaries and land disputes in Georgia.

Baldwin founded the University of Georgia and served as president of its board of trustees.

Counties in Georgia and Alabama and an agriculture college in Georgia are named for him.

Abraham Baldwin led a quiet life and won the respect of many.

"Make it your ambition to lead a quiet life, to mind your own business and to work with your hands, just as we told you, so that your daily life may win the respect of outsiders. . . ."

1 Thessalonians 4:11, 12

Father, someone is watching our lives. Help us to be aware of our influence.

Blanton Winship, governor
November 23, 1869–October 9, 1947

After graduating from the University of Georgia law school, Blanton Winship joined the army in 1898 as a volunteer in the Spanish-American War. He was commissioned and assigned to the judge advocate's department and made major in 1904. In 1906, Winship served on the commission that rewrote the legal code of Cuba. In 1914, during the occupation of Vera Cruz, Mexico, Winship was administrator of civilian affairs.

Although a lawyer in the judge advocate's corps at the outbreak of World War I, Winship was assigned to General John J. Pershing. He requested a field command and eventually was decorated for his combat leadership. After World War I, he headed the army claims settlement division, processing over 100,000 war claims. Then he served as judge advocate of the occupation army in Germany.

"For the Lord gives wisdom, and from his mouth come knowledge and understanding."

Proverbs 2:6

His toughest military and legal assignment came when he was counsel for the military board that tried war hero General Billy Mitchell. In 1928, Winship became the military adviser to President Coolidge, where he served until 1930. In 1931, he was promoted to major general and became the army's Judge Advocate General.

After his retirement from the military, President Franklin Roosevelt named Winship governor of the Territory of Puerto Rico. In that post, he became the first governor to anticipate the potential for tourism. In 1937, Winship barely survived an assassination attempt.

He resigned in 1939 and returned to active duty with the army. In 1944, Blanton Winship retired from public life.

Father, for faithful service and integrity, we give You thanks.

November 24

Anna Louise Strong, social activist
November 24, 1885–March 29, 1970

After Anna's graduation from the University of Chicago, where she wrote her doctoral dissertation on prayer, she worked initially in Seattle, organizing a program with her clergyman father called Know Your City. The program's aim was to help citizens know the beauty of Seattle. Later she would organize similar campaigns in other cities.

Anna became engaged to Roger Baldwin, a future director of the American Civil Liberties Union. Because of opposition from her father and her own doubts about Baldwin's spiritual commitment, Anna broke the engagement.

She returned to Washington to run for the state legislature but was defeated. Then conservatives nominated her for the Seattle school board. However, Strong, who considered herself a socialist, wrote a series of articles in the *Seattle Daily Call* urging young men not to enlist for military service. Outraged conservatives organized a recall campaign and removed her from office in March 1918.

Anna Strong alienated powerful ladies in Seattle when she began supporting laborists during the great strike

"I saw the wicked buried—those who used to come and go from the holy place and receive praise in the city where they did this."

Ecclesiastes 8:10

289

of 1919. Her editorial in the *Seattle Union Record*, which concluded, "We are starting on a road that leads—NO ONE KNOWS WHERE!" led to open ostracism and threats on her life.

In the early twenties, she went to Russia and became involved in their revolution. She taught Trotsky English and defended Lenin in her book *The First Time in History*. For the next twenty years she lived in Russia, frequently traveling to the United States to lecture and raise funds.

She was also a correspondent in the Spanish Civil War and in China, joining the opposition forces against Chiang Kai-shek. When the Germans invaded Russia in World War II, Strong found herself stranded in the United States. She wrote a book defending Stalin, consulted on an MGM movie, and wrote a novel. In 1944, Anna returned to Russia as a journalist with *Atlantic Monthly* and traveled with the Red Army fighting in Poland.

After the war, Anna moved to China and wrote about Mao Tse-tung. At his urging "to spread the news of the revolution," she returned to Russia but was expelled as a spy in 1949. Anna Strong lived in the United States until her exoneration in 1955. In 1965, on her eightieth birthday, she was honored by Mao and the Red Guard for her work reporting news from China.

Her last desire was to return to the United States to oppose the Vietnam War. She died a loyal Communist.

Father, what went wrong? How could an authority on prayer end up a Communist propagandist? Are there seeds of spiritual dissension in our lives? If so, show them to us.

November 25

Kate Gleason, developer
November 25, 1865–January 9, 1933

Kate Gleason had an unusual father. He had an interest in women's emancipation and a zeal to teach his children the marvels of engineering. When Kate was eleven, her half-brother died, and she convinced her father that she could take his place in the family's tool shop.

After brief stints in college, Kate went to work for her father, selling beveled gear planers for the growing automobile industry. Henry Ford mistakenly thought Kate had designed the gear planer and praised it as "the

"She considers a field and buys it; out of her earnings she plants a vineyard."

Proverbs 31:16

most remarkable machine work ever done by a woman." Kate's real contribution was as the sales manager for the device; she helped build her father's little machine tool factory into the country's leading producer of gear-cutting equipment.

Following a series of family disagreements, Kate went into business for herself. She financially resurrected one of her father's competitors and served as president of the First National Bank of East Rochester while its president worked for the war. In this position, Gleason learned of the need for suburban housing.

Kate decided to adapt some of the techniques she had learned for mass production in the automobile industry to home building. By 1921, Miss Gleason was selling $4,000 concrete prefabricated homes for a low down payment and $40 a month. She designed a way to make housing more affordable for middle-class families. She conducted similiar experiments in Beaufort, South Carolina, and in Sausalito, California.

When Kate Gleason died, she was one of the nation's few female general contractors.

Father, teach us to be innovative in our efforts to help others.

November 26

Sarah Grimké, abolitionist
November 26, 1792–December 23, 1873

Sarah Grimké was a brilliant child who read most of the books in her father's library, including the law books. One biographer said, "If she had been born of the other sex, she would have made the greatest jurist of the land."

As it was, Sarah found herself on a collision course with Southern reality. She found slavery "a millstone around my neck, and marred my comfort from the time I can remember myself." Sarah used prayer to combat the situations out of her control. As a child, anytime a slave was to be whipped, Sarah began praying. Later she said, "My prayers were answered in very unexpected ways."

Sarah became a felon as a twelve-year-old when she broke a South Carolina law drafted for the legislature by her lawyer father: She taught slaves to read. When Jus-

"So God created man in his own image, in the image of God he created him; male and female he created them."

Genesis 1:27

tice Grimké found his daughter and a slave reading together, he was incensed. "Slaves have no use for reading, my dear . . . it only makes them restless and rebellious."

Years later, "restless and rebellious" were the phrases Southerners used to describe Sarah before she fled the South in 1821. After becoming a Quaker, she joined the abolition movement. In 1836, she wrote *Epistle to the Clergy of the Southern States*, in which she skillfully exegeted the Old and New Testaments to prove that the Bible could not be used to justify slavery.

Then Sarah joined her sister to write an irrefutable documentation of slavery, *American Slavery As It Is*, which became a blockbuster best-seller (100,000 copies sold in twelve months) in America and England. Another author slept with the book under her pillow every night while she wrote *Uncle Tom's Cabin*. Harriet Beecher Stowe's writing was greatly influenced by the Grimkés.

Finally, Sarah Grimké did much to ignite the intellectual beginnings of the women's movement with her book, *Letters on the Equality of the Sexes and the Condition of Women*, published in 1838.

Key Thought: From William Francis's eulogy at Sarah's funeral: "We will more truly live because she has lived among us. May her hope and peace be ours."

November 27

Adelaide Addison Pollard, hymn writer
November 27, 1862–December 20, 1934

Adelaide Pollard was born Sarah Pollard, but she didn't like the name and changed it to Adelaide. It is amazing that a woman with such determination could write the gospel classic, "Have Thine Own Way, Lord."

Adelaide graduated from the Boston School of Oratory and taught school in Chicago for a number of years. She became involved in the evangelistic ministry of Alexander Dowie and was particularly interested in his teaching on healing, since she had been healed of diabetes.

Later, Adelaide felt called to go to Africa as a missionary. However, as the time came for her to leave, it became clear that the necessary funds were not available. This sent Miss Pollard, who was very frail, into a deep depression.

"So I went down to the potter's house, and I saw him working at the wheel. But the pot he was shaping from the clay was marred in his hands; so the potter formed it into another pot, shaping it as seemed best to him."

Jeremiah 18:3, 4

As she sat in a prayer meeting, too depressed to concentrate, Adelaide kept hearing a prayer she had overheard: "It's all right, Lord! It doesn't matter what You bring into our lives; just have Your own way with us!" In the midst of her great disappointment, Adelaide found peace. After returning home from the service, she meditated on the passage in Jeremiah 18 and wrote:

Have Thine own way, Lord! Have Thine own way!
Thou are the Potter, I am the clay!
Mold me and make me after Thy will,
While I am waiting, yielded and still.

Have Thine own way, Lord! Have Thine own way!
Search me and try me, Master today!
Whiter than snow, Lord, Wash me just now,
As in Thy presence Humbly I bow.

"Father, have thine own way, Lord! Have thine own way. Hold over my being absolute sway! Fill with thy Spirit, until all shall see: Christ only, always, living in me."

Miss Pollard sought an alternative to her plans and spent eight years teaching at the Missionary Training School in Nyack, New York. Eventually, she did go to Africa for a few months, but with the outbreak of World War I, she left for Scotland. After the war, she returned to New England and continued her religious work until she was seventy-two.

November 28

Irwin Edman, writer
November 28, 1896–September 4, 1954

Irwin Edman spent his entire adult life on the campus of Columbia University. He received his B. A. in 1917, Ph.D. in 1920, and turned his doctoral dissertation into a book, *Human Traits and Their Social Significance.* The text pioneered a new course in general education, Contemporary Civilization, a curricular innovation later adopted by other universities.

Edman, a philosopher, loved to travel. He went to Brazil, Syria, and Sweden and lectured in foreign universities such as Oxford and the Sorbonne. Edman deliberately compensated for his single status by what he called "diffused domesticity"—close friendships with a

"For as he thinketh in his heart, so is he."

Proverbs 23:7 KJV

wide variety of people: poets, writers, journalists, and judges. Moreover, he kept in touch with former students long after their graduations.

Edman made his classroom exciting. He considered philosophy "a disciplined personal testament, an individual's way of summing up for himself the decisive factors in human destiny and the basic meaning to be found in existence."

In his *Four Ways of Philosophy* (1937), Edman suggested that "mankind stands at the pinnacle of nature and looks beyond to the world of Truth, Goodness, and Beauty . . . as this world's unrealized, never to be completely realized, good."

Dr. Edman's most popular book, *Philosopher's Holiday* (1935), chronicled the interesting people Edman met in his travels. In *The Mind of Paul* (1935), he recreated the world of Paul's imagination.

Edman lived out his singleness as a charming philosopher, equally gifted with a brilliant intellect and a warm wit, with faith and great insight into the meaning of life.

Father, for those who teach us how to expand our capacity to think, we give You thanks.

November 29

Louisa May Alcott, writer
November 29, 1832–March 6, 1888

Louisa Alcott's writing, which eventually included 270 books and articles, began with stories called *Flower Fables*. She had written the tales to entertain her sisters, and published them in 1855 for five dollars. Three decades later, this single adult was one of the most widely read authors in America. Her book *Little Women*, based on her own life with three sisters, became an American literary classic.

Some women in her era wrote to amuse themselves; Louisa wrote to provide for her family because her father could not adequately meet their needs. At times, she sewed ten hours a day, lived on pennies, and wrote her articles late at night. Alcott's characters fought for personal and social autonomy. She created heroines who won recognition for the talents of women.

Louisa served as a nurse in Georgetown during the Civil War before she was sent home with typhoid fever.

"She watches over the affairs of her household and does not eat the bread of idleness."

Proverbs 31:27

As a result of her experiences, she wrote the popular *Hospital Sketches*, which helped establish her literary reputation. At some point, it became apparent to her that she had to "forego the fulfillment and security of marriage so that the Alcott family might have her undivided attention."

The first part of *Little Women* was written in about six weeks and was published in September 1868; the second part followed in the spring of 1869.

Miss Alcott was the first woman to register to vote in Concord when Massachusetts gave women the right to vote on school taxes and bond suffrage in 1879.

In 1880, as a forty-eight-year-old single, Louisa Alcott became a parent, adopting her niece after her sister May died.

Father, encourage us to commit ourselves to things that will live beyond our lifetimes.

November 30

Jonathan Swift, writer and clergyman
November 30, 1667–October 19, 1745

Jonathan Swift graduated from Trinity College in Dublin and then Oxford. He was ordained in the Church of Ireland in 1694 and assigned a small church near Belfast. Soon a former employer, Sir William Temple, invited Swift to work for him as literary executor. For three years, Swift lived on Temple's estate and wrote. His first works, *Pindaric Odes* and *The Battle of the Books*, come from this period of intense creativity.

After Temple's death, Swift pastored and served as a chaplain to the second Earl of Berkeley, the lord justice of Ireland. Although he received a doctor of divinity degree from Trinity College, his desire for advancement in the Church of Ireland was thwarted.

Jonathan Swift lived in England between 1700 and 1704 and nurtured friendships with writers Alexander Pope, Joseph Addison, and Richard Steele. He published the first volume of his satires, *A Tale of the Tub, The Battle of the Books,* and *The Mechanical Operation of the Spirit,* in 1704. Three years later, Swift published his best narrative poem, *Baucis and Philemon,* and then his greatest irony, *The Argument to Prove That the Abolishing of Christianity in England May, As Things Now Stand, Be Attended With Some Inconveniences.*

"How painful are honest words! But what do your arguments prove?"

Job 6:25

In 1713, after having aligned himself with the Tories, Swift was appointed dean of St. Patrick's in Dublin (although he wanted an English assignment). In 1720, he published anonymously *Proposal for the Universal Use of Irish Manufactures,* in which he urged the Irish not to use English goods; within a few years he was an Irish hero. Six letters that he wrote under the name M. B. Draper, protesting the English governance of Ireland, won more support for Swift.

Today, Swift is best remembered for *Gulliver's Travels,* a political commentary on the social conditions of England in the eighteenth century.

Jonathan Swift wrote and performed his pastoral duties so well that he became very wealthy. When he died, he left his fortune to provide an institution for the mentally ill.

Here are a few Swiftisms:

- Vision is the art of seeing things invisible.
- We have just enough religion to make us hate, but not enough to make us love one another.
- The sight of you is good for sore eyes.
- Lord, I wonder what fool it was that first invented kissing.
- May you live all the days of your life.

Father, for the man, for his gift with words, we give You thanks. Help us to live all the days of our lives.

December 1

Ann Preston, physician
December 1, 1813–April 18, 1872

When Ann Preston heard that the Female Medical College would be opened in Philadelphia in 1850, she wasted no time in submitting an application. She had long been awaiting such an opportunity. Ann had cared for her invalid mother and six brothers, been involved with the antislavery movement, and had helped a slave escape through the Underground Railroad. Ann Preston, at the age of thirty-seven, was ready for a challenge.

In 1852 she graduated but, to satisfy her intellectual curiosity, continued to audit classes the next year. In 1853, she was appointed to teach physiology and hy-

"Be wise in the way you act toward outsiders; make the most of every opportunity."

Colossians 4:5

giene. Through a series of lectures in Baltimore, New York, and Philadelphia, she improved the public image of female physicians.

Since women could not practice in hospitals, Ann Preston dedicated her energies to building a facility for women physicians. In 1861, the Women's Hospital of Philadelphia opened, with Ann as manager and consulting physician. In 1866, she became the first dean of the Female Medical College.

However, in 1867, the Philadelphia County Medical Society published a statement that disapproved of women physicians. Ann carefully prepared a response that won praise and led to the society rescinding its policy.

Without the work of Ann Preston, women might have been denied clinical training and public recognition.

Father, it takes a great deal of effort to debunk prejudice. Thank You for the courage of Ann Preston in opening the door for women to serve in the field of medicine. Help us to examine ourselves for prejudice.

December 2

Mary Slessor, missionary
December 2, 1848–January 13, 1915

A mill in Dundee, Scotland, was hardly the place to look for a woman who would eventually be called "white queen of the cannibals," but that was the start of the working career of a single adult named Mary Slessor. At eleven, Mary began working twelve-hour days to support her family. She read as she worked, and in her twenties, she was deeply moved when she read of the death of David Livingstone in 1873. She applied to be a missionary teacher for a new work in Calabar.

Mary brought a fresh perspective to missions, refusing to live as a European. Instead, she built a house like her African neighbors', adopted an African diet, and got rid of her shoes.

Eventually, Mary pushed deeper into the jungles and set up a base in the Oioyung area. She declared that her home and land were a sanctuary for refugees from murder and witchcraft plots and began taking in children who had been abandoned or orphaned. She settled feuds between tribes. When one chief boldly declared that "No word of a woman could prevent war!" she responded, "You forget the woman's God!"

"I am with you and will watch over you wherever you go."

Genesis 28:15

Mary Slessor challenged the old tribal tradition of killing twins. Known as "White Ma who loved babies," she adopted one baby whose sister was found dead in the bush. Mary named the infant Janie after her own sister in Scotland.

Eventually, the British government recognized Mary's influence in the region and made her their consular agent, later decorating her for her political administration and compassion.

Characteristically, Mary wrote friends in Scotland: "Don't think there is any great change in me because I received this honor. I am still Mary Slessor; nothing more and none other than the unworthy, unprofitable, but most willing servant of the King of Kings."

How could this woman with the Scottish brogue have survived Africa? Didn't she miss her homeland? Her response was, "Life apart from Christ is a terrible thing." She had not been alone; God had been with her. Otherwise she never would have survived among the cannibals.

Her last words were, "Do not weep, do not weep; the Lord is taking me home."

Father, how mightily You used this Scottish millworker. Give me a heart willing to say yes to Your best.

December 3

Belle Bennett, women's leader
December 3, 1852–July 20, 1922

"I'll do it!" Belle Bennett said to the Lord one night three years after her conversion. "Almost without knowing what I did," she explained later, "I responded to the urgings of His Spirit."

"I consider my life worth nothing to me."

Acts 20:24

Belle grew up in a prominent Kentucky family. She could have had her choice of suitors. After attending a revival in a Presbyterian church at the age of thirty-one, she began to commit herself to making a difference.

The Methodist Church had just begun sending single women to the mission field. Serving on the selection committee, Belle was alarmed by the lack of missionary preparation; the church needed a place to train missionaries. She decided if single women were going to the field, surely married women could help support them financially. Belle became a fund-raiser par excellence, traveling across the United States speaking in Methodist churches. Women gave diamond rings, watches, and family heirlooms to the cause, and ground was broken on April 28, 1891, for what eventually became Scarritt College.

Over the years, Belle continued to provide leadership for the women's movement. At the time, women could not be ordained, serve, or speak in annual or general conferences. By 1906, Belle was traveling across the country, reminding members, "Both men and women were created in God's image, and to both God came in the flesh of Jesus Christ."

Until 1909, Belle was the most respected woman in the Methodist Episcopal Church because of her work in missions and deaconess programs. But the Methodist hierarchy turned against her on this issue.

In 1914, the issue was debated and defeated. By 1918, after women's involvement in the war effort, the measure to give women voting rights in general conference (the highest council of the church) passed.

"Don't congratulate me!" Belle said of the victory. "We are not so foolish as to count the battle won!"

In 1921, Belle was elected to represent Kentucky Methodists at the 1922 general conference. However, she was too ill to attend. For thirty-five years she had given herself to the Methodist Church with no compensation, often paying her own expenses.

Key Point: "Obedience is the key that unlocks the treasure house of God."

Belle Bennett

December 4

Edith Cavell, nurse
December 4, 1865–October 12, 1915

Edith Cavell completed her studies at London Hospital and, after two years of practical experience, was sent to supervise nurses during an outbreak of typhoid fever in Kent. Her kind, gentle ways won her a great reputation. Many people called her "the poor man's Nightingale."

In 1907, Dr. Antoine Depage, a Belgian surgeon, invited Edith to open a school of nursing in Belgium. Previously only nuns had done nursing there, so Edith had to convince girls, particularly of the more privileged social classes, that nursing had dignity and social status.

As her program was winning a reputation, war swept

"Be still before the Lord and wait patiently for him; do not fret when men succeed in their ways, when they carry out their wicked schemes."

Psalm 37:7

across Europe and Germany occupied Belgium. The brutalities of war made a deep impression on Edith, and she spoke out against them. When warned that such statements endangered her, she responded, "In times like these, when terror makes might seem right, there is a higher duty than prudence."

Edith decided to make her hospital a refuge for Allied soldiers trying to escape.

On August 5, 1915, police raided the hospital and arrested Miss Cavell and her assistant. The American embassy tried to furnish her legal counsel, but the Germans would not permit it.

On October 8, she and thirty-three others were tried. Edith confessed that she had admitted French soldiers to her hospital and that she had helped them escape. "It was my duty," she reminded them, as a nurse "to save lives."

On October 11, Edith was sentenced to be shot by a firing squad. Again, American diplomats tried to reason with the Germans to save Edith's life.

"The life of one German soldier seems to us much more important than that of all the old English nurses!" the American ambassador was told. Edith would not be spared.

At daybreak, Edith arrived on the rifle range at *Tir National*. She opened her Prayer Book and wrote, "Died at 7 A.M. on October 12, 1915. With love to my mother. E. Cavell." Moments later she was dead.

Father, teach us to be still and wait patiently for You.

December 5

Christina Rossetti, poet
December 5, 1830–December 29, 1894

Christina Rossetti's first poems were written when she was twelve. Before she was twenty, her poetry had been published under the pen name of Ellen Alleyne. Her father's death in 1854 motivated her to give increased attention to her mother and deepened her faith.

When Christina was twenty, she broke off a two-year engagement with a painter when he became a Roman Catholic. She then fell in love with Charles Cayley but broke that engagement because of his lack of faith. The two relationships influenced her writing: Lost love was

"Remember your word to your servant, for you have given me hope. My comfort in my suffering is this: Your promise preserves my life."

Psalm 119:49, 50

a common theme in her work. Rossetti found the world a painful place and looked forward to death as a chance to reconcile both with God and with those she had loved and lost.

Rossetti is remembered for three books of poetry: *Goblin Market and Other Poems* (1862), *The Prince's Progress and Other Poems* (1866), and *A Pageant and Other Poems* (1881), and for *Sing-Song: Nursery Rhyme Book* (1872), which became a classic for Victorian children. Her work combines a sensuous attraction to physical beauty with strong religious faith.

From 1871 to 1873, Christina battled Graves' disease, from which she nearly died. After her recovery, her writing was almost exclusively devotional in nature.

After a long bout with cancer, she died in 1894 in London. She wrote,

> Better by far you should forget and smile
> Than that you should remember and be sad.

Father, life is not always easy. The world seems to be a place where our hearts can too easily be broken. Give us strength for this day.

December 6

Frederick Townsend Martin, author
December 6, 1849–March 8, 1914

Born into a wealthy family, Fred Martin loved to travel, but as he toured the world, he became concerned about the needs of the poor. Martin used his money to support programs for relieving the suffering of the poor in both the United States and abroad. In New York, he invested generously in the Bowery Mission; in England, he donated large sums to London's East End.

Martin concluded that the age of great wealth was passing, and so would the social order. In his 1911 book, *The Passing of the Idle Rich,* he demonstrated his belief that social decay always follows wealth and excessive living. He contended the fallout could be avoided if the wealthy used their resources to help others.

Another problem Martin discovered during his travels was that there were no permanent residences in the major capitals for American diplomats. He founded the American Embassy Association to win public favor for

"Seek justice, encourage the oppressed. Defend the cause of the fatherless, plead the case of the widow."

Isaiah 1:17

Key Thought: Of whom much is given, much shall be required. We

301

government appropriations to buy homes for the diplomatic missions. The effort was a success.

Frederick Martin ministered to the poor and to the wealthy, finding no contradiction in his charity.

December 7

Willa Cather, novelist
December 7, 1873–April 24, 1947

Willa Cather believed that if she had not lived in Nebraska as a child her impact as a writer would not have been as great. Willa was only nine when her family left Virginia for a fresh start on the prairie. Her decision to become a writer occurred after her freshman English teacher mailed one of her essays on Thomas Carlyle to a magazine and it was published. As a university junior, she supported herself writing for the *Nebraska State Journal.*

After graduation, Willa worked as a writer in Pittsburgh but quit after five years to teach English and Latin. During that time she published her first book, *April Twilights.* Next, Miss Cather became an editor at *McClure's Magazine* and moved to New York City. Soon she was known as one of the best women editors in the country.

In 1908, a letter from Willa's friend Sarah Orne Jewett changed her life: "You must find your own quiet center of life, and write from that to the world." Miss Jewett urged Willa to quit *McClure's,* otherwise, "you can write about life, but not life itself."

As a result, Willa resigned her post. By this time, she had distanced herself enough from her early days in Nebraska that she could write with objectivity. She believed that the history and color of a land began in the hearts of its men and women, so she wrote out of her nostalgia for the pioneers.

Ironically, her best work was not about Nebraska, but the Southwest. She fictionalized the life of Archbishop Lany, the first bishop in the territory of New Mexico after its annexation. The work, *Death Comes to the Archbishop,* won Willa Cather a permanent niche in American literature.

"Commemorate this day, the day you came out of Egypt, out of the land of slavery, because the Lord brought you out of it with a mighty hand."

Exodus 13:3

Key Point: We may never know the impact of a well-written letter. Without Sarah Orne Jewett's prodding, would Miss Cather have achieved literary prominence?

December 8

Ruth Fanshaw Waldo, advertising executive
December 8, 1885–August 30, 1975

After four years in the field of social work, Ruth Waldo wanted a change. When she received a job offer from the Walter Thompson Advertising Agency as an apprentice copywriter in 1915, she jumped at the chance. During her first years with the agency, Miss Waldo developed a reputation as a skilled wordsmith. This was in the early thirties, when the advertising industry was undergoing great changes: color photography, million-dollar ad budgets, and new attempts to reach the consumer, particularly women.

In 1930, Ruth began to oversee all advertising directed to women. She hired women copywriters and insisted they wear hats at work. She and her staff made advertising copy into household phrases. Her most famous was for Pond's: "She's lovely! She's engaged! She uses Pond's!" With such slogans, she made corporate clients happy and increased the sales of many products, particularly cosmetics.

Ruth's hobby was "getting along with people, especially difficult people."

In 1944, she became the first woman vice president of the J. Walter Thompson Agency. Her success in that position opened the door for other women executives.

Ruth Waldo became a Quaker in 1953 and spent a great deal of time working with peace-related issues.

> "Tarshish did business with you because of your great wealth of goods; they exchanged silver, iron, tin and lead for your merchandise."
>
> **Ezekiel 27:12**

> *Father, for those who open professions to others, we thank You.*

December 9

Grace Murray Hopper, admiral
December 9, 1906–

The next time you're annoyed by a computer, remember you may have a single adult to thank. At thirty-seven, Grace Hopper entered the United States Naval Reserve Midshipman's School at Northampton, Massachusetts. She had a Ph.D. in mathematics from Yale and had taught at Vassar but wanted to be involved in the war effort.

> "Make it your ambition to lead a quiet life, to mind your own business and to work with your hands, just as we told you, so that

The navy assigned her to the Harvard team building the first United States computer, the Mark I. Tired of computer codes, Miss Hopper invented the first compiler to make computers talk in human symbols. Then she co-invented COBOL, one of the most widely used computer languages. Her work with computers included stints at both Remington Rand and the Sperry Corporation.

Grace was recalled to active duty by the navy in 1967 to standardize the computer languages used by the military and to convince navy personnel to use them. By 1973, she had been promoted to commodore.

Her biggest hurdle was the protest, "but we've always done it this way."

Admiral Hopper rejected such thinking. "I'm going to shoot somebody for saying that someday. In the computer industry, with changes coming as fast as they do, you just can't afford to have people saying that."

Hopper received honorary doctorates from three universities and has published more than fifty scholarly articles that have influenced the design and programming of modern-day computers. Yet, when asked about her greatest accomplishment, she will answer, "Teaching young people." How has she handled her status?

> I never intended to be a celebrity, just an officer in the Navy. I realize I'm awfully lucky the Navy ordered me to that first computer; otherwise, I'd still be a college teacher. It's much more fun being a commodore in the Navy. I just remember my commission says I'm an officer and a gentleman. So I endeavor to behave like a gentleman.

your daily life may win the respect of outsiders."

1 Thessalonians 4:11, 12

Key Thought: Grace Hopper retired as the oldest person on active duty in the military. No wonder she earned the nickname "Amazing Grace."

December 10

Emily Dickinson, poet
December 10, 1830–May 15, 1886

Ironically, America's greatest woman poet was unread during her lifetime. Of the 1,700 poems Emily Dickin-

"A word aptly spoken is like apples

son wrote, only seven were published prior to her death.

Emily lived with her family in Amherst, Massachusetts. Neither Emily nor her younger sister, Lavinia, ever married, probably due to the overbearing influence of their father, a prominent New England lawyer. Emily lived with her family and seldom left home. Her longest sojourn was an unhappy year at Mount Holyoke.

Certainly there were men in her life. Benjamin Norton, a lawyer in her father's office, became her literary preceptor, encouraging her to write. Emily's close involvement with another man—a married minister—left her in great psychological pain. The reverend's move to the West influenced a large number of poems—611 in three years.

Eventually she sent some of her work to Thomas Wentworth Higginson, a well-known and respected essayist and critic. Although he advised her not to publish (he thought her poems "too delicate"), he did become her friend and mentor and encouraged her to keep writing.

Emily's poetry survived because she wrote in a language described as "spare and fresh." Her life illustrates a point many of us need to learn: Our ultimate contribution to the world is not always evident. It may be years before our work is recognized for the bud of genius.

> If I can stop one heart from breaking
> I shall not live in vain
> If I can ease one life the aching
> or cool one pain
> Or help one fainting robin
> Unto his nest again
> I shall not live in vain.
> We never know how high we are
> Till we are called to rise
> And then if we are true to plan
> Our statures touch the skies.

There is no indication that Emily Dickinson had a personal commitment to Christ. One biographer noted, "She found Jehovah cruelly distant and inscrutable, and she rejected the church and questioned its doctrines, particularly the immortality of the soul." She once said, "I have a horror of death; the dead are so soon forgotten. But when I die, they'll have to remember me."

of gold in settings of silver."

Proverbs 25:11

Father, we are glad that we have found You to be the source of life and the hope of life eternal. Let us not only be remembered for our life's work but for our faith in You.

December 11

Annie Jump Cannon, astronomer
December 11, 1863–April 13, 1941

Annie Cannon's fascination with stars began as a child. She attended Wellesley College, studying physics and astronomy. After her mother's death, she enrolled as a special student in astronomy at Radcliffe, where she took part in experiments to confirm the discovery of X rays.

In 1896, at the invitation of Edward C. Pickering, Annie joined the staff of the Harvard University observatory, specializing in the study of variable stars and stellar spectra. In 1910, her scheme of classifying spectra became the standard for all observatories.

In 1911, she began what one biographer called "the greatest compilations of astronomical information ever achieved by one person." Her catalog listed 225,330 stars. By the end of her academic career, she had classified the spectra of almost 400,000 stars.

No meeting of the American Astronomical Society was complete without Cannon's participation. Star Cottage, her home in Cambridge, was a mecca for astronomers from around the world. Honors came to her from societies and institutions everywhere. She was the first woman ever honored with a doctorate of science from Oxford.

Annie Cannon was an active Methodist who loved children and entertained them regularly, despite her busy schedule.

"He determines the number of the stars and calls them each by name."

Psalm 147:4

Father, much of the work of Miss Cannon is beyond our level of scientific understanding. But we thank You for sharing Your secrets and wonders with her and for her ability to interpret them to us.

December 12

Charlotte D. Lottie Moon, missionary
December 12, 1840–December 24, 1912

Lottie Moon was one of the first women to receive a master's degree. One scholar called her "the most educated woman in the South." As the principal of a girls' school in Cartersville, Georgia, Lottie heard a sermon that changed her life. She walked down the aisle of the

" 'But if the charges brought against me by these Jews are not true, no one has the

church and said, "I have long known that God wanted me to go to China. I am now ready to go."

On July 7, 1873, Lottie Moon sailed for China as a missionary for the Southern Baptist Convention. She lived on her own, quickly adopting Chinese ways and clothing. She organized Bible studies for women and later established a girls' school, which was a major departure from the Chinese tradition that discouraged education for women.

In her work, Lottie traveled across the countryside, teaching in houses. Some Baptists protested that she was preaching, and that was a man's job. She wrote the mission executives, "If the men do not like the way I am 'sharing the gospel,' let them send some men to do it better."

Lottie angered many by her outspokenness on the development of mission policy. Males expected silence from women, especially single women, but Lottie made sure her position was heard by mission executives. Her long letters back to women in Baptist churches became objects of interest and eventually evolved into a curriculum for organizing women's missionary societies. They also gained her strong grass-roots support for her ideas.

For many years, Lottie Moon loved Crawford Toy, a professor at Southern Seminary and Harvard. In fact, at one point she wrote her family and told them to plan a spring wedding. However, because of Toy's theological liberalism, he could not join Lottie in China as a Baptist missionary, and because of her love for China, she would not leave to be with him at Harvard.

Lottie fought the Chinese government for the rights of Christians to practice their faith and evangelize. Today she is recognized as a forerunner in the development of women's rights in China.

Lottie Moon starved herself to death, giving away her food to Chinese students. At the time of her death, she weighed fifty pounds.

right to hand me over to them. I appeal to Caesar!' After Festus had conferred with his council, he declared: 'You have appealed to Caesar. To Caesar you will go!' "

Acts 25:11, 12.

Father, one woman opened the doors of northern China to the Gospel. Her impact is only now beginning to be understood. Lottie Moon demonstrated that single adults could be effective on the mission field.

Phillips Brooks, preacher
December 13, 1835–January 23, 1893

Phillips Brooks changed the way generations of American ministers preached, yet he is usually remembered for a Christmas carol he wrote: "O Little Town of Bethlehem."

Brooks experienced many failures as a single adult. He joined the faculty of Boston Latin School but quit abruptly because he could not maintain discipline. At the time, he was struggling with a decision that would have been unacceptable for many of his Harvard friends: He wanted to enter the ministry.

During the Civil War, Brooks faithfully visited Confederate prisoners in Philadelphia and became concerned with the needs of free blacks. He preached to black congregations on Sunday afternoons and used his own pulpit to challenge Philadelphians on their racial attitudes. He frequently called for public support of the Emancipation Proclamation.

Brooks's reputation as a pulpiteer earned him calls from many churches. In July 1869, he accepted a call to pastor Boston's Trinity Church. When a new sanctuary was built, Brooks insisted that large balconies be included, since all the pews were reserved for families who paid rent for them.

Today in Boston's Trinity Church, there is a statue of Brooks. He stands in his pulpit, and Christ stands behind him, His hand resting on Brooks's shoulder. Brooks was one of America's greatest preachers.

He gave this advice to single adults:

> You never become truly spiritual by sitting down and wishing to become so. You must undertake something so great that you cannot accomplish it unaided. Begin doing something for your fellow man and if you do it with all your power, it will almost immediately bring you face to face with problems you cannot solve: you need God and you need to go to God.

"The shepherds said to one another, 'Let's go to Bethlehem and see this thing that has happened, which the Lord has told us about.' "

Luke 2:15

Father, help me to learn that the only way to get rid of my past is to make a future from it.

Frances Ridley Havergal, hymn writer
December 14, 1836–June 3, 1879

Frances Havergal gave the world one hundred hymns and forty tunes. She is best known for two: "I Gave My Life for Thee" and "Take My Life and Let it Be." Frances read seven languages, including Greek and Hebrew, but at fourteen, she told her future stepmother how willing she would be to give up everything if she could only find Christ as her Savior.

The woman replied, "Why cannot you trust yourself to your Savior at once?"

In that moment, "Then and there, I committed my soul to my Savior . . . I did trust the Lord Jesus."

Frances lived a devout Christian life, teaching Sunday school and singing in churches, but she wanted a deeper experience. At twenty-two, she knew the Gospels by memory, as well as the epistles, Revelation, Psalms, Isaiah, and eventually the minor prophets.

In 1852, Frances became ill; she was an invalid the rest of her life. What others would have called a tragedy, she called a blessing. "It has already comforted me," she wrote, "to think that God might be leading me through some dark ways, so that I might afterward be His messenger to some of His children in distress."

When her American publishers went bankrupt, owing her a great deal of money, she responded, "I have not a fear, or a doubt, or a care, or a shadow upon the sunshine of my heart." Later, when valuable stereotype plates of her music were destroyed in a fire, she accepted the loss with calm.

Some said Frances wore herself out ministering to others. When they suggested that she slow down, she replied, "Never mind! It's home the faster! God's will is delicious; He makes no mistakes."

No wonder Frances Havergal's hymns are still relevant a century and a half later.

> **"But if we walk in the light as He is in the light, we have fellowship with one another, and the blood of Jesus Christ His Son cleanses us from all sin."**
>
> **1 John 1:7** NKJV

> Take my life and let it be
> Consecrated Lord, to Thee;
> Take my hands and let them move
> At the impulse of Thy love,
> At the impulse of Thy love.

Take my love—my God, I pour
At Thy feet its treasure store;
Take myself and I will be
Ever, only, all for Thee;
Ever, only, all for Thee.

Lord, let these words be the prayer of our hearts.

December 15

Lewis Redner, organist
December 15, 1830–August 29, 1908

Lewis Redner was a successful real estate broker in Philadelphia when he met Phillips Brooks. He had been the organist at three churches and now served at Holy Trinity Church, where Brooks pastored. In addition to his music responsibilities, Redner was the superintendent of the Sunday school for nineteen years. During his tenure, attendance increased from thirty-six children to more than a thousand.

Redner often held music committee meetings at the home he shared with his sister, Mrs. Sarah Sagers. Brooks would often attend, but since he was not a musician, he sat in the corner and read. However, whenever he heard a tune he liked, he yelled out, "I like that!"

For Christmas 1868, Brooks had written a little poem inspired by his visit to Bethlehem on Christmas Eve the previous year. Lewis Redner composed the music, and "O Little Town of Bethlehem" soon became part of the Christmas tradition—a Christmas carol originally intended for children, written by two bachelors, and loved by millions.

"Do not be afraid. I bring you good news of great joy that will be for all the people. Today in the town of David a Savior has been born to you."

Luke 2:10, 11

Father, thank You for the talents You gave Lewis Redner. Remind us when we hear his carol of Your gift to us in Your Son who came to a little town called Bethlehem.

December 16

Amy Carmichael, missionary
December 16, 1867–January 18, 1951

The death of Amy Carmichael's father sent the young Irish girl on a spiritual pilgrimage that forever changed her life. Initially, she went to Japan as a missionary, but failed because she had great difficulty with the language and suffered a nervous breakdown. Then she felt called to Ceylon, but that too was a failure.

Next she went to India, but found the Hindu caste

"Anyone who loves his father or mother more than me is not worthy of me."

Matthew 10:37

310

system and Islamic influence formidable opponents. "Feeling like a fish out of water" after five discouraging years in India, she discovered the "temple children," children of five and six who had been given up by their parents for ritual prostitution in the temples. In 1901, Amy Carmichael found a purpose for her life: rescuing such children. This commitment put her on a collision course not only with the children's parents but also with Amy's missionary colleagues.

By 1904, Amy was caring for seventeen children and had launched the Dohnavur Fellowship, a safe refuge for them. Many of the girls became Christians and joined the rescue work through an organization Amy named Sisters of the Common Life.

Amy Carmichael wrote this about singleness:

> On this day many years ago I went away alone to a cave in the mountain called Arima. I had feelings of fear about the future, that was why I went there—to be alone with God. The devil kept whispering, "It's all right now, but what about afterwards? You are going to be very lonely." And he painted pictures of my loneliness—I can see them still. And I turned to my God in a kind of desperation and said, "Lord, what can I do? How can I go on to the end?" And He said, "None of them that trust in Me shall be desolate." That word has been with me ever since. It has been fulfilled to me. It will be fulfilled to you.

By 1930, Amy had founded thirty nurseries for children; by 1945, thousands of children had been rescued. She was called *Amma,* or "Mother," by her Indian friends.

Today Amy Carmichael is mainly remembered for her thirty-five books.

Father, for a life freely given for others, we give You thanks. Help us, too, to find our purpose in life.

December 17

John Greenleaf Whittier, poet and editor
December 17, 1807–September 7, 1892

Although he had little formal education, John Greenleaf Whittier read widely, and before his twentieth birthday, his writing had attracted the attention of abolitionist editors and supporters. Whittier's strong Quaker faith stimulated his involvement in social causes and reform, particularly those against slavery. His *Legends of New England in Prose and Poetry,* published in 1831, established his literary reputation and gave him a platform to air his antislavery feelings.

For some thirty-four years, Whittier hammered away against slavery. After the Civil War, his writing emphasized religious values and the beauty of New England. His poems, set to music, were popular hymns among the country folk of New England. His greatest works were "Snow-Bound," "Telling the Bees," "The Barefoot Boy," and "Maud Muller."

"Remember that you were slaves in Egypt and the Lord your God redeemed you from there."

Deuteronomy 24:18

Key Thought:
"I know not where
  His islands lift,
Their fronded
  palms in air;
I only know I can-
  not drift
Beyond His love
  and care."

December 18

John Hemphill, congressman
December 18, 1803–January 4, 1862

John Hemphill, after graduation from Jefferson College, taught school and studied law. He was admitted to the South Carolina bar in 1829, practiced law in Sumter, South Carolina, from 1831 to 1838, and edited a pro-states' rights paper for two years.

After fighting in the Florida Seminole War in 1836, John settled in Texas in 1838. From 1840 to 1842, Hemphill was a state judge. As a delegate to the Texas constitutional convention in 1845, he was a strong advocate of statehood.

John Hemphill served as chief justice of the Texas Supreme Court from 1846 to 1858. In 1859, he was elected as a states'-rights Democrat to the United States

"For I am the Lord, your God, who takes hold of your right hand and says to you, Do not fear; I will help you."

Isaiah 41:13

312

Senate and was expelled after a blistering speech in January 1861 on the right of a state to secede from the Union.

On January 6, 1861, he and thirteen senators met and recommended immediate secession. He was a strong member of the provisional Confederate Congress and died in 1862 in Richmond.

Father, there are so many issues and causes that demand our attention. Give us insight to know where to invest ourselves.

December 19

Carter Woodson, historian
December 19, 1875–April 3, 1950

The oldest child of former slaves, Carter Woodson hungered for an education but was largely self-taught until the age of seventeen. After several years of working in the West Virginia coal mines, he entered high school at twenty-one and later attended Berea College and the University of Chicago. Before graduation, he taught in the Philippines and studied at the Sorbonne. In 1912, he completed his Ph.D. in history.

Woodson taught nine years at M Street High in Washington, then served as dean of the school of liberal arts at Howard University until 1920.

His major contribution was in the study of Negro history, where he argued that black children need to develop pride in their cultural history.

To foster that, in 1915, he organized the Association for the Study of Negro Life and History and a year later founded the *Journal of Negro History*, a scholarly periodical. In 1921, he started Associated Publishers to publish black historical materials. In 1937, he launched a popular historical magazine for blacks, *Negro History Bulletin*.

Woodson also started the annual celebration of Negro History Week in 1926.

His many books and articles contributed to the appreciation of black history, and he assisted many young black historians financially so they could complete their education and research.

"For the eyes of the Lord range throughout the earth to strengthen those whose hearts are fully committed to him."

2 Chronicles 16:9

Father, thank You for this good man who never believed that one person could not make a difference.

313

Jessie Hubbell Bancroft, physical education specialist
December 20, 1867–November 13, 1952

Jessie Bancroft's lifelong interest in physical education began as a teen, when she attended a lecture on exercise. Because of concerns about her own health, she took private instruction, then attended the Minneapolis School of Physical Education and later Winona State Normal School.

Employment was not easy for Jessie to find because the field of physical education was dominated by men. As an alternative, she organized "parlor classes" in her home to teach physical exercise. She also gave programs in churches and schools. After traveling through the Midwest for two years, she attended the Harvard Summer School of Physical Education.

In 1893, Jessie became director of physical training for the Brooklyn public schools and held that position for ten years. She later became assistant director of physical training for the New York City schools in 1903 and held that position for twenty-five years.

Without a college degree, Bancroft instituted major changes in physical education. She developed exercises to be taught by classroom teachers, instituted a system of games and exercise according to grades, and opened the first public school gymnasium. Jessie also worked to incorporate children's anthropometric measurements into the design of classroom furniture and introduced sight and hearing tests for elementary students.

Bancroft wrote seven books and numerous articles. Her *Games for the Playground, Home and Gymnasium* was considered the most comprehensive book on games published in her day. Jessie Bancroft was founder of the American Posture League. Her research on foot measuring was used to develop new standards in the shoe industry, furniture making, and subways.

"For physical training is of some value."

1 Timothy 4:8

Father, we need to be reminded that our bodies are the temple of the Holy Spirit. Give us the courage to exercise regularly.

December 21
Henrietta Szold, Zionist leader
December 21, 1860–February 13, 1945

Henrietta Szold's father, a Baltimore rabbi, tutored his precocious daughter in Hebrew, French, German, the Bible, and philosophy. Although she had a limited formal education, her brilliance made her an effective teacher in a Baltimore girls' school for some fifteen years.

Eventually Henrietta founded one of the first schools for Jewish immigrants, teaching English, American history, bookkeeping, and dressmaking. Outside the classroom, she found time to raise money to support the project and foster the adjustment of immigrants to American society. Henrietta helped form Hebrew Zion as one of America's first Zionist organizations.

In 1893, Miss Szold became editor of the Jewish Publication Society, a post she held for almost a quarter of a century. She was instrumental in the organization's successful preservation and restoration of Jewish culture. She revised the five-volume English edition of *A History of the Jews* and edited five editions of the *American Jewish Year Book*. She also wrote for the *Jewish Encyclopedia*.

After falling in love with a professor who broke her heart by marrying another woman, Henrietta went off to Europe. A side trip to Palestine increased her commitment to Zionism and gave Henrietta a cause in which she could invest her heart.

She became involved in the Hadassah movement to support the agricultural development of Palestine. In 1912, she formed the Hadassah Women's Zionist Organization and moved to Palestine. From 1927 to 1930, she was a ranking member of the Palestine Zionist Executive of the World Zionist Organization, for what in essence was the Jewish government in Palestine.

Miss Szold served from 1931 to 1933 in the *Vaad Leumi*, or national council of the Knesset. Under her able direction, a system of social service was developed for Palestinian Jews, and she established a social work training program in Jerusalem.

In 1933, she took an active role in resettling German Jews who were escaping the Nazis, making three heroic trips to Germany to rescue Jews. By the start of World

"Proclaim liberty throughout all the land unto all the inhabitants thereof."

Leviticus 25:10 KJV

Key Thought: In a day of great violence in the land of Israel and across the Middle East, one must consider Miss Szold's definition of Zionism:

War II, Miss Szold had resettled 13,000 German and Polish children.

Henrietta Szold consistently fought against the growing influence of the orthodox in Palestine, a land she insisted must be for *all* Jews.

"no necessary antagonism between the hopes of the Jews and the rights of the Arabs."

December 22

Robert Ogden Tyler, soldier
December 22, 1831–December 1, 1874

Lieutenant Robert Tyler, a graduate of West Point, began his military career in Salt Lake City in 1854. After his promotion to first lieutenant, he transferred to Washington,where he took part in several skirmishes with Indians. Next, Tyler served in the Sioux country in Minnesota.

With the outbreak of the Civil War, Tyler traveled south to Fort Sumter in April of 1861. Later he established a supply depot in Alexandria, Virginia, then joined the First Artillery, which was appointed to defend the nation's capital.

By November 1862, after seeing action in battle, Tyler was promoted to brigadier general. He was credited with major contributions in the North's decisive victory at Gettysburg and highly praised for pushing back the assault of Confederate General Richard Ewell at Spotsylvania. Tyler was wounded during the battle; after recovering, he returned to his military command. By March 1865, Robert Tyler had been elevated to major general.

In 1866, he transferred to the regular army and served in the quartermaster's department. Due to his war injuries, his health declined; and after a year's leave to travel in the far West for the sake of his health, Tyler returned home and died in Boston. His diary, *Memoir of Brevet Major General Robert Ogdum Tyler*, was published posthumously in 1878.

General Tyler was known for his strictness and his justice.

"For I myself am a man under authority, with soldiers under me. I tell this one, 'Go,' and he goes; and that one, 'Come,' and he comes."

Luke 7:8

Father, we will be remembered for something. Help us to make decisions today that will lead to positive memories.

316

December 23

William Henry Moody, Supreme Court justice
December 23, 1853–July 2, 1917

Once admitted to the Massachusetts bar, William Moody became involved in politics. In 1890, he was appointed United States district attorney for eastern Massachusetts; five years later, Moody was elected to the United States House and re-elected four times.

In 1902, he became secretary of the navy in the administration of Theodore Roosevelt. He established two naval bases that have had long-term strategic significance: Guantanamo in Cuba and Subic Bay in the Philippines.

Based on his success, Roosevelt appointed Moody attorney general in 1904. He was successful in obtaining a decision from the Supreme Court that barred corporation officers from using the Fifth Amendment to withhold legal documents in civil cases. However, Moody's greatest accomplishment was instituting the famous suit by the government against Standard Oil Company. William Henry Moody was a trustbuster.

In 1906, Roosevelt appointed him an associate justice of the United States Supreme Court, where he served until ill health forced him to resign in 1910.

William Henry Moody may have been the only single adult to have served in all three branches of the federal government: legislative, executive, and judicial.

"Now Daniel so distinguished himself among the administrators and the satraps by his exceptional qualities that the king planned to set him over the whole kingdom."

Daniel 6:3

Key Point: William Henry Moody was a man who could get things done. That was the key to his impeccable record in government service.

December 24

Hortence Powdermaker, anthropologist
December 24, 1896–June 15, 1970

While studying at Goucher College, Hortence Powdermaker "discovered" the slums of Baltimore and the emerging labor movement. After graduation, she went to work for the Amalgamated Clothing Workers of America. She soon asked to be moved to the field and was successful in organizing union locals in Cleveland and Rochester. After a few years she moved to England to do graduate work at the London School of Economics.

"No one whose hope is in you will ever be put to shame . . ."

Psalm 25:3

In London she studied with famed anthropologist Bronislaw Malinowski and found anthropology "to be what I had been looking for without knowing it." Malinowski invited her to become part of his family of students, and under his influence, she completed her dissertation on leadership in primitive societies.

Anxious to have a field experience, Hortence went to live among the Lesu in New Ireland, Australia. As a female, she was able to develop friendships with the women of the villages.

Life in Lesu, published in 1934, led to Hortence's appointment to Yale, where she worked with Edward Sapir, who introduced her to psychology. Miss Powdermaker conducted extensive research on blacks in the deep South, particularly in Indianola, Mississippi. Her *After Freedom* was the first study of a modern American community.

After founding the anthropology department at Queens College and teaching at Yale, Hortence turned her attention to the study of Hollywood. Powdermaker's *Hollywood: Dream Factory* (1950) was the first serious study of this key American institution and the impact of film on American culture.

Hortence Powdermaker believed she could have been more successful in anthropology if she had been male. Because she regretted not having been a mother, she adopted a Korean child, Won Mo Kim, who became a gifted violinist.

Key Thought: Hortence Powdermaker had a diversity of interests. As single adults, are we well-rounded?

December 25

Jesus of Nazareth, Savior
ca. 5 B.C.–ca. A.D. 30

In His final words to His disciples, Jesus declared: "All authority in heaven and on earth has been given to me. Therefore go and make disciples of all nations, baptizing them in the name of the Father and of the Son and of the Holy Spirit, and teaching them to obey everything I have commanded you" (Matthew 28:18–20).

As single adults, we can take comfort in Jesus' final words before His ascension: "And surely I am with you always, to the very end of the age" (Matthew 28:20).

"Therefore, since we have a great high priest who has gone through the heavens, Jesus the Son of God, let us hold firmly to the faith we profess. For we do not have

John recorded some of Jesus' greatest words of comfort. To His disciples, who were troubled by thoughts of life without Him, Jesus said:

> Do not let your hearts be troubled. Trust in God; trust also in me. In my Father's house are many rooms; if it were not so, I would have told you. I am going there to prepare a place for you. And if I go and prepare a place for you, I will come back and take you to be with me that you also may be where I am.
>
> John 14:1–3

"I am the way and the truth and the life," Jesus said (John 14:6). Millions of single adults have accepted that truth. To some, He was merely a Judean carpenter, a social reformer, a good teacher. To a few, He was a revolutionary. But to those who believe, He is the Christ, Redeemer, Comforter, and coming King.

To all, Jesus was a single adult. Had He not lived, most of the accomplishments in this book would never have been attempted. He made it possible for single adults who know Him to accomplish great things for God.

a high priest who is unable to sympathize with our weaknesses, but we have one who has been tempted in every way, just as we are—yet was without sin. Let us then approach the throne of grace with confidence, so that we may receive mercy and find grace to help us in our time of need."

Hebrews 4:14–16

Key Thought: Just as He called single adults in His day to follow Him, so this day, December 25, He still calls: "Come, follow me."

December 26

Eva March Tappan, writer
December 26, 1854–January 29, 1930

Eva Tappan grew up in a single-parent home and followed her schoolteacher mother through a series of schools. It surprised no one that Eva became a teacher. She completed her Ph.D. in English at the University of Pennsylvania in 1896.

Tappan first wrote English textbooks, but later she turned to writing books for children. In 1904, she resigned to devote more time to writing and to care for her aged mother.

Her first book, *Charles Lamb, the Man and the Author*, was followed by *The Days of Alfred the Great.* Her

"But if a widow has children or grandchildren, these should learn first of all to put their religion into practice by caring for their own family and so repaying their parents and grandparents, for

319

informal, lucid style, her ability to paint word pictures, and her tightly organized structure won her a wide readership.

Eva enjoyed history, and two of her books were texts for public schools: *Our Country's Story* (1902) and *The Story of Our Constitution* (1922). She made the past come alive through other books such as *The Days of Queen Elizabeth* and *The Days of Queen Victoria.*

Tappan wanted to teach students to enjoy biography. *American Hero Stories* (1906), *Old World Hero Stories* (1911), and others made a strong impression on many schoolchildren and stimulated their interest in history.

Eva Tappan's writing career provided the financial stability she needed to care for her invalid mother. After her mother died, she maintained her writing and stayed close to home.

this is pleasing to God."

1 Timothy 5:4

Father, through writing, Eva Tappan touched the lives of generations of schoolchildren. Prod us to use our talents for the building of Your kingdom.

December 27

Meg Greenfield, journalist
December 27, 1930–

Few single adults have made such a contribution to the field of journalism as columnist Meg Greenfield. Born in Seattle, Meg began her career in journalism in Washington, D.C., writing for *Reporter* magazine in 1957 and advancing to the position of the magazine's Washington editor in 1965.

In 1968, Meg Greenfield began writing on the editorial staff of the *Washington Post*, and in 1979 she became editor of the editorial page. Miss Greenfield won the 1978 Pulitzer Prize for editorial writing.

However, her influence extends far beyond the pages of the *Washington Post*. Since 1974 she has also been a columnist for *Newsweek* magazine and has had a profound influence on the way people think about public issues.

The above Scripture passage talks about God's words to John. The last phrase also symbolizes the writing of Meg Greenfield: Millions of people have found her words trustworthy, too.

"Write this down, for these words are trustworthy and true."

Revelation 21:5

Father, remind us that excellence isn't accidental. It takes years of pouring ourselves into our work.

December 28

Thomas Dowse, bibliophile
December 28, 1772–November 4, 1856

When Thomas Dowse and his parents fled from Charlestown, Massachusetts, ahead of the advancing British troops, they resettled in the village of Sherborn. Thomas's childhood was marked by his incredible appetite for reading. "A regular bookworm!" townsfolk laughed. By age eighteen, Thomas Dowse had read almost every book in the town, apparently in compensation for his lameness, a result of a fall from a tree.

He learned his father's trade of wool-pulling and leather-dressing and worked at those until he was seventy-four. Because of his financial success, Dowse was able to devote long hours to reading, and through careful buying, he accumulated a library worth a small fortune.

A fan of Sir Walter Scott, Dowse said, "Lameness drove us both to books—him to making them, and me to reading them."

Shortly before his death, Dowse gave his large library to the Massachusetts Historical Society and the art he owned to the Boston Athenaeum. Patrons of both institutions enjoy his donations to this day.

One biographer observed of Thomas Dowse, "He kept no company, he joined no clubs, belonged to no mutual admiration societies, talked little, wrote less, and published nothing." But he did know a good book when he saw it.

"And Mephibosheth lived in Jerusalem, because he always ate at the king's table, and he was crippled in both feet."

2 Samuel 9:13

Key Point: Could a biographer say the same thing of you that was said of Thomas Dowse?

December 29

Joseph F. Guffey, senator
December 29, 1870–March 6, 1959

Joseph Guffey began his political career at twenty-four when he was appointed supervisor of city delivery in the Pittsburgh post office through the influence of his uncle. In 1894, he used his family contacts to begin working for a utilities holding company. He invested heavily in oil and coal leases but went bankrupt. Guffey then borrowed money from his family and bought oil leases in east Texas, which eventually made him wealthy.

"The plans of the diligent lead to profit as surely as haste leads to poverty."

Proverbs 21:5

Although he owed a great deal to his uncle, Guffey distanced himself politically by supporting Woodrow Wilson. By 1920, Guffey was a member of the Democratic National Committee.

In 1934, Guffey was elected Pennsylvania's first Democratic senator in fifty-eight years. In 1936, he used his strong ties with unions to help Roosevelt win the state's electoral votes. He was an early believer that blacks, who had traditionally voted Republican since the Civil War, could be attracted to the Democratic Party. At his urging, the Democratic National Committee set up a special office to target black voters. Guffey became head of the Democratic machine in Pennsylvania and wielded great political power through patronage appointments. He declared, however, "ours isn't a machine . . . it's an organization for service."

Guffey's major legislative victory was the Guffey-Vinson Act of 1937, which helped stabilize the price of bituminous coal and set a price base in the oil business.

Joseph Guffey was one of the first to support Roosevelt's plan to seek a third term. In 1946, he was defeated in a Republican landslide; although he was the incumbent, he lost by 600,000 votes.

Key Point: You win some and you lose some. Whichever, it is still your choice to react or to respond.

December 30

William Haddock Park, public health officer
December 30, 1863–April 6, 1939

Although William Haddock Park had established himself in a good nose-and-throat practice in New York, he wondered if there wasn't more to life. He discussed his future with Dr. T. Mitchell Prudden, the consulting bacteriologist for the city of New York, and Prudden urged him to join him in the city lab to study diphtheria.

For two years, Park, although still in private practice, did his research. His results, published in 1892, confirmed the role of the Klebs-Loffler bacillus in diphtheria and won Park international recognition.

Park and his assistants focused on the role of healthy members of a household in spreading diphtheria and the impact of that on public health. In the fall of 1895,

"The royal officer said, 'Sir, come down before my child dies.' Jesus replied, 'You may go. Your son will live.' "

John 4:49, 50

Park and Anna Williams developed a diphtheria antitoxin that neutralized diphtheria in the infected individual and protected the uninfected.

Dr. Park researched poliomyelitis, meningitis, scarlet fever, tuberculosis, and pneumonia. He was an early advocate of improved milk sanitation, and his work helped reduce diarrhea as a major cause of infant mortality.

Dr. William Park carried on an active teaching load for forty-two years and contributed significantly to the development of the discipline of bacteriology. His text *Pathogenic Micro-organisms* (co-authored with Williams) was a standard text for the nation's medical schools.

Father, the lifework of William Park cannot be easily dismissed. His research saved millions of lives. Remind us of that the next time we think one person cannot make a difference.

December 31

Orry George Kelly, designer
December 31, 1897–February 26, 1964

As a small boy, Orry Kelly loved to draw. After he completed school, he worked for a bank, but when he had the chance to join a stage company, he took it.

Arriving in New York in 1923, Orry opened his first studio and created hand-painted Spanish shawls. In 1932, he moved to Hollywood and secured a position as a costume designer for Warner Brothers. He also worked at Twentieth Century-Fox, Universal, and MGM studios.

His designs were worn by Bette Davis, Rosalind Russell, Marilyn Monroe, and other leading Hollywood stars. His career was capped by winning the Academy Award for the clothes in the movie *An American in Paris*.

"He has filled them with skill to do all kinds of work as craftsmen, designers, embroiderers in blue, purple and scarlet yarn and fine linen, and weavers—all of them master craftsmen and designers."

Exodus 35:35

Father, the ability to see clothes in a bolt of cloth, the ability to take sketches and make them reality, is from You. Thank You for all those who contribute to the beautiful clothes we wear.

PRESENTE!

Americans have strange thoughts about the deceased: Give them a tombstone, a bronze on a wall, a moment of remembrance. Dust them off occasionally, but let them sleep on.

I have been told that Latin Americans have a different view of death. They believe that those men and women of faith who have died are not dead at all but continue on in the struggle against sin and oppression. At funerals, the name of the deceased is called out, and the congregation responds, *"Presente!"*

The writer of Hebrews would understand. In his roll call of the faithful in chapter 11, he says, "And by faith he still speaks, even though he is dead" [v. 4].

Today, *A Singular Devotion* is a roll call of single adults who have made a difference. My hope is that reading this book has given you some new friends, that your vision has been stretched, and that you can hear down through the corridor of history the courageous, the heroic, even the plodders, calling us to join in and use this season of our lives to make a difference.

John Delaney, in *Saints Are Now*, recalls a person saying of Mother Teresa, "When she is dead she will be made a saint."

"I completely disagree with the remark," says Delaney. "Saints are not made in death but during their lifetimes, by the lives they lead. Recognition of sainthood often comes *after* their deaths, but the elements of that sainthood are forged by their deeds and actions during their lifetimes."

You are the only one who can be you and get it right. Give your dream a chance.

> Therefore, since we are surrounded by such a great cloud of witnesses, let us throw off everything that hinders and the sin that so easily entangles, and let us run with perseverance the race marked out for us.
>
> Let us fix our eyes on Jesus, the author and perfecter of our faith, who for the joy set before him endured the cross, scorning its

shame, and sat down at the right hand of the throne of God.

Consider him who endured such opposition from sinful men, so that you will not grow weary and lose heart.

Hebrews 12:1–3

May the lives of these single adults—whether saint or hero, celebrity or stranger—give you the courage to join the lengthy procession of single adults who made and are making a difference.

There is a saying in the Jewish neighborhood in which I live that sums up the theme of this book—

"May their memory to us be a blessing."

Bibliography

American Council of Learned Societies, ed. *Concise Dictionary of American Biography.* New York: Scribner's, 1980.

Baltzell, W. K. *Baltzell's Dictionary of Musicians.* Boston: Oliver Ditson Company, 1910.

Benet's Reader's Encyclopedia. 3d ed. New York: Harper & Row, 1987.

Bowden, Henry Warner. *Dictionary of American Religious Biography.* Westport, Conn.: Greenwood, 1977.

Chamber's Biographical Dictionary. Rev. ed. New York: Cambridge University Press, 1986.

Coleman, Kenneth, and Charles Stephen Gunn, ed. *Dictionary of Georgia Biography.* Athens, Ga.: University of Georgia Press, 1983.

Congress, A to Z. Washington, D.C.: Congressional Quarterly, 1988.

Contemporary Authors. Detroit, Mich.: Gale Research, 1981.

DeGregorio, William A. *The Complete Book of U.S. Presidents.* New York: Dembner Books, 1984.

Dictionary of Literary Biography. Vol. 12: *American Realists and Naturalists.* Vol. 10: *Modern British Dramatists, 1900–1945.* Vol. 9: *American Novelists, 1910–1945.* Detroit, Mich.: Gale Research, 1982.

Ewen, David. *Composers Since 1900: A Biographical and Critical Guide.* New York: H. W. Wilson, 1969.

———. *Musicians Since 1900: Performers in Concert and Opera.* New York: H. W. Wilson, 1978.

Hammack, Mary L. *A Dictionary of Women in Church History.* Chicago: Moody Press, 1984.

Harmon, Nolan B. *The Encyclopedia of World Methodism.* 3 vols. Nashville, Tenn.: United Methodist Publishing House, 1974.

Hitchcock, H. Wiley, and Stanley Sadie, ed. *New Grove Dictionary of American Music.* 4 vols. New York: Macmillan, 1986.

Hustad, Donald P. *Dictionary-Handbook to Hymns for the Living Church.* Carol Stream, Ill.: Hope Publishing Company, 1978.

James, Edward T., ed. *Notable American Women, 1607–1950.* 3 vols. Cambridge, Mass.: Belknap Press, 1971.

Johnson, Allen, *Dictionary of American Biography.* 17 vols. New York: Scribner's, 1964.

———. *Dictionary of American Biography: Supplements.* 8 vols. New York: Scribner's.

Kinsman, Claire D., and Mary Ann Tennehouse. *Contemporary Authors.* 12 vols. Detroit, Mich.: Gale Research, 1974.

Kuritz, Stanley J., and Howard Haycraft, ed. *American Authors: 1600–1900.* New York: H. W. Wilson, 1938.

———. *Twentieth Century Authors.* New York: H. W. Wilson, 1942.

McGraw-Hill Encyclopedia of World Biography. 18 vols. New York: McGraw Hill, 1983.

McHenry, Robert, ed. *Famous American Women: A Biographical Dictionary from Colonial Times to the Present.* New York: Dover Press, 1980.

McMullin, Thomas A., and David Walker. *Biographical Dictionary of American Territorial Governors.* Westport, Conn.: Meckler Publishing, 1984.

Magill, Frank N. *Great Lives from History: Britain and Commonwealth Series.* Pasadena, Calif.: Salem, 1987.

Moritz, Charles, ed. *Current Biography: 1978.* New York: H. W. Wilson, 1978.

Moyer, Elgin. *Wycliffe Biographical Dictionary of the Church.* Chicago: Moody Press, 1983.

O'Neil, Lois Decker, *Women's Book of World Records.* New York: Anchor, 1979.

Powell, William S., ed. *Dictionary of North Carolina Biography.* Chapel Hill, N.C.: University of North Carolina Press, 1979.

Raven, Susan, and Alisa Weir. *Women of Achievement: 35 Centuries of History.* New York: Harmony, 1981.

Reeves, Winona Evans, ed. *The Blue Book of Nebraska Women.* Lincoln, Neb.: University of Nebraska Library, 1916.

Rood, Karen L., ed. *American Literary Almanac: 1608 to Present.* New York: Facts on File, 1988.

Sicherman, Barbara, and Carol Hurd Green, ed. *Notable American Women, The Modern Period.* Cambridge, Mass.: Belknap Press, 1980.

Smith, Leslie, ed. *Dictionary of National Biography.* 27 vols. New York: Oxford University Press, 1917.

Sobel, Robert, ed. *Biographical Dictionary of the U.S. Executive Branch, 1774–1977.* Westport, Conn.: Greenwood Press, 1977.

Sobel, Robert, and John Raimo, ed. *Biographical Dictionary of the Governors of the United States, 1789–1977.* Westport, Conn.: Meckler, 1978.

Stokley, Jim, and Jeff D. Johnson, ed. *An Encyclopedia of East Tennessee.* Oak Ridge, Tenn.: Children's Museum of Oak Ridge, 1981.

Thompson, Oscar. *The International Cyclopedia of Music and Musicians.* Edited by Bruce Bohle. New York: Dodd, Mead, 1985.

Tuttle, Lisa. *Encyclopedia of Feminism.* New York: Facts on File, 1986.

Uglow, Jennifer S., ed. *The Continuum Dictionary of Women's Biography.* New York: Continuum, 1989.

Van Doren, Charles, ed. *Webster's American Biographical Dictionary.* Springfield, Mass.: Merriam, 1974.

Vernoff, Edward, and Rima Shore. *The International Dictionary of 20th Century Biography.* New York: New American Library, 1987.

Wakelyn, Jon L. *Biographical Dictionary of the Confederacy.* Westport, Conn.: Greenwood Press, 1977.

Watkins, Josephine Ellis, comp. *Who's Who in Fashion.* New York: Fairchild, 1975.

Who Was Who in the American Revolution. Indianapolis, Ind.: Bobbs-Merrill, 1976.

Willard, Frances, and Mary Livermore. *A Woman of the Century: Biographical Sketches of Leading American Women.* Reprint. Detroit, Mich.: Gale Research, 1967.

Wilson, Daniel J. *Thinkers of the Twentieth Century.* 2d ed. Edited by Roland Turner, Chicago: St. James, 1987.

Wilson, Vincent, Jr. *The Book of Distinguished American Women.* Brookeville, Md.: American Historical Research Associates, 1983.

Witt, Elder, ed. *Congressional Quarterly: Guide to the U.S. Supreme Court.* Washington, D.C.: Library of Congress, 1979.

Autobiographies and Biographies

Allen, Alexander V. G. *Phillips Brooks: 1835–1893, Memories of His Life With Extracts From His Letters and Note Books.* 2 vols. New York: E. P. Dutton, 1907.

Allen, Catherine B. *The New Lottie Moon Story.* Nashville, Tenn.: Broadman, 1980.

Armitage, Merle. *Stella Dysart of Ambrosia Lake.* New York: Duell, Sloan and Pearce, 1959.

Bakeless, John. *Background to Glory: The Life of George Rogers Clark.* Philadelphia, Pa.: J. P. Lippincott, 1957.

Baldwin, Ethel May, and David V. Benson. *Henrietta Mears and How She Did It.* Glendale, Calif.: Gospel Light, 1966.

Bishop, Selma L. *Isaac Watts: Hymns and Spiritual Songs, 1707–1748.* London: Faith Press, 1962.

Blackburn, Joyce. *Martha Berry: Little Woman With a Big Dream.* Philadelphia, Pa.: J. P. Lippincott, 1968.

Bonhoeffer, Dietrich. *Life Together.* Translated by John W. Doberstein. New York: Harper and Row, 1954.

Burgess, Alan. *The Small Woman: The Story of Gladys Aylward of China.* Ann Arbor, Mich.: Servant, 1975.

Curtis, George Ticknor. *The Life of James Buchanan.* Vol. 1. New York: Harris and Butler, 1883.

Davis, Kenneth S. *The Politics of Honor: A Biography of Adlai Stevenson.* New York: Putnam's, 1967.

DeBardeleben, Mary, comp. *Lambuth-Bennett Book of Remembrance.* Nashville, Tenn.: Publishing House of the Methodist Church, South, 1922.

Dimmitt, Marjorie. *Isabella Thoburn College.* Asheville, N.C.: Author, 1962.

Dooley, Thomas. *The Edge of Tomorrow.* New York: New American Library, 1958.

Duff, L. David. *The Ramsey Covenant: A Story About Evelyn Ramsey, M.D.* Kansas City, Mo.: Beacon Hill, 1985.

"Elizabeth Cole: Missionary Featured at the Church of the Nazarene." Department of World Missions, Church of the Nazarene biographical release, n.d.

Elliot, Elisabeth. *A Chance to Die: The Life and Legacy of Amy Carmichael.* Old Tappan, N.J.: Fleming H. Revell Co., 1987.

Fineman, Irving. *Woman of Valor: The Story of Henrietta Szold.* New York: Simon and Schuster, 1961.

Fowler, Robert Booth. *Carrie Catt: Feminist Politician.* Boston, Mass.: Northeastern University Press, 1986.

Green, Wendy. *Getting Things Done: A Biography: Eva Burrows.* Reading, England: Marshall-Pickering, 1988.

Hall, Sherwood. *With Stethoscope in Asia.* McClean, Va.: MCI Association, 1978.

Harrison, Lowell H. *George Rogers Clark and the War in the West.* Lexington, Ky.: University of Kentucky Press, 1976.

Hasler, Richard A. *Journey With David Brainerd.* Downer's Grove, Ill.: Inter-Varsity, 1976.

Hopkins, Hugh Evan. *Charles Simeon of Cambridge.* Grand Rapids, Mich.: Eerdmans, 1977.

Howard, Fred. *Wilbur and Orville: A Biography of the Wright Brothers.* New York: Knopf, 1987.

Howell, Beth Prim. *Lady on a Donkey.* New York: E. P. Dutton, 1960.

Jay, Ruth Johnson. *Mary Slessor: White Queen of the Cannibals.* Chicago: Moody, 1985.

Kelen, Emery. *Hammarskjöld.* New York: Putnam, 1966.

Kirk, Russell, *John Randolph of Roanoke.* Chicago: Henry Regnery Company, 1964.

Latourette, Kenneth Scott. *Beyond the Ranges: An Autobiography.* Grand Rapids, Mich.: Eerdmans, 1967.

Lean, Garth. *On the Tail of a Comet: The Life of Frank Buchman.* Colorado Springs, Colo.: Helmers and Howard, 1988.

Leibholz, G. "Memoir." In *The Cost of Discipleship.* Rev. ed. New York: Macmillan, 1968.

Lerner, Gerda. *The Grimké Sisters From South Carolina: Pioneers for Women's Rights and Abolition.* New York: Schocken, 1971.

Letters From Lillian. Springfield, Mo.: Assemblies of God, Division of Foreign Missions, 1983.

MacDonell, Mrs. R. W. *Belle Harris Bennett: Her Life Work.* Nashville, Tenn.: Cokesbury, 1928.

Marton, Kati. *Wallenberg.* New York: Ballantine, 1982.

Maxwell, Margaret E. *Sharlott Hall: A Passion for Freedom.* Tucson, Ariz.: University of Arizona, 1982.

A Memorial of Louis Sandford Schuyler. New York: Pott, Young and Company, 1879.

Morrison, Samuel Eliot. *John Paul Jones: A Sailor's Biography.* New York: Time Books, 1959.

"Outfiguring the Navy." *American Way* (May 1984), pp. 39–43.

Padwick, Constance E. *Henry Martyn.* Chicago: Moody, 1980.

Reid, Charles. *Malcolm Sargent: A Biography.* London: Hamilton, 1968.

Roberts, Brian. *Cecil Rhodes: Flawed Colossus.* New York: Norton, 1987.

Rogers, Sherbrooke. *Sarah Josepha Hale: A New England Primer, 1788–1879.* Grantham, N.H.: Thompson and Rutter, 1985.

Rudolph, L. C. *Francis Asbury.* Nashville, Tenn.: Abingdon, 1966.

Sawyers, June. "Way We Were: 'Suitcase Mary' Leads a Crusade for Needy Girls." *Chicago Tribune* (April 7, 1988), Tempo Section, p. 31.

Sherwood, J. M., ed. *Memoirs of Rev. David Brainerd.* New York: Funk and Wagnalls, 1884.

Smith, Amanda. *An Autobiography: The Story of the Lord's Dealings with Mrs. Amanda Smith.* Chicago: Meyer and Brothers, 1893.

Smith, Bryon Caldwell. *Love Life of Bryon Caldwell Smith.* New York: Antigone, 1930.

Smith, Norma. "The Woman Who Said No to War." *MS* (March 1986), pp. 86–89.

Sorrill, Bobbie. *Annie Armstrong: Dreamer in Action.* Nashville, Tenn.: Broadman, 1984.

Strong, Anna Louise. *I Changed Worlds: The Remaking of an American.* New York: Hull, 1935.

ten Boom, Corrie. *A Prisoner and Yet.* London: Christian Literature Crusade, 1954.

———. *Tramp for the Lord.* Fort Washington, Pa.: Christian Literature Crusade, 1974.

ten Boom, Corrie, with C. C. Carlson. *In My Father's House.* Old Tappan, N.J.: Fleming H. Revell Co., 1976.

Thompson, Evelyn Wingo. *Luther Rice: Believer in Tomorrow.* Nashville, Tenn.: Broadman, 1967.

Tucker, Ruth A., and Walter Liefeld. *Daughters of the Church.* Grand Rapids, Mich.: Zondervan, 1989.

Urquhart, Brian. *Hammarskjöld.* New York: Knopf, 1972.

Van Dorn, Carl. *Jonathan Swift.* New York: Viking, 1930.

White, Mel. *Aquino.* Dallas, Tex.: Word, 1989.

Whitman, Alden. *Portrait: Adlai Stevenson: Politician, Diplomat, Friend.* New York: Harper and Row, 1965.

Wolf, Earl C. ed. *The Best of Bertha Munro.* Kansas City, Mo.: Beacon Hill, 1987.

Collected Biographies

Bowie, Walter Russell. *Women of Light.* New York: Harper and Row, 1963.

Burrage, Henry S. *Baptist Hymn Writers and Their Hymns.* Portland, Maine: Brown, Thurston and Company, 1988.

Duncan, Canon. *Popular Hymns.* London: Skeffington and Sons, n.d.

Erdman, Walter. *Sources of Power in Famous Lives.* Nashville, Tenn.: Cokesbury, 1939.

Forrest, Diane. *The Adventurers: Ordinary People with Special Callings.* Nashville, Tenn.: Upper Room Books, 1983.

Hardesty, Nancy A. *Great Women of Faith.* Nashville, Tenn.: Abingdon, 1980.

Harrison, Lowell H. *Kentucky's Governors, 1792–1985.* Lexington, Ky.: University of Kentucky Press, 1985.

Johnston, Julia H. *Fifty Missionary Heroes Every Boy and Girl Should Know.* New York: Fleming H. Revell Co., 1913.

Kubiak, Dan. *Ten Tall Texans: Biographical Sketches.* Austin, Tex.: Balcones Company, 1985.

Lawson, J. Gilchrist. *Deeper Experiences of Famous Christians.* Anderson, Ind.: Warner Press, 1911.

Mable, Norman. *Popular Hymns and Their Writers.* London: Independent Press, 1951.

McClendon, James William, Jr. *Biography as Theology.* Nashville, Tenn.: Abingdon, 1974.

Martin, Hugh. *They Wrote Our Hymns.* London: SCM, 1961.

Ninde, Edward. *Story of the American Hymn.* Nashville, Tenn.: Abingdon, 1921.

Peale, Norman Vincent, and William Thomas Buckley. *The American Character.* Old Tappan, N.J.: Fleming H. Revell Co., 1988.

Pennock, Meta Rutter, ed. *Makers of Nursing History.* New York: Lakeside Publishing, 1940.

Posin, Dan Q. *Dr. Posin's Giants: Men of Science.* Evanston, Ill.: Row, Peterson, 1961.

Reynolds, William. *Hymns of Our Faith.* Nashville, Tenn.: Broadman, 1964.

Richey, Elinor. *Eminent Women of the West.* Berkeley, Calif.: Howell-North, 1975.

Silverman, Sydel. *Women Anthropologists: A Biographical Dictionary.* Westport, Conn.: Greenwood Press, 1988.

Thompson, Ronald. *Who's Who of Hymn Writers.* London: Epworth, 1967.

Vare, Ethlie Ann, and Greg Potacek. *Mothers of Invention: From the Bra to the Bomb, Forgotten Women and Their Unforgettable Ideas.* New York: Morrow, 1988.

Verdesi, Elizabeth Howell, and Sylvia Thorson-Smith. *A Sampler of Saints.* New York: Committee on Women's Concerns and the Council on Women and the Church, Presbyterian Church, U.S.A., 1988.

Wilson, Dorothy Clarke. *Twelve Who Cared: My Adventures With Christian Courage.* Chappaqua, N.Y.: Christian Herald Books, 1977.

Yost, Edna. *American Women of Science.* New York: Stokes, 1943.

Histories

Ambrose, Stephen. *Duty, Honor, Country: A History of West Point.* Baltimore, Md.: Johns Hopkins University Press, 1966.

Cobb, Alice. *"Yes, Lord, I'll Do It": Scarritt's Century of Service.* Nashville, Tenn.: Scarritt College, 1987.

Dannett, Sylvia G. L., ed. *Noble Women of the North.* New York: Yoseloff, 1959.

Emurian, Ernest K. *Living Stories of Famous Hymns.* Grand Rapids, Mich.: Baker Book House, 1955.

Folmsbee, Stanley, Robert E. Corlew, and Enoch L. Mitchell, eds. *Tennessee: A Short History.* Knoxville, Tenn.: University of Tennessee Press, 1969.

A History of the Yellow Fever Epidemic of 1878, in Memphis, Tennessee. Memphis, Tenn.: Howard Association, 1879.

LaPointe, Patricia. *From Saddlebags to Science.* Memphis, Tenn.: University of Tennessee Center of Health Sciences, 1984.

McBeth, Leon. *Women in Baptist Life.* Nashville, Tenn.: Broadman, 1979.

McPherson, James M. *Ordeal by Fire: The Civil War and Reconstruction.* New York: Knopf, 1982.

Morgan, Murray. *Skid Road: An Informal Portrait of Seattle.* New York: Viking, 1951.

Spence, Clark C. *Montana: A History.* New York: Norton, 1978.

Archives

Baylor, R. E. B. Papers. Baylor University, Waco, Texas.

Burn, Harry T. Papers. Tennessee State Library and Archives, Nashville, Tennessee.

Flexner, Bernard. Papers. Louisville Public Library, Louisville, Kentucky.

Flexner, Jeannie. Papers. Louisville Public Library, Louisville, Kentucky.

Jones, Amanda Theodosia. Papers. Junction City Library, Junction City, Kansas.

Malone, Walter. Papers. Memphis State University, Memphis, Tennessee.

Scholl, William M. Papers. Illinois College of Podiatry, Chicago, Illinois.

Thrasher, Lillian. Papers. Archives, Assembly of God Headquarters, Springfield, Missouri.

White, Eartha Mary Magdalene. Papers. University of North Florida, Jacksonville, Florida.

Newspapers

Cincinnati Enquirer. September 4–18, 1878.

Kansas City Star. "Texan Found in Pool: Ex-Politican Is Revived, Hospitalized." July 31, 1988, p. 4A.

New York Times. October 10, 1947, p. 25.

Orlando Sentinel. "Resnik Liked a Job Label With No Frills." January 29, 1986, p. A-9.

Washington Post. March 7, 1959, p. D-2.

Miscellaneous Sources

Bish, Diane. Material on Diane Bish supplied by Joy of Music, Ft. Lauderdale, Florida.

Traylor, Jerry. Material on Jerry Traylor supplied by Jerry Traylor Company, North Parkesburg, West Virginia.

Index